Touchstone

DOUBLE OVERTIME

Stephen Cole

Touchstone
A Division of Simon & Schuster, Inc.
1230 Avenue of the Americas
New York, NY 10020

Copyright © 2011 by Stephen Cole

First Touchstone hardcover edition October 2011

TOUCHSTONE and colophon are registered trademarks of Simon & Schuster, Inc.

For information about special discounts for bulk purchases, please contact Simon & Schuster Special Sales at 1-800-268-3216 or CustomerService@simonandschuster.ca.

The Simon & Schuster Speakers Bureau can bring authors to your live event. For more information or to book an event contact the Simon & Schuster Speakers Bureau at 1-866-248-3049 or visit our website at www.simonspeakers.com.

Designed by PGB

Manufactured in the United States of America

10 9 8 7 6 5 4 3 2 1

ISBN 978-1-4391-9614-4
ISBN 978-1-4391-9615-1 (ebook)

To Trent Frayne and Evan Frustaglio

Contents

Foreword

Hello, Canada, and hockey fans in the United States and Newfoundland. Welcome to *Double Overtime*. Make yourself a sandwich, get something to drink. The book is going to start in...oh, about six pages.

Before then a story: My first publishing job was at McClelland & Stewart. I was a copywriter, back in the mid-'80s. M&S operated in those days out of a redbrick building on Hollinger Road in the eastern suburbs of Toronto; a winding, 15-minute bus ride from the Woodbine subway station. The building amounted to a dozen cramped offices surrounding a gloomy warehouse filled with books. "Filled" wasn't necessarily a good thing, mind you. You wanted books moving out of a warehouse, after all.

Landmark piles drew the name of luckless sponsors: the reckless sales managers who called for pyramids, 5,000 high, of unwanted books. Slipping past the Himalayas–Mount Neale and Mount Asboth collecting wool-thick dust at its peak–you came to back shelves devoted to agency stock and old hardcover favorites. Copies of once-popular titles ready for order and shipping.

Orders that never came, it seemed. Books sat there like forgotten playthings in the *Toy Story* attic. Everything was in alphabetical order, except, curiously, one shelf, hidden in a bottom row at the far end, devoted to hockey. There was a welcoming chair there, like on the set of the old CBC kids' show *The Friendly Giant*. And if you got down on hands and knees and looked, lots of hockey books: Trent Frayne's *Mad Men of Hockey* and *Famous Hockey Players* from Dodd, Mead; Scott Young's *A Boy at the Leafs' Camp* (Little Brown). Plus all of M&S's hockey backlist: *The Game of Our Lives* by Peter Gzowski; as well as Scott Young's books with Punch Imlach and Conn Smythe, volumes with great, grabby titles: *Heaven and Hell in the NHL* and *If You Can't Beat 'Em in the Alley*.

And what was this? Editions of *Hockey Heroes*, by Ron McAllister, from 1949, with stories on (speaking of great titles) Dit Clapper and Hap Day, along with the 1953 offering, *the hockey book*, by Bill Roche, a collection of oral histories, which, despite the collection's demure, lowercase title, is widely held to be the first essential hockey book.

Ladies and gentlemen, boys and girls–hockey fans!–those books, maybe 25 in all, amounted to my graduate degree in hockey. Thanks to whomever left them there and for providing a folding chair for visitors to curl up in.

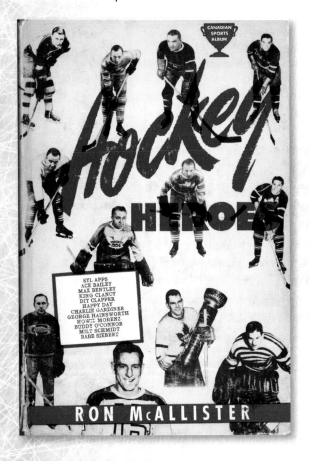

I consulted these books at lunch and on bus and subway rides to and from work. They were sampled randomly, a chapter at a time and often out of chronological order. Eating a sandwich at noon, say, I would read in Roche's book of how in the early 1930s, Toronto Maple Leafs owner Conn Smythe owned a horse, Shoeless Joe, that raced illegally at Saratoga in New York. Someone–not saying who–slipped the horse a mickey. At a subsequent NHL governors' meeting at the Royal York Hotel in Toronto, Smythe, sensing an impolite welcome perhaps, arrived late, hoping to slip quietly into the last vacant chair. As soon as he settled in, his lifelong antagonist, Boston owner Art Ross cleared his throat and bellowed:

"Mr. President, I insist that a saliva test of all those present be taken before proceeding any further with the business at hand."

Coming home from work, I'd read in Peter Gzowski's book on the Edmonton Oilers how, in 1980 the author was traveling on the Edmonton team bus when Mark Messier, then shaggy-haired and 19, hopped aboard, wearing a contraption just catching on with teenagers, the Walkman. Messier bopped down the aisle, bending and swaying.

"Pretty good sound, eh?" a teammate asked, begging a listen.

Messier offered the player his new toy. The teammate slipped on the headphones. The machine was without batteries. Totally dead.

When I was asked to write a hockey book—the premise being 30 teams, 30 essays—I quickly, instinctively, decided to dedicate whatever I came up with to Trent Frayne, my favorite hockey writer (although I'd enjoyed his juvenile hockey titles as a kid, I came to prize his elegantly crafted hockey essays even more as an M&S employee).

I hoped with my book to somehow transplant the joy I experienced ransacking the treasure trove of M&S hockey books for stories and information. Hoped that what you're holding now might, like Frayne's best essays, make our sport come alive with scholarship, rough humor and opinion.

There are undoubtedly more opinions here than Mr. Frayne would believe healthy. What can I say? The furthest I ever got in hockey is referee and I grew up to be a film critic and father of two boys. I have grown accustomed to making authoritative, sometimes stern, judgments on fleeting evidence.

Furthermore, let me say I wrote these stories believing I was addressing an imaginary figure curled up in a chair like the one waiting for me in the M&S warehouse. Only this chair is in a bar. A hockey game is playing on the TV overhead. A fan comes in, falls in next to me and asks, "What's the score?"

"Well, let me tell you . . ." I begin.

Upon reflection, many of these stories began as bar or kitchen-party arguments. I watched the Leafs-Kings 1993 semifinal series in a Brooklyn tavern–our Congress Street apartment didn't have cable, alas. Late one evening, I was the bar's last customer, drinking more than I wanted and leaving big, paper-money tips in hopes the bartender wouldn't call it a night.

"Last call," my server finally said, checking his watch. This was after Toronto's Wendel Clark tied it late. Overtime loomed. My Leafs might soon be in the Stanley Cup final.

"You can't...I'm a Leafs fan, this is a historic occasion," I begged and then told the obliging worker the history of the team. How the Leafs were a Canadian institution.

"You mean everyone in Canada loves them?" he asked.

"Oh no, half the country, maybe more, hates them," I said and then proceeded to tell the other half of this book's Toronto Maple Leafs chapter. (By the way, as Leaf fans know, Gretzky scored for the Kings early on in OT, causing me to wander home down Court Street, rubber-legged and morose.)

The Carolina story began when my brother Rob and I were visiting back home in Ottawa, draining our parents' fridge, momentarily kids again, watching a playoff game in the rec room. The Hurricanes were playing. The announcer mentioned Raleigh. "Isn't that where Andy Griffith and what's his face, Gomer live?" my brother said. "Shaz-a-yum," I responded. Gomer's signature cry. Rob laughed. Five years later, here's the rest of that story.

What I didn't know when I began this volume was that the guy or girl next to me in a bar would contribute to the book. What happened was, late in the editorial process, a public-minded Simon & Schuster employee, Lynda Kanelakos, suggested that it might be interesting to invite fans to offer up personal photos of their favorite NHL teams. Sounds great, I figured. And so we waded into the image-hosting photo website, Flickr, home to five billion or so pictures, sorting through thousands of candid, surprising hockey photos, looking for shots that might decorate this volume.

Next, there came the pesky task of getting permission from all the would-be photographic contributors. Happily, almost everyone wanted their shots in the book.

I'm grateful all these photos made it. Watching old, pre-expansion games for the St. Louis chapter, I couldn't help feel something was missing. The hockey was great–the Richards, Howe, Beliveau, Keon, Bobby Hull and

Orr. But the crowds were too sedate. Their applause seemed canned. In any case, the camera never scanned the stands.

The game was on the ice.

But it isn't, is it? Not completely. Never was. Hockey is played in our heads and hearts–something Trent Frayne and Peter Gzowski understood well. Fans make the game better. Make teams better. Red Kelly, the great Red Wing-Maple Leaf, once told me that it was always difficult playing in Montreal because, "you were playing against 15,000 fans as well as the Canadiens."

Playoffs have become rabid public spectacles where crowds emerge as almost as big a story as the performers: hockey Beatlemania every spring. That sunk home watching Calgary play Tampa in the 2004 Stanley Cup final. Calgary took to the streets celebrating their team and community. Citizens were glad to be caught red-faced on TV and cell phone cameras that scattered their images far and wide.

The public ceremony is repeated every season. Indeed, when a long overtime has ended, how many of us salute the victor with one last email or Facebook remark before hitting the hay.

And so we social network even when we're asleep.

Fan photographs, I believe, make this a more interesting and authentic hockey experience. And I hope you enjoy seeing Guy Lafleur flying on a Montreal tenement wall and Steve Yzerman turned into a Detroit skyscraper as much as I do.

My thanks to Lynda and to everyone who agreed to share their photographic hockey memories.

And thanks to all the writers, coaches, managers and players who inspired these stories.

Now it's time to drop the puck. On with the book!

Stephen Cole, Toronto, May 21, 2011

www.doubleovertime.ca

DOUBLE OVERTIME

ANAHEIM DUCKS

ALTERNATE NICKNAME: Quackers (a pejorative).

FRANCHISE STARTED: Expansion team, 1993.

Baby Duck.

UNIFORMLY SPEAKING: At first, they were the Disney-owned Mighty Ducks and wore the same jerseys as the hockey-playing kids in Uncle Walt's Mighty Ducks film trilogy. (See Duckling, left.) The color scheme was jade, aubergine and gray, what you'd expect in an EL Lay health spa. In 2006, the team adopted a darker look.

HOW COOL?: Baby Duck: 8.0. Hockey-puck black: 7.1.

THE AGONY: The part in *Mighty Ducks 2* where our heroes lose 12–1 to Team Iceland.

THE ECSTASY: The Ducks win the Stanley Cup in 2007.

FANATIC: Stashing away fans: Duck winger George Parros and admirer. (See banditos, left.)

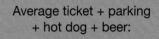

Average ticket + parking + hot dog + beer:
$66.99
(21st highest in the NHL)

Ducks Amuck

The only hockey team to be preceded by a trailer, the Mighty Ducks first appeared in a 1992 movie, the story of a Minnesota pee wee, Gordon Bombay (played by Emilio Estevez), whose life is ruined when he misses a penalty shot. So he becomes an overachieving lawyer with "JUST-WIN" vanity plates. Cops catch him driving drunk, and he's sentenced to community service: coaching a pee-yoo hockey team— think *The Bad News Bears* on skates.

In the first movie, Bombay's team receives magic uniforms from a sporting-goods Santa, Mr. Ducksworth. Suddenly, they're Mighty Ducks, airborne at last when Bombay gives a pep talk: "Have you guys ever seen a flock of ducks flying in perfect formation? Pretty awesome…. Ever seen a duck fight? No way. Why? Because the other animals are afraid. They know if they mess with one duck, they gotta deal with the whole flock."

In *D2* (1994), the Mighty Ducks represent the United States against Team Iceland, coached by Wolf "The Dentist" Stansson, the baddest oral surgeon since Laurence Olivier in

Marathon Man. Before the big game, the Ducks again get new-and-improved uniforms—the same aubergine and jade jerseys the NHL Mighty Ducks wear. Yes, they win again. *D3* (1996) is more of the same. And in all three movies, the good green (read health, munificence and youth) guys face off against— and defeat—black-uniformed villains.

Disney made a fortune off their hockey teams' backs. The trilogy grossed $124 million, and Mighty Ducks sweaters flew off the shelves, winning an ESPY Award as the most fashionable uniform in all sports.

In 2005, Disney sold the Mighty Ducks of Anaheim to an electronics conglomerate, who hired on as GM Brian Burke, a charismatic former hockey player and lawyer who himself could be a character from a movie— a brawling, self-opinionated Irish sergeant, second in command to

John Wayne in a John Ford cavalry picture.

Like Gordon Bombay, Burke gave his team a

fashion makeover. Except he turned Anaheim into … *Wolf Stansson's Team Iceland!* Bye-bye aubergine. Even the "Mighty" disappeared from Mighty Ducks. The newly christened Anaheim Ducks wore bad-guy black and flew below the belt. Burke traded for Chris Pronger—no evil dentist, but a great player and mean as a toothache. Another swap brought

George Parros in cruise missile control.

4

George Parros, an enforcer with the look of a WWF villain.

And forget about Gordon Bombay's PG pacifism. Burke's Ducks played like they'd just heard the big speech from *Patton*. You know, the R-rated one that goes: "Now I want you to remember that no bastard ever won a war dying for his country. He won it by making the other poor bastard die for his country."

Wearing Darth Vader pajamas, the Anaheim Ducks flew through the 2007 playoffs. Oh, they were good. And bad, effectively mean, handing out double doses of punishment along the boards—Brad May and Ryan Getzlaf taking out Vancouver's Willie Mitchell, then, later in the same series, Pronger and Rob Niedermayer harassing

Jannik Hansen to set up an overtime winner. Next round, against Detroit, Pronger was suspended for elbowing Tomas Holmstrom. Against Ottawa, he was penalized a game for knocking Dean McAmmond silly.

For Mighty Duck purists, there was a sentimental moment: When Ryan Getzlaf, their best forward, threw the Stanley Cup over his head (see below), his face took on the Scrooge McDuck scowl from Anaheim's good old aubergine crest.

Scrooge McDuck: Ryan Getzlaf.

BOSTON BRUINS

ALTERNATE NICKNAMES: Broons, B's.

FRANCHISE STARTED: 1924.

UNIFORMLY SPEAKING: Owner Charles Adams owned a grocery chain with a brown-and-yellow motif. The Bruins nickname was the result of a rigged contest: fans were asked to provide the name of an animal, and it had to have "size, strength, agility, ferocity and cunning...in the color brown." Couldn't be anything but a bear, right? Doesn't matter, all Bruins uniforms are great.

HOW COOL?: Black home jersey: 10.0. Throwback yellow: 10.0. White away: 9.0.

Bruin cubs.

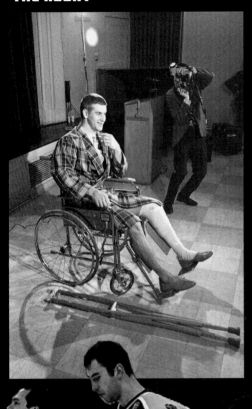

FANATIC: Excess, thy name is Boston Bruin, Zdeno Chara, one of the tallest (6'7"), fittest, fasting-shooting players in NHL history. Zdeno's father was a Greco-Roman wrestler on Czechoslovakia's 1976 Olympic team. Dad made an obstacle course in the backyard to encourage his son's development. Trees were outfitted with pull-up bars and punching bags. Every time he passed a tree, Little Zee had to do a series of pull-ups or work the bag. The Charas also encouraged language skills. Zdeno speaks seven: Slovak, Czech, Polish, Swedish, Russian, German and English. As a result of spending seven hours a day in off-season training, Chara is a four-time winner of the NHL All-Star game hardest-shot competition. In the 2011 contest, he shot a puck 105.9 miles per hour. What did you do with your 2008 summer holiday? Zdeno climbed Mt. Kilimanjaro.

The Big Z, Zdeno Chara, number 33.

Average ticket + parking
+ hot dog + beer:
$87.15
(7th highest in the NHL)

Profiles in Courage

That's President John Fitzgerald Kennedy watching brothers Bobby and Ted in a pickup hockey game in Hyannis Port, Massachusetts, a month before Christmas 1960. Children Caroline and John are on his right. Ethel, Bobby's wife, is second on his left. The venue is Joseph Kennedy Memorial Rink, named after JFK's older brother, a pilot whose plane exploded in World War II.

Hockey in Boston, like its greatest political family, is the story of valor and often tragically shortened careers—a tale tied together with physical and emotional scars as wide as the blue line.

The story begins at the university the Kennedys attended: Harvard, where hockey was played as far back as 1898. Rivalries with Yale, Princeton and Dartmouth ensued. Because of hockey's Ivy League tradition, Boston was the home of the NHL's first American team, in 1924. That ice sports were popular here is evident in the Bruins' first sales pitch: fans were allowed a free skate after games.

To broaden its fan base, Boston extolled players' working-stiff bona fides. Historian Aidan O'Hara elaborates, "Notes in a 1926 game program point out 'Lionel Hitchman is a salesmen in the off season … Jimmy Herberts is a mariner.'" A 1927 program had Eddie Shore in perpetual servitude, "[selling] automobiles when he isn't shoveling a million tons of coal into a locomotive."

Soon the Bruins, playing out of Boston Garden,[1] were carelessly tough, working-class heroes. That aura remains. Whenever a crime movie puts on a Boston South End accent, it inevitably turns to hockey.[2]

Speaking of heroes, here are seven profiles in battered-Bruin courage.

---

[1] The Boston hockey rink was christened Boston Madison Square Garden. The "Madison Square" quickly vanished from public use.

[2] Robert Mitchum's character gets rubbed out on his way to a Bruins game in *The Friends of Eddie Coyle* (1972). *Mystic River* (2003) begins with kids playing ball hockey. Bruins sweaters and references pop in *The Town* (2010) and *Good Will Hunting* (1997).

Bobby Orr

It's impossible for those who were young when they first saw Bobby not to become foolish talking about him. He was a defenseman who led the NHL in scoring; a seeming contradiction with one sporting parallel: Babe Ruth topped the majors in homers as a pitcher in 1918. In 1969–70, Orr won the Norris, Art Ross, Hart and Conn Smythe trophies. He was 21, but looked five years younger, like a supermarket bag boy. He was a 12-year-old's daydream—a downhill skier transplanted to a rink, flying past waving opponents. Like a kid's jeans, his legs always seemed to need a patch at the knees. There were seven surgeries. He came back, good as new, after six. He was the best hockey player of his generation—beautiful as your first girlfriend.

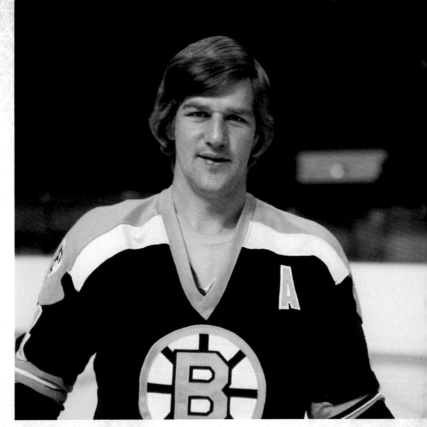

Eddie Shore

The best player of his era, Shore was the son of a wealthy Saskatchewan rancher who lost his fortune to bad investments, teaching Eddie to look out for number two (his Boston numeral). His School of Hard Knocks diploma arrived in his first NHL season, 1926–27, when the Montreal Maroons carved Eddie's head into a Halloween pumpkin. "Here's a poultice for your face," GM Art Ross said later, handing him a check for $500.

Shore played 55 minutes a game, exhibiting incredible endurance. He once missed the team's train to Montreal, so he drove there through a snowstorm—16 hours on the road, staring out the side window, his head a block of ice because his windshield wipers jammed, arriving for a game against the Canadiens that Boston won 1–0.

Shore scored the goal.

Teammate Billy Coutu cut off Shore's ear in practice. Eddie visited doctors, holding the tattered shell against his head until he found a surgeon who agreed to sew it back. Of course, he refused the expense of an anesthetic.

Later, Shore bought and starred on the minor-league Springfield Indians while playing for Boston. Five games, seven nights, two paychecks. After he quit the NHL, he continued managing Springfield, ignoring five heart attacks. His madness ripened. He was Kurtz up river. Eddie forced players to tap dance to improve their dexterity; strung goalies up with a noose to encourage a standup style; crowding 80, he punched out a reporter who bothered him.

The Kraut Line

Milt Schmidt, Woody Dumart and Bobby Bauer grew up in Kitchener, Ontario, becoming famous in the minors as the Kraut Line. The trio roomed together in Boston, where their nickname took on a new meaning when Hitler invaded Europe. They considered what to do at night, in trains rattling between NHL cities. The boys were in their prime, having taken Boston to Cup wins in 1939 and 1941. After Pearl Harbor, the trio enlisted in the Royal Canadian Air Force, returning to Kitchener to tell their folks. As he left, Schmidt asked his mom, "Mind if I change my name to Smith?" They had a last game in Montreal and, given everything, they worried what would happen. On February 11, 1942, the Kraut Line scored 22 points. Boston beat Montreal 8–1. Montreal and Bruin players lifted them off the ice on their shoulders as the crowd sang "Auld Lang Syne." Schmidt never bothered changing his name.

Ray Bourque

Everyday Ray, the ordinary guy as star. Never flashy, always there, 30–35 minutes a game from 1979–2000 for the Bruins, before taking a spring ski holiday in Colorado to win the Stanley Cup with the Avalanche in 2000. If Eddie Shore had a good shrink, he might have been Ray Bourque.

Cam Neely

Say Bobby Orr's and Terry O'Reilly's parents never met. Instead, Bobby's dad and Terry's mom fell in love and had a child. He would have been Cam Neely's twin (1986–96). Cam scored 50 goals in three different seasons, the last time on legs so bad he only played 49 games.

Terry O'Reilly

A career Bruin (1971–85), O'Reilly worked harder than anyone else. Encouragement made him better. It was as if he channeled the will of the Garden crowd. He was a fighter-captain who could score—as unlikely a sum of talents as Bobby Orr, when you think of it.

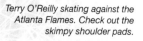
Ray Bourque before a game.

Terry O'Reilly skating against the Atlanta Flames. Check out the skimpy shoulder pads.

Don Cherry

Proof that God has a soft spot for old hockey players, Don was a minor leaguer who became a hockey star coach for the Bruins (1974–79) by daring to take a lunch bucket to the Stanley Cup banquet. Later, he evolved into a superstar hockey analyst by daring to be himself, becoming the poet laureate of Canadian tap rooms. Here's a couple of his poems, culled from radio and TV:

The Taxi Squad (Spring 2009)

It was back in the '60s
— I forget what '60 it was —
We were in the minor leagues
We were going to go to Rochester
Joe Crozier bought a new car
A Dodge Charger
And he says to me,
"You're not going to make
The Toronto Maple Leafs.
I don't want to send
My new car out to Vancouver.
I want you to drive it
From Peterborough
To Vancouver."
Give me that again?
He said, "I want you to drive my car."
Well, I thought, what's the difference?
I'm not going to make the Leafs
So I skipped training camp
I said, "Yes, I'll go if you give me Brian"
— Kilrea had a bad back —
We got in the car and it took us
Four or five days
Then we stopped and had some
Chinese food

Mom and Pops (Fall 2008)

My mother heard me say "beer" all the time
And she phones me and says,
"It sounds so bummy—'beer'—
I don't want you saying 'beer' all the time"
So 26 years ago I said
I was going out to have a few pops

Fight Over a Woman (Fall 1989)

It was a tip shot
A guy tried to get it over the blue line
And a guy tipped it
Went right over my head
And it hit this poor lady in the face
When you come to the games
Keep your eyes on the puck
I'm telling you
I've seen some awful smacks
And it's always a woman yapping away
Ron MacLean: No, lots of fans…
What are you talking… both genders
Get involved in talking about the game.
Look at the game, but don't blame women, men or anyone else
Don: What a wimp

No Doubting Thomas

Boston Bruins have another Stanley Cup. And one more inspirational, never-give-up hero. The Bruins won the 2011 Cup courtesy of Tim Thomas, a long shot overachiever with a "battle-fly" stance who did not nail down a starting goalie's job in the NHL until age 32. Before that, he'd paid more dues than Boston Teamsters Local 25, stopping pucks in Finland, Sweden, Houston, Hamilton, Providence and Detroit (the IHL Vipers, not the Wings). A blue-collar kid whose parents hocked their wedding rings and moved from Flint to De-troit, Michigan, to give their son a hockey chance, Thomas developed an unorthodox, combative style that mirrored his aggressive yet carefree nature. He made the 2011 playoffs a joy to watch, throwing himself at shooters, smiling on the job—a 37-year-old kid playing ball hockey for the Stanley Cup. In two months, he washed away a lifetime of Bruin nightmares—from too many men on the ice (he beat Montreal!) to the four-game collapse in 2010 (beat Philly, too). Tim Thomas will never have to buy another beer in New England.

BUFFALO SABRES

ALTERNATE NICKNAMES: Sabs, Swords.

FRANCHISE STARTED: Woolworth's heir Seymour H. Knox III lettered at Yale in hockey. He and brother Northrup R. Knox tried unsuccessfully to purchase an NHL expansion team in 1967. The brothers, and Western New York, were finally rewarded with a franchise in 1970.

UNIFORMLY SPEAKING: Fabulously rich, polo-playing Seymour threw a wing on the Albright-Knox Art Gallery in 1962. Subsequent owners haven't always been philanthropists. Nevertheless, like most rich kids, the Sabres still have too many clothes to wear. Here, in logo-motion, on the back of fans and players, is a history of the Sabres' ever-changing, often-curious, crest.

HOW COOL?: Was that Seymour Knox or See More Uniforms? Don't go changing to try and please us, Buffalo. We love you just the way you are. Original jersey: Home: 7.8. Away: 7.4.

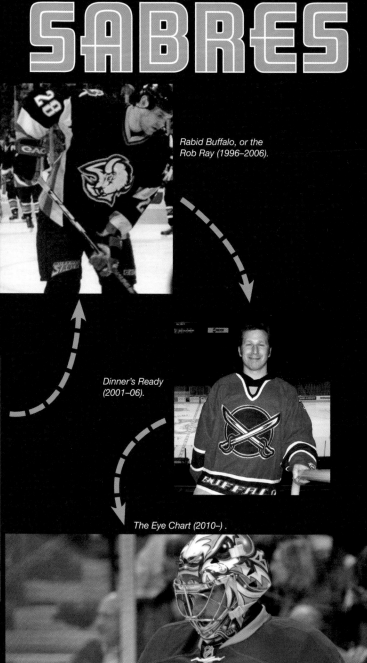

Rabid Buffalo, or the Rob Ray (1996–2006).

Dinner's Ready (2001–06).

The Eye Chart (2010–).

Classic original jersey featuring General Custer's crossed-swords logo (1970–96; 2010–).

40. Lindy Ruff (1979–89)
39. Tim Horton (1972–74)
38. Tyler Myers (2009–)
37. Tony McKegney (1978–83)
36. Stu Barnes (1999–2003)
35. Donald Audette (1990–98, 2001)
34. Ric Seiling (1977–86)
33. Alexei Zhitnik (1995–2004)
32. Jim Lorentz (1972–78)
31. Jay McKee (1995–2006)
30. Rob Ray (1989–2003)
29. Larry Playfair (1978–86, 1988–90)
28. Brian Campbell (1999–2008)
27. Thomas Vanek (2005–)
26. Miroslav Satan (1997–2004)
25. Jerry "King Kong" Korab (1973–80, 1983–85)
24. Roger Crozier (1970–76)
23. Tom Barrasso (1983–88)
22. Pierre Turgeon (1987–91)
21. Don Edwards (1976–82)

20. Dale Hawerchuk (1990–95)
19. Bill Hajt (1973–87)
18. Mike Foligno (1981–90)
17. Chris Drury (2003–07)
16. Daniel Briere (2003–07)
15. Phil Housley (1982–90)
14. Michael Peca (1995–2000)
13. Dave Andreychuk (1982–93, 2000–01)
12. Don "Luuuuuuuce" (1971–81)
11. René Robert (1972–79)
10. Jim Schoenfeld (1972–81, 1984–85)
9. Ryan Miller (2002–)
8. Alexander Mogilny (1989–95)
7. Craig Ramsay (1971–85)
6. Mike Ramsey (1979–93)
5. Danny Gare (1974–81)
4. Rick Martin (1971–81)
3. Pat LaFontaine (1991–97)
2. Gilbert Perreault (1970–87)
1. Dominik Hasek (1992–2001)

3—Buffalo Memorial Auditorium, Buffalo, N. Y.

OB-H2470

FANATIC: Sabres play-by-play man Rick Jeanneret is an excitable shouter with lots of trademark calls—"On the top shelf where Mama hides the cookies" being his most famous. Our favorites include "There have been more cheap shots in this game than in a Mexican cantina during happy hour!" and "Holy Zhitnik!"

Average ticket + parking + hot dog + beer:
$61.43
(25th highest in the NHL)

Stand Tall, Buffalo

The economy is in the tank. The football Bills are doing tricks to survive, leasing their services to Toronto once a year. The Sabres' next-to-last owner, John Rigas, was arrested for bank, wire and securities fraud. Sometimes, it seems being a Buffalo sports fan is a ceaseless incoming tide of bad memories. At the turn of the century, Buffalo was twice screwed by the law: First, the Sabres lost the Stanley Cup in June 1999, when Brett Hull scored a triple-overtime goal that, under existing NHL rules, shouldn't have counted. Six months later, in January 2000, the Bills dropped a playoff game in Nashville on a last-second kickoff return, during which a Titans player threw a forward pass from the 24-yard line to the 26 that was ruled a lateral. Some millennium! If it seems like it's always snowing on Buffalo, that's because it is. Nine months after the Bills–Tennessee football game, dubbed the Music City Miracle, 35 inches of snow hit Buffalo just before Thanksgiving. Thanks a lot, God. But enough—let's stop torturing ourselves. Here, in honor of number 11, Gilbert Perreault, are ten-plus-one great Buffalo hockey men and memories.

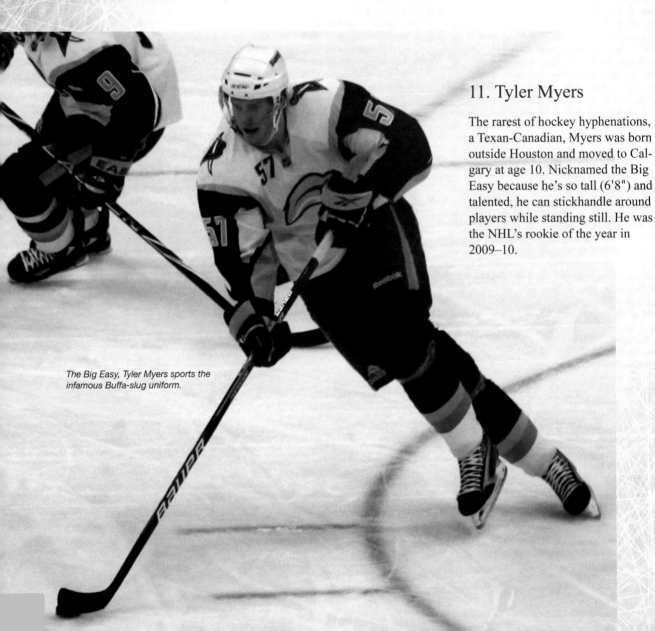

The Big Easy, Tyler Myers sports the infamous Buffa-slug uniform.

11. Tyler Myers

The rarest of hockey hyphenations, a Texan-Canadian, Myers was born outside Houston and moved to Calgary at age 10. Nicknamed the Big Easy because he's so tall (6'8") and talented, he can stickhandle around players while standing still. He was the NHL's rookie of the year in 2009–10.

10. Danny Gare

So good he broke up the French Connection, moving René Robert back to the point on power plays, Gare established the prototype of the diminutive, endlessly chugging Sabre forward. See also Michel Briere, Derek Roy, Nathan Gerbe and Tyler Ennis.

9. Alexander Mogilny

Ovechkin's boyhood hero and hockey's first Alexander the Great. In the 1992–93 season, Mogilny scored 76 goals in 77 games for the Sabres, most of them in spectacular fashion, sending Sabres' play-by-play man Rick Jeanneret into apoplectic delirium.

Alexander Mogilny doing his Rob Ray impersonation.

8. Pat LaFontaine

This brilliant playmaker combined with Alexander Mogilny for a magical 1992–93 season, collecting 53 goals and 95 assists. A master of the breakaway, if La-la-la-la-Fontaine, as Sabres' announcer Rick Jeanneret called him, were playing in today's shootout NHL, teams would be forced to employ both goalie coaches and psychiatric counselors.

7. The Buffalo chicken wing

It was Good Friday, 1964. The Anchor Bar on Main Street received a shipment of chicken wings instead of the chicken backs they used in their spaghetti. "They were looking at you, like saying, 'I don't belong in the sauce,'" owner Frank Bellissimo told *New Yorker* writer Calvin Trillin. Frank asked his wife, Teressa, to do something with them. She deep fried 'em, threw some hot sauce on the side, thought a bit, then added a few celery stalks and, the perfect finish, blue cheese salad dressing. It being Good Friday, and the Bellissimos being good Catholics, the dish was served after midnight. And the glorious, great-with-a-Genesee Buffalo chicken wing was born. The Anchor still serves 'em. As do hundreds of other local restaurants. Including the Pearl Street Grill and Brewery, blocks from the HSBC Arena.

6. Buffalo chicken-maker, Rob Ray

The hockey player as factory worker, punching other team's tough guys instead of the clock. The Sabres' blue-collar fans appreciated his hard work, both in the corners and the community.

Rob Ray doing his Alexander Mogilny impersonation.

5. Ryan Miller

In 2009–10, Miller proved he was the best goalie in the world, winning the Vezina Trophy along with the MVP award at the Olympics.

4. Dominik Hasek

Mercurial, unorthodox, floppy yet unflappable, Hasek had the fastest reflexes of any goalie ever. His hands were so quick he could defeat the wall in a game of handball. NHL MVP in 1997 and 1998 and Vezina Trophy winner six seasons from 1994–95 to 2000–01, all of them with Buffalo. He was incredible. He was The Dominator.

Dominic Hasek often got rid of his stick so he could free up both hands in the crease.

3. The 7– 6 game

Heroism and valor are possible in defeat. In the 2006 play-offs, Buffalo came within a game of reaching the Stanley Cup final, despite having four of their top six defenseman and three forwards sidelined with injuries. The Sabres never gave up, however. In a playoff encounter with the Ottawa Senators, Buffalo came from behind five times, including a tying goal with 11 seconds left, to defeat the Sens 7–6 on a Chris Drury snap shot in overtime.

2. Beating the Russians

On January 4, 1976, the Buffalo Sabres trounced the Soviet Wings, becoming the first NHL team to defeat a Russian hockey team. The score was 12–6, although the Sabres actually scored 13 times, as defender Jocelyn Guevremont accidentally put one in his own net. The French Connection was particularly well connected this afternoon. Rick Martin was on the ice for eight goals, and one of his slap shots ripped the Russian goalie's glove out of his hand. Little Danny Gare showed off his devastating wrist shot, snapping a goal past a startled Soviet netminder from the outer edge of the right circle. Gare would score two more goals against the Central Red Army in the Sabres' memorable, and even more impressive, 6–1 defeat of what was the Russian national team on January 3, 1980.

1. The French Connection

They were all born in Quebec, with silver skates on their feet—Gilbert Perreault, Richard Martin and René Robert. The French Connection turned the old Memorial Auditorium into hockey heaven from 1972–79. Perreault (given number 11 because it was Sabre GM Punch Imlach's lucky number) was a lightning-fast, endlessly creative skater who, two or three times a game, turned a rink-long dash into a thrilling slalom run. The late Rick Martin could skate with Perreault and outshoot anybody. If the two seemed like brothers, that's because they slept in adjoining bedrooms in junior hockey—Gilbert boarded at Martin's home during his last season with the Montreal Junior Canadiens. René Robert was a playmaking right winger who was also useful in the corners. The trio were hockey's most exciting forward unit in the 1970s.

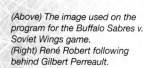

(Above) The image used on the program for the Buffalo Sabres v. Soviet Wings game.
(Right) René Robert following behind Gilbert Perreault.

CALGARY FLAMES

C of red: scenes from outside the Calgary Saddledome during the Flames' 2004 Cup run.

ALTERNATE NICKNAMES: None.

FRANCHISE STARTED: Team started in Atlanta in 1972. "Flames" referred to the fire that consumed Atlanta during the American Civil War. Either that, or the urgent passion Rhett felt for Scarlett in *Gone With the Wind*.

UNIFORMLY SPEAKING: The Calgary Flames' jersey is much the same as the old Atlanta jersey, except the burning *A* is now a burning *C*. The team's old red-orange sweater, with a white *C* (1980–94), was too American football-y. Adding black to the color scheme in 1994 helped. The best Flames uniform yet is the Heritage Classic throwbacks the team wore against Montreal in the 2011 outdoor game—a hybrid of the Calgary Tigers of the 1920s and the current Calgary outfit.

HOW COOL?: Home: 7.6. Away: 6.4. Heritage Classic: 8.8.

"So, you live with your folks?" Atlanta Flames' Willi Plett played for both the Atlanta (1975–80) and Calgary Flames (1980–82)

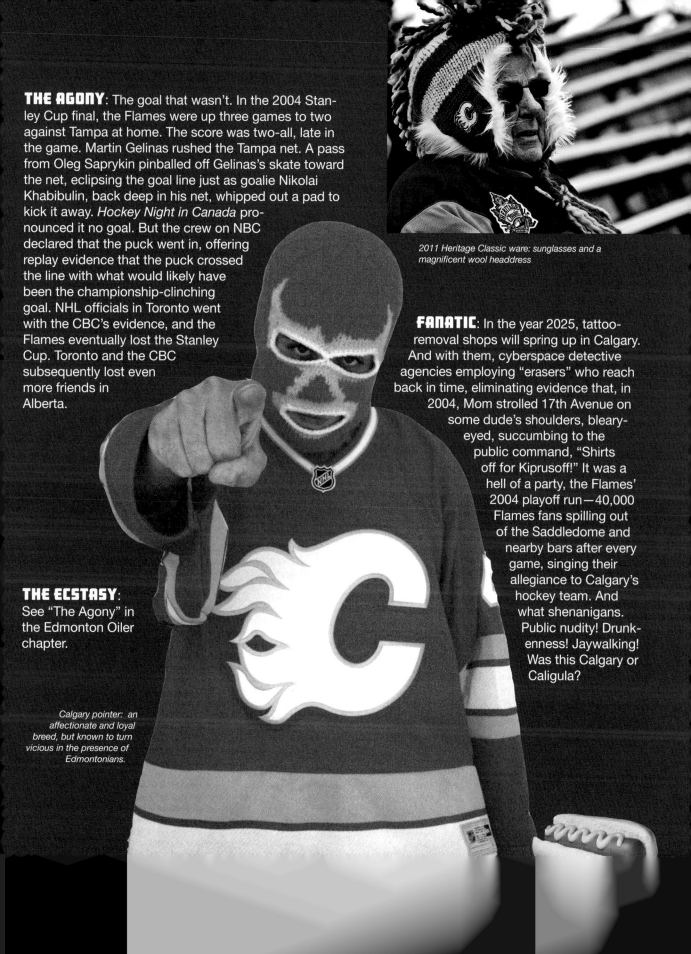

THE AGONY: The goal that wasn't. In the 2004 Stanley Cup final, the Flames were up three games to two against Tampa at home. The score was two-all, late in the game. Martin Gelinas rushed the Tampa net. A pass from Oleg Saprykin pinballed off Gelinas's skate toward the net, eclipsing the goal line just as goalie Nikolai Khabibulin, back deep in his net, whipped out a pad to kick it away. *Hockey Night in Canada* pronounced it no goal. But the crew on NBC declared that the puck went in, offering replay evidence that the puck crossed the line with what would likely have been the championship-clinching goal. NHL officials in Toronto went with the CBC's evidence, and the Flames eventually lost the Stanley Cup. Toronto and the CBC subsequently lost even more friends in Alberta.

2011 Heritage Classic ware: sunglasses and a magnificent wool headdress

FANATIC: In the year 2025, tattoo-removal shops will spring up in Calgary. And with them, cyberspace detective agencies employing "erasers" who reach back in time, eliminating evidence that, in 2004, Mom strolled 17th Avenue on some dude's shoulders, bleary-eyed, succumbing to the public command, "Shirts off for Kiprusoff!" It was a hell of a party, the Flames' 2004 playoff run—40,000 Flames fans spilling out of the Saddledome and nearby bars after every game, singing their allegiance to Calgary's hockey team. And what shenanigans. Public nudity! Drunkenness! Jaywalking! Was this Calgary or Caligula?

THE ECSTASY: See "The Agony" in the Edmonton Oiler chapter.

Calgary pointer: an affectionate and loyal breed, but known to turn vicious in the presence of Edmontonians.

The Hundred-Mile Diet

No team in the NHL is more of a regional operation than the Calgary Flames. Going into the 2009–10 season, its GM and coach, along with three of four assistant coaches, were Prairie boys. Eleven players hailed from Canada's western provinces. Aside from goalie Miikka Kiprusoff, a Finn, the core of the Flames—captain Jarome Iginla, along with assistants Dion Phaneuf and Robyn Regehr—hailed from Alberta and Saskatchewan. Their big off-season acquisition, Jay Bouwmeester, was, like Iginla and Phaneuf, Edmonton-born.

This Big Four—Iginla, Phaneuf, Regehr and Bouwmeester—were also organically grown, graduates of junior teams with small-town western values: Kamloops, Red Deer and Medicine Hat.

Wait, there's more. The coaches of Calgary's AHL farm team, the Abbotsford Flames, were all westerners in 2009–10. As were 20 of the team's 32 top farmhands.

This isn't business as usual in the modern, multicultural NHL. Even Montreal, once the most homegrown of NHL teams, went into 2009–10 with two Americans and a Russian assistant captain. The Toronto Maple Leafs had an American GM, Brian Burke, and coach, Ron Wilson. Furthermore, the Leafs employed but a single Ontario player, John Mitchell, in their 2009 opening-day lineup. Minnesota Wild opened without a Minnesotan. The Boston Bruins? Nary a single New Englander.

Because 2009–10 was a lost season for Calgary—the team could hit and bump, but couldn't score, didn't make the playoffs, and felt compelled to trade Phaneuf, an Oil Patch Kid with perfect hockey genes (dad Paul was in construction; mom Amber was a former figure skater)—it may be argued that the Flames' Hundred-Mile Hockey Diet contained too much roughage. Unhappy fans may suggest that the team had too many gritty, unselfish westerners. That it needed a couple of stylish puck-hogging centers from Ontario or Quebec. That's only a reasonable conclusion, however, if you believe western players share a common DNA with the Flames' 2009–10 management team, GM Duane and coach Brent Sutter, two of six NHL hockey–playing brothers from Viking, Alberta. The Sutters weren't gaudy goal scorers. Duane, Brent, Brian, Darryl, Rich and Ron Sutter were fearless, unrelenting character actors—110-percenters who went into corners like they were looking for the guy who stole their car.

The Sutters were so effective they became an adjective for NHL scouts, who inevitably described flinty defensive forwards as "Sutter-like" wingers.

But can a team have too many Sutters? Too many western Canadians? What is a typical western hockey player? Is he any different—tougher, better, worse—than his central Canadian counterpart? Let's not compare mythologies; let's compare statistics. With the help of hockey historian Paul Patskou and stats guru Norm Pawluck, that's exactly what we've done, manufacturing all-star teams from Canada's western provinces as well as Ontario and Quebec over the last 90 years. We've then asked the ghost of Foster Hewitt, hockey's first and most famous play-by-play man, to decide who would've prevailed in a hypothetical seven-game Dominion Cup playoffs—an every-decade hockey variation of the Canadian Football League's Grey Cup.

Let's get it on, then: the Western Monarchs vs. Eastern Bastards—er, Eastern Royal Canadians.

May the best provinces win!

Western union: Alberta boys Dion Phaneuf and Jarome Iginla before the 2009 NHL All-Star game.

1929 Dominion Cup

Foster Hewitt at the microphone.

Western Monarchs

		POS	H	W	PROV	S/O	GA		HOF
Goalie	Cecil "Tiny" Thompson	G	5'10"	180	AB	12	1.15		x
						G	**A**	**PIM**	
Defense	Eddie Shore	D	5'11"	194	SK	12	17	96	x
	Ivan "Ching" Johnson[1]	D	5'11"	210	MB	10	6	146	x
	Harold "Bullet Joe" Simpson	D	5'10"	175	MB	3	2	25	x
	Mervyn "Red" Dutton	D	6'0"	185	MB	1	3	139	x
1st Line	Frederick "Bun" Cook	LW	5'11"	180	SK	13	5	70	x
	Andy Blair	C	6'2"	177	MB	12	15	41	
	Bill Cook	RW	5'10"	172	SK	15	8	41	x
2nd Line	Paul Thompson	LW	5'11"	180	AB	10	7	38	
	Norm "Dutch" Gainor	C	6'1"	170	MB	14	5	30	
	Harry Oliver	RW	5'8"	146	MB	17	6	23	
Extra Change	Chuck Gardiner	G	6'0"	176	MB				x
	Herb Gardiner	D	5'10"	190	MB				x
	Herbie Lewis	LW	5'9"	160	AB				x
	TOTALS		**5'11"**	**179**		**119**		**649**	**10**

[1] Ivan Ching Johnson missed all but a few games in the 1928-29 season with a broken collarbone, so we used his previous seasons' totals – a clear violation of statistical analysis. But how could you not include the defenceman who made hockey popular in New York?

Eastern Royal Canadians

		POS	H	W	PROV	S/O	GA		HOF
Goalie	Roy "Shrimp" Worters	G	5'3"	135	ON	13	1.15		x
						G	**A**	**PIM**	
Defense	Frank "King" Clancy	D	5'7"	155	ON	13	2	89	x
	Lionel "The Big Train" Conacher	D	6'2"	195	ON	5	2	132	x
	Albert "Battleship" Leduc	D	5'9"	190	PQ	9	2	79	
	Sylvio Mantha	D	5'10"	173	PQ	9	4	56	x
1st Line	Irvine "Ace" Bailey	LW	5'10"	160	ON	22	20	78	x
	Howie Morenz	C	5'9"	165	ON	17	10	47	x
	Carson Cooper	RW	5'7"	160	ON	18	9	14	
2nd Line	Nels "Old Poison" Stewart	LW	6'0"	200	PQ	21	8	74	x
	Frank Boucher	C	5'10"	175	ON	10	16	8	x
	Frank "The Shawville Express" Finnigan	RW	5'9"	165	PQ	15	4	71	x
Extra Change	George Hainsworth	G	5'6"	150	ON				x
	Cy Wentworth	D	5'11"	175	ON				
	Aurele Joliat	LW	5'7"	136	ON				
	TOTALS		**5'10"**	**167**		**152**		**648**	**10**

Here's how to read your starting lineups

GA	goals-against average
S/O	shut outs
G	goals
A	assists
PIM	penalties in minutes
HOF	Hall of Fame

Series: West leads 1–0

Foster's Call:

"Hello, Canada, and hockey fans in the United States and Newfoundland, this is Foster Hewitt reporting from Victoria's Patrick Arena, where the West has prevailed four games to three over the East in what was a spirited, highly entertaining playoff affair. Both teams were in good form, but in the end, the West's Tiny Thompson stood a little taller than the East's 5'3" Shrimp Worters in net, allowing the Prairie boys to defeat Howie Morenz, Ace Bailey and the high-scoring Easterners. It certainly helped that the West had the best player on the ice, Alberta's Eddie Shore."

Incidental Color:

In the fourth game, which took place in the Ottawa Auditorium, hometown defender King Clancy punched Eddie Shore in the face when the western rear guard was on the ice. Shore climbed to his feet, shouting, "I'd like to see you do that again." "Sure thing, Eddie," Clancy responded. "First, you get back down on your hands and knees."

1939 Dominion Cup

Western Monarchs

		POS	H	W	PROV	S/O	GA			HOF
Goalie	Cecil "Tiny" Thompson	G	5'10"	180	AB	7	1.80			x
						G	**A**	**PIM**		
Defense	Eddie Shore	D	5'11"	194	SK	4	14	47		x
	Art Coulter	D	5'11"	195	MB	4	8	90		x
	Walter "Babe" Pratt	D	6'2"	190	MB	2	19	20		x
	Murray "Muzz" Patrick	D	6'2"	215	BC	1	11	64		
1st Line	Johnny Gottselig	LW	5'11"	158	SK	16	23	15		
	Neil Colville	C	5'11"	180	AB	18	19	12		x
	Alex Shibicky	RW	6'0"	185	MB	24	9	24		
2nd Line	David "Sweeney" Schriner	LW	5'11"	175	AB	13	31	20		x
	Clint Smith	C	5'8"	165	MB	21	20	2		x
	Lorne Carr	RW	5'9"	160	SK	20	16	18		
Extra Change	Truk Broda	G	5'9"	165	MB					x
	Tommy Anderson	D	5'10"	175	AB					
	Mel "Sudden Death" Hill	C	5'10"	175	MB					
	TOTALS		**5'11"**	**180**		**136**		**312**	**8**	

Eastern Royal Canadians

		POS	H	W	PROV	S/O	GA			HOF
Goalie	Dave Kerr	G	5'10"	160	ON	6	2.12			
						G	**A**	**PIM**		
Defense	Aubrey "Dit" Clapper	D	6'2"	200	ON	13	13	22		x
	Earl Seibert	D	6'2"	200	ON	4	17	57		x
	Reginald "Red" Horner	D	6'1"	195	ON	4	10	85		x
	Reginald "Hooley" Smith	D	5'10"	155	ON	15	25	4		x
1st Line	Hector "Toe" Blake	LW	5'10"	162	ON	24	23	10		x
	Syl Apps	C	6'0"	185	ON	15	25	4		x
	Johnny "Black Cat" Gagnon	RW	5'5"	150	PQ	12	22	23		
2nd Line	Woody Dumart	LW	6'0"	190	ON	13	14	2		x
	Milt Schmidt	C	6'0"	185	ON	15	17	13		x
	Bobby Bauer	RW	5'7"	160	ON	13	3	4		x
Extra Change	Normie Smith	G	5'7"	165	ON					
	Ehrhardt "Ott" Heller	D	6'0"	175	ON					
	Bill Cowley	C	5'10"	165	ON					x
	TOTALS		**5'10"**	**175**		**134**		**224**	**10**	

Foster's Call:

"Hello, Canada, and hockey fans in the United States and Newfoundland, this is Foster Hewitt reporting from the Montreal Forum, where the East just pulled off a remarkable comeback, stringing together three straight wins to take the series in seven games. The West jumped ahead with wins in games two and three on double-overtime goals by bench player Mel 'Sudden Death' Hill, but the East's strength up the middle—Syl Apps, Milt Schmidt and Bill Cowley—was finally too much for Eddie Shore and company."

Incidental Color:

Canadian prime minister William Lyon Mackenzie King dropped the puck prior to game two at Maple Leaf Gardens. Asked who would win, the PM carefully replied, "The team with the best defense; for surely it is what we prevent rather than what we do that counts most in life."

Series: Tied one-all

1949 Dominion Cup

Western Monarchs

		POS	H	W	PROV	S/O	GA		HOF
Goalie	Chuck Rayner	G	5'11"	190	SK	7	2.90		x
						G	**A**	**PIM**	
Defense	"Black Jack" Stewart	D	5'11"	180	MB	4	11	96	x
	Ken Reardon	D	5'11"	180	MB	3	13	103	x
	Glen Harmon	D	5'8"	175	MB	8	12	44	
	Fernie Flaman	D	5'10"	190	SK	4	12	122	x
1st Line	Harry Watson	LW	6'1"	207	SK	26	19	0	x
	Sid Abel	C	5'11"	170	SK	28	26	49	x
	Gordie Howe	RW	6'1"	205	SK	12	25	57	x
2nd Line	Doug Bentley	LW	5'8"	145	SK	23	46	38	x
	Max Bentley	C	5'9"	158	SK	19	22	18	x
	Bill Mosienko	RW	5'8"	160	MB	17	25	6	x
Extra Change	Turk Broda	G	5'9"	188	MB				x
	Jimmy Thomson	D	6'0" .	188	MB				
	Elmer Lach	C	5'10"	165	SK				x
	TOTALS		5'10"	178		151		543	12

Eastern Royal Canadians

		POS	H	W	PROV	S/O	GA		HOF
Goalie	Bill Durnan	G	6'0"	190	ON	10	2.10		x
						G	**A**	**PIM**	
Defense	Bill Quackenbush	D	5'11'	180	ON	6	11	0	x
	Emile "Butch" Bouchard	D	6'2"	205	PQ	3	3	42	x
	Doug Harvey	D	5'11"	190	PQ	3	13	87	x
	Leonard "Red" Kelly	D	6'0"	195	ON	5	11	10	x
1st Line	Ted Lindsay	LW	5'8"	163	ON	26	28	97	x
	Jim Conacher	C	5'10"	155	ON	26	23	155	
	Maurice "Rocket" Richard	RW	5'10"	180	PQ	20	18	110	x
2nd Line	Roy Conacher	LW	6'1"	175	ON	26	42	6	x
	Milt Schmidt	C	6'0"	185	ON	10	22	25	x
	Howie Meeker	RW	5'9"	165	ON	7	7	46	
Extra Change	Harry Lumley	G	6'0"	200	ON				X
	Gus Mortson	D	5'11"	195	ON				x
	Gaye Stewart	LW	5'11"	170	ON				
	TOTALS		5'11"	182		142		578	11

Series: 2-1 West

Foster's Call:

"Hello, Canada, and hockey fans in the United States and Newfoundland, Foster Hewitt reporting here from the Winnipeg Amphitheatre—the Ampf—where the West has finished off the East four games to two to take what was a real barn burner of a tournament—a civil war, you might say, brother against brother—with skirmishes breaking out between Ted Lindsay and Gordie Howe, linemates in Detroit during the regular season, of course, and Montreal's Rocket Richard and Kenny Reardon, best of friends usually, but in this series, mortal enemies."

Incidental Color:

The East appeared headed for victory after Richard scored four in game two in Montreal, his only goals of the series, but then the West stormed back. The turning point was game four, in Regina, when Howe appeared to stumble behind the net, catching Lindsay with an errant stick. Lindsay, who injured Howe earlier in the series, missed the remainder of the playoff with a fractured ankle.

1959 Dominion Cup

Western Monarchs

		POS	H	W	PROV	S/O	GA		HOF
Goalie	Terry Sawchuk	G	5'11"	190	MB	5	3.09		x
						G	**A**	**PIM**	
Defense	Tom Johnson	D	6'0"	180	MB	10	29	76	x
	Bill Gadsby	D	6'0"	190	AB	5	46	56	x
	Bob Turner	D	6'0"	178	SK	4	24	66	
	Jack Evans	D	6'0"	180	AB	1	8	75	
1st Line	Vic Stasiuk	LW	6'1"	185	AB	27	33	65	
	Norm Ullman	C	5'10"	185	AB	22	36	63	x
	Gordie Howe	RW	6'1"	205	SK	32	46	57	x
2nd Line	Johnny Bucyk	LW	6'0"	215	AB	24	36	36	x
	Larry Popein	C	5'9"	170	SK	13	21	28	
	Andy Bathgate	RW	6'0"	183	MB	40	48	48	x
Extra Change	Glenn Hall	G	5'11"	190	SK				x
	Fernie Flaman	D	5'10"	190	SK				
	Eddie Litzenberger	RW	6'3"	194	SK				
	TOTALS		6'0"	188		183		551	8

Eastern Royal Canadians

		POS	H	W	PROV	S/O	GA		HOF
Goalie	Jacques Plante	G	6'0"	175	PQ	9	2.16		x
						G	**A**	**PIM**	
Defense	Marcel Pronovost	D	5'11"	180	PQ	11	21	44	x
	Doug Harvey	D	5'11"	190	PQ	4	16	61	x
	Pierre Pilote	D	5'10"	178	PQ	7	37	79	x
	Leonard "Red" Kelly	D	6'0"	195	ON	8	13	34	x
1st Line	Dickie Moore	LW	5'10"	185	PQ	41	55	61	x
	Jean Beliveau	C	6'3"	205	PQ	45	46	67	x
	Bernard "Boom Boom" Geoffrion	RW	5'9"	170	PQ	22	30	30	x
2nd Line	Alex Delvecchio	LW	5'11"	180	ON	19	35	6	x
	Henri Richard	C	5'7"	160	PQ	21	33	20	x
	Jerry Toppazzini	RW	6'0"	180	ON	21	33	51	
Extra Change	Gump Worsley	G	5'7"	165	PQ				x
	Leo Boivin	D	5'7"	177	ON				x
	Maurice "Rocket" Richard	RW	6'0"	175	PQ				x
	TOTALS		5'10"	180		208		453	13

Foster's Call:

"Hello, Canada, and hockey fans in the United States, Foster Hewitt reporting from Maple Leaf Gardens, where the East has survived a determined challenge from their western rivals, taking the series four games to three. The East won the final game as they did the series—taking advantage of power-play opportunities. The East scored 11 goals with a man advantage. Really, they just threw out Montreal's power play and that did the trick—Doug Harvey and Boom Boom Geoffrion on the points, with Dickie Moore, John Belly-veau and the Rocket, Maurice Richard, who only played on the power play this series, up front."

Incidental Color:

After the decisive Saturday-night win in Toronto, Doug Harvey drove the team bus across the border into Buffalo, where the bars were still open.

Series: 2-2 tie

1969 Dominion Cup

Western Monarchs

		POS	H	W	PROV	S/O	GA		HOF
Goalie	Glenn Hall	G	5'11"	190	SK	8	2.97		x
						G	**A**	**PIM**	
Defense	"Terrible" Ted Green	D	5'11"	185	MB	8	38	99	
	Ted Harris	D	6'2"	175	MB	7	18	102	
	Jim Neilson	D	6'2"	205	SK	10	34	95	
	Dallas Smith	D	5'11"	175	MB	4	24	74	
1st Line	John Ferguson	LW	6'0"	198	BC	29	23	185	
	Red Berenson	C	6'0"	195	SK	35	47	43	
	Gordie Howe	RW	6'1"	205	SK	44	59	58	x
2nd Line	John Bucyk	LW	6'0"	215	AB	24	18	18	x
	Norm Ullman	C	5'10"	185	AB	35	42	41	x
	Johnny McKenzie	RW	5'9"	170	AB	29	27	99	
Extra Change	Cesare Maniago	G	6'2"	175	BC				
	Ed Van Impe	D	5'10"	210	SK				
	Garry Unger	C	5'11"	170	AB				
	TOTALS		6'0"	188		233		814	4

Eastern Royal Canadians

		POS	H	W	PROV	S/O	GA		HOF
Goalie	Ed Giacomin	G	5'11"	180	ON	2	2.55		x
						G	**A**	**PIM**	
Defense	Bobby Orr	D	6'0"	200	ON	21	43	133	x
	Tim Horton	D	5'10"	180	ON	11	29	111	x
	Pat Stapleton	D	5'8"	180	ON	6	50	44	
	Jean-Claude Tremblay	D	5'10"	170	PQ	7	32	18	
1st Line	Bobby Hull	LW	5'10"	180	ON	58	49	48	x
	Phil Esposito	C	6'1"	185	ON	49	77	79	
	Yvan Cournoyer	RW	5'7"	172	PQ	43	44	31	x
2nd Line	Frank Mahovlich	LW	6'1"	205	ON	49	28	38	x
	Stan Mikita	C	5'7"	169	ON	30	67	52	x
	Rod Gilbert	RW	5'9"	175	PQ	28	44	22	x
Extra Change	Gerry Cheevers	G	5'11"	180	ON				x
	Serge Savard	D	6'3"	210	PQ				x
	Jean Ratelle	C	6'1"	175	PQ				x
	TOTALS		5'11"	183		304		576	12

Foster's Call:

"Hello, Canada, and hockey fans in the United States, Foster Hewitt reporting from Edmonton Gardens, where the East has once again taken care of business, winning four out of five encounters against a game but outmatched West team. Really, it was a case of too much Bobby—Orr and Hull, that is. They were really skating, giving the big western defense—Ted Harris, Teddy Green and Jim Neilson—fits. As was little Yvan Corn-wire, Montreal's Roadrunner, who scored a hat trick in the final game."

Incidental Color:

Glenn Hall's backup, Cesare Maniago finished game two in Montreal, allowing five goals. East defender Bobby Orr contributed a goal and four assists, prompting *Globe and Mail* sportswriter Dick Beddoes to lead off his game story, "Render unto Cesare Maniago the things that are Cesare Maniago's, and unto Bobby Orr the things that are Bobby Orr's."

Series: 3–2, East

1979 Dominion Cup

Western Monarchs

		POS	H	W	PROV	S/O	GA		HOF
Goalie	Glen "Chico" Resch	G	5'9"	195	SK	2	2.50		
						G	**A**	**PIM**	
Defense	Ron Greschner	D	6'2"	205	SK	17	36	66	
	Brad Maxwell	D	6'2"	195	MB	9	28	148	
	Phil Russell	D	6'2"	200	AB	8	23	122	
	Harold Snepsts	D	6'3"	210	AB	7	24	130	
1st Line	Clark Gillies	LW	6'3"	210	SK	35	56	68	x
	Bryan Trottier	C	5'11"	195	SK	47	87	50	x
	Lanny McDonald	RW	6'0"	190	AB	43	42	32	x
2nd Line	Brian Sutter	LW	5'11"	180	AB	41	39	165	
	Bobby Clarke	C	5'10"	176	MB	16	57	68	x
	Dave "Tiger" Williams	RW	5'11"	190	SK	19	20	398	
Extra Change	John Davidson	G	6'3"	205	AB				
	Jimmy Watson	D	6'0"	190	BC				
	Robert "Butch" Goring	C	5'10"	165	MB				
	TOTALS		6'0"	193		244		1247	4

Ontario-Quebec All-Stars

		POS	H	W	PROV	S/O	GA		HOF
Goalie	Ken Dryden	G	6'4"	207	ON	5	2.30		x
						G	**A**	**PIM**	
Defense	Denis Potvin	D	6'0"	205	PQ	31	70	58	x
	Larry Robinson	D	6'4"	225	ON	16	45	33	x
	Serge Savard	D	6'3"	210	PQ	7	26	30	x
	Guy Lapointe	D	6'0"	185	PQ	13	42	43	x
1st Line	Bill Barber	LW	6'0"	185	ON	33	46	30	x
	Marcel Dionne	C	5'8"	185	PQ	59	71	30	x
	Guy Lafleur	RW	6'0"	180	PQ	52	77	28	x
2nd Line	Steve Shutt	LW	6'0"	180	ON	37	40	51	x
	Darryl Sittler	C	6'0"	190	ON	36	51	69	x
	Mike Bossy	RW	6'0"	185	PQ	69	57	25	x
Extra Change	Bernie Parent	G	5'10"	170	PQ				x
	Brad Park	D	6'0"	190	ON				x
	Bob Gainey	LW	6'2"	190	ON				x
	TOTALS		6'0"	192		358		369	14

Foster's Call:

"Hello, Canada, and hockey fans in the United States, Foster Hewitt reporting from the Montreal Forum, where the East has once again come out on top, outlasting the West four games to three in what was a real super, super series. It started off looking like it was going to be another cakewalk for the East, as their big defensemen completely shut down the opposition, leading the team to easy wins in Montreal and Quebec City. But the West switched from Chico Resch to John Davidson in net in Winnipeg, and Davidson, along with Bryan Trottier and Bobby Clarke, came on, winning three of the next four, really making it a tight series. And it took some overtime magic by Darryl Sittler with a breakaway goal to allow the East a hard-earned win."

Incidental Color:

The East's team changed its name to the Ontario-Quebec All-Stars, triggering a furor in Parliament. The All-Stars were roundly booed during the western swing. In the National Assembly in Quebec City, there were calls for the team to be called the Quebec-Ontario All-Stars during games played in Montreal and Quebec City.

Series: 4-2, East

1989 Dominion Cup

Western Monarchs

		POS	H	W	PROV	S/O	GA		HOF
Goalie	Grant Fuhr	G	5'10"	184	AB	1	3.83		x
						G	**A**	**PIM**	
Defense	James Patrick	D	6'2"	200	MB	11	36	41	
	Glen Wesley	D	6'1"	207	AB	19	35	61	
	Dave Manson	D	6'2"	202	SK	18	36	352	
	Dave Babych	D	6'2"	215	AB	6	41	54	
1st Line	Glenn Anderson	LW	5'11"	175	BC	16	48	93	x
	Mark Messier	C	6'1"	190	AB	36	61	130	x
	Cam Neely	RW	6'1"	218	BC	37	38	190	x
2nd Line	Geoff Courtnall	LW	6'0"	195	BC	42	38	112	
	Steve Yzerman	C	5'11"	185	BC	65	90	61	x
	Brett Hull	RW	5'10"	200	MB	43	33	4	x
Extra Change	Mike Vernon	G	5'9"	167	AB				
	Brad McCrimmon	D	5'11"	193	SK				
	Joe Sakic	C	5'11"	195	BC				x
	TOTALS		6'0"	195		294		1098	7

Ontario-Quebec All-Stars

		POS	H	W	PROV	S/O	GA		HOF
Goalie	Patrick Roy	G	6'2"	190	PQ	4	2.47		x
						G	**A**	**PIM**	
Defense	Ray Bourque	D	5'11"	220	PQ	18	43	52	x
	Scott Stevens	D	6'2"	225	ON	7	61	265	x
	Paul Coffey	D	6'0"	200	ON	33	83	195	x
	Kevin Lowe	D	6'2"	200	PQ	7	18	99	
1st Line	Steve Larmer	LW	5'10"	190	ON	43	44	54	
	Wayne Gretzky	C	6'0"	185	ON	54	114	26	x
	Mario Lemieux	RW	6'4"	235	PQ	85	114	100	x
2nd Line	Luc Robitaille	LW	6'1"	204	PQ	46	52	64	x
	Dale Hawerchuk	C	5'11"	185	ON	41	55	28	x
	Rick Tocchet	RW	6'0"	214	ON	45	36	183	
Extra Change	Kirk McLean	G	6'0"	182	ON				
	Steve Duchesne	D	5'11"	195	PQ				
	Kevin Dineen	RW	5'11"	190	PQ				
	TOTALS		6'0"	201		383		1066	8

Foster's Call:

"Hello, Canada, and hockey fans in the United States, Foster Hewitt reporting from Copps Coliseum in Hamilton, where the East has pulled out a real squeaker, winning the series and the final match by the identical score of four to three. Speaking of three, the East threw out three centers on the same line—Mario Lemieux, Dale Hawerchuk and, of course, Wayne Gretzky—late in the third period, and they all combined on the final goal, a real beauty by Lemieux, with a little under two minutes left to play."

Incidental Color:

The first star of the game in all three western wins, Mark Messier refused to answer reporters' questions about Wayne Gretzky during the series. "After it's all done, he's my friend," he said. "Right now, I don't want to talk about him. Don't want to hear his name. I don't even want to hear anyone humming '99 Bottles of Beer on the Wall.'"

Series: 5-2, East

1999 Dominion Cup

Western Monarchs

		POS	H	W	PROV	S/O	GA		
Goalie	Eddie Belfour	G	6'0"	215	MB	5	1.99		
						G	**A**	**PIM**	
Defense	Scott Niedermayer	D	6'1"	194	BC	11	35	46	
	Darryl Sydor	D	6'1"	211	AB	14	34	50	
	Wade Redden	D	6'2"	209	SK	8	21	54	
	Derek Morris	D	6'0"	221	AB	7	27	73	
1st Line	Paul Kariya	LW	5'10"	180	BC	39	62	40	
	Joe Sakic	C	5'11"	195	BC	41	55	29	
	Theoren Fleury	RW	5'6"	180	SK	40	54	86	
2nd Line	Rod Brind'Amour	LW	6'1"	205	BC	24	50	54	
	Steve Yzerman	C	5'11"	185	BC	29	45	42	
	Jarome Iginla	RW	6'1"	209	AB	28	23	58	
Extra Change	Byron Dafoe	G	5'11"	175	BC				
	Sheldon Souray	D	6'4"	233	AB				
	Mark Messier	C	6'1"	205	AB				
	TOTALS		6'0"	201		246		532	

Ontario-Quebec All-Stars

		POS	H	W	PROV	S/O	GA		
Goalie	Martin Brodeur	G	6'2"	210	PQ	4	1.79		
						G	**A**	**PIM**	
Defense	Ray Bourque	D	6'1"	194	PQ	10	47	34	
	Rob Blake	D	6'4"	225	ON	12	23	128	
	Eric Desjardins	D	6'1"	205	PQ	15	36	38	
	Chris Pronger	D	6'6"	220	ON	13	36	133	
1st Line	Brendan Shanahan	LW	6'3"	220	ON	31	27	123	
	Eric Lindros	C	6'4"	245	ON	40	53	120	
	Claude Lemieux	RW	6'0"	215	PQ	27	24	102	
2nd Line	Luc Robitaille	LW	6'1"	205	PQ	39	35	54	
	Keith Primeau	C	6'5"	235	ON	30	32	75	
	Steve Thomas	RW	5'11"	185	ON	28	45	33	
Extra Change	Curtis Joseph	G	5'11	193	ON				
	Scott Stevens	D	6'2"	225	ON				
	Joe Nieuwendyk	C	6'2"	195	ON				
	TOTALS		6'2"	212		249		840	

Foster's Call:

"Hello, Canada, and hockey fans in the United States, Foster Hewitt reporting from the Calgary Saddledome, where the fast-skating West has ended a three-game Dominion Cup losing streak in sterling fashion, shutting out the East 1–0 in the sixth and deciding game. Tournament star Eddie 'The Eagle' Belfour earned the shutout, his second of the tournament. Martin Brodeur recorded two shutouts for the East as well, but let in the only goal this night, a blazing second-period wrist shot just under the crossbar from Joe Sakic. The line of Kariya, Sakic and Fleury really put on a show this series, skating miles every night."

Incidental Color:

Curtis Joseph served as backup to Martin Brodeur for the East when Patrick Roy bowed out of the series. "Sorry, the only time I sit on a bench is in church," the goalie said.

Series: 5-3, East

Verdict on the Hundred-Mile Diet

What can we learn from our imaginary Dominion Cup with regard to western hockey players? Only that they're just as good as but no better than their central-Canadian counterparts, winning four of nine encounters. Yeah, that's one less. But the West has won 13 of the last 25 Memorial Cups—Canada's junior hockey championship. (And they're picking up steam. The 1972 Super Series between Canada and Russia included only one westerner, Manitoba's Bobby Clarke. In the 2010 Olympics, 10 western Canadian players made the team, compared to 12 from central Canada.)

At the same time, there is no statistical evidence to suggest that western players are bigger and tougher than Central Canadians—at least not anymore. Stats show that was the case up until 1979, but after that, the East was bigger and meaner (as measured by penalty minutes) in 1989 and 1999, while the West was larger and more liverish

2009 Dominion Cup

Western Monarchs

		POS	H	W	PROV	S/O	GA		
Goalie	Chris Mason	G	6'0"	200	AB	6	2.41		
						G	**A**	**PIM**	
Defense	Mike Green	D	6'1"	204	AB	31	42	68	
	Scott Niedermayer	D	6'1"	194	BC	14	45	70	
	Duncan Keith	D	6'0"	187	MB	8	33	60	
	Brent Seabrook	D	6'3"	220	BC	8	18	62	
1st Line	Ryan Smyth	LW	6'3"	215	AB	26	33	62	
	Ryan Getzlaf	C	6'4"	220	SK	25	66	121	
	Jarome Iginla	RW	6'1"	209	AB	35	54	37	
2nd Line	Patrick Marleau	LW	6'2"	220	SK	38	33	18	
	Jonathan Toews	C	6'2"	211	MB	34	35	91	
	Danny Heatly	RW	6'4"	220	AB	39	43	88	
Extra Change	Cam Ward	G	6'1"	185	SK				
	Shea Weber	D	6'4"	234	BC				
	Brenden Morrow	LW	5'11"	210	SK				
	TOTALS		**6'2"**	**209**		**264**		**677**	

Ontario-Quebec All-Stars

		POS	H	W	PROV	S/O	GA		
Goalie	Martin Brodeur	G	6'2"	210	PQ	5	2.41		
						G	**A**	**PIM**	
Defense	Dan Boyle	D	5'11"	190	ON	16	41	52	
	Chris Pronger	D	6'6"	220	ON	13	36	88	
	Drew Doughty	D	6'1"	203	ON	6	21	56	
	Brian Campbell	D	5'11"	185	ON	7	45	22	
1st Line	Rick Nash	LW	6'4"	238	ON	40	39	52	
	Eric Staal	C	6'4"	205	ON	40	35	50	
	Corey Perry	RW	6'3"	206	ON	32	40	109	
2nd Line	Simon Gagne	LW	6'0"	195	PQ	34	40	42	
	Jeff Carter	C	6'3"	200	ON	46	38	68	
	Martin St. Louis	RW	5'9"	177	PQ	30	50	14	
Extra Change	Steve Mason	G	6'4"	212	ON				
	Stephane Robidas	D	5'11"	180	PQ				
	Joe Thornton	C	6'3"	235	PQ				
	TOTALS		**6'2"**	**204**		**269**		**553**	

Foster's Call:

"Hello, Canada, and hockey fans in the United States. Foster Hewitt reporting from the MTS Centre in Winnipeg, where the West has made it two in a row, winning by the closest of margins, four games to three. The final game was a fast, close, crowd-pleasing affair, with the West coming back to tie it two-all late in the second on a goal by Jonathan Toews, then pulling away for good in the third on a tip-in by Jarome Iginla. Both goals were set up by the ever-steady Scott Niedermayer, who, along with the youngster Toews, were, I thought, the stars of the tournament."

Incidental Color:

There was a widespread call for Sidney Crosby to be deemed eligible for the Ontario-Quebec All-Stars, since the Maritimer played junior in Quebec. A compromise was reached, allowing Crosby to play in 2019, when he'll be 32.

**Series:
5-4, East**

in 2009. Goals scored? Again, it's close: the West scored more often in 2009, the East won out in 1989, with 1999 being a tie.

Presumably, the Flames stocked up on western talent, believing there was a competitive dividend, that Albertans would battle for provincial honor the way Spartans fought at the Battle of Thermopylae—"with your shield or on it!" and all that. Isn't that how, and why, the mostly French

Montreal Canadiens succeeded from the 1950s through 1980? Not quite. Montreal had exclusive rights to the best French-Canadian players until the late '60s, while the West's best players are up for grabs by any 1 of 30 NHL teams. Winnipeg's Jonathan Toews ended up in Chicago. Regina's Ryan Getzlaf, in Anaheim.

Shopping and eating at home in today's NHL will lead to perpetual hunger pangs—always missing the playoffs

CAROLINA
HURRICANES

ERNATE NICKNAMES: 'Canes.

NCHISE STARTED: In 1972, as the New
and Whalers of the World Hockey Association.
me the Hartford Whalers upon joining the
in 1979. Relocated to North Carolina in 1997.

FORMLY SPEAKING: Hurricane Fran pul-
ed North Carolina in 1996. A 12-foot ocean
n surge and 16 inches of rain carried away a
e station on Topsail Island. The hockey Hur-
es arrived the following year with a swirling,
red, category-three cyclone weather-map

U COOL?: The *Hockey News* once suggested
the Hurricanes logo looks like a toilet flushing.
e: 5.6. Away: 5.8.

Hurricane Corey Stillman (61)

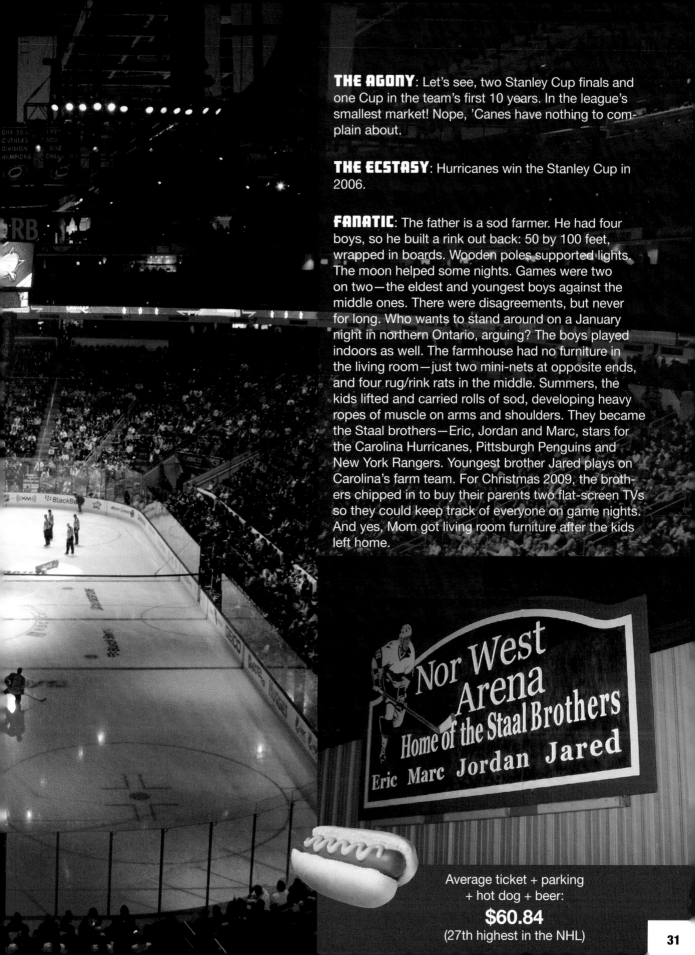

THE AGONY: Let's see, two Stanley Cup finals and one Cup in the team's first 10 years. In the league's smallest market! Nope, 'Canes have nothing to complain about.

THE ECSTASY: Hurricanes win the Stanley Cup in 2006.

FANATIC: The father is a sod farmer. He had four boys, so he built a rink out back: 50 by 100 feet, wrapped in boards. Wooden poles supported lights. The moon helped some nights. Games were two on two—the eldest and youngest boys against the middle ones. There were disagreements, but never for long. Who wants to stand around on a January night in northern Ontario, arguing? The boys played indoors as well. The farmhouse had no furniture in the living room—just two mini-nets at opposite ends, and four rug/rink rats in the middle. Summers, the kids lifted and carried rolls of sod, developing heavy ropes of muscle on arms and shoulders. They became the Staal brothers—Eric, Jordan and Marc, stars for the Carolina Hurricanes, Pittsburgh Penguins and New York Rangers. Youngest brother Jared plays on Carolina's farm team. For Christmas 2009, the brothers chipped in to buy their parents two flat-screen TVs so they could keep track of everyone on game nights. And yes, Mom got living room furniture after the kids left home.

Average ticket + parking
+ hot dog + beer:
$60.84
(27th highest in the NHL)

31

Shaz-a-yum!
The Stanley Cup Comes to Mayberry

That's Sheriff Andy Taylor and his boy, Opie, in Raleigh, North Carolina. The statues are based on characters from the CBS-TV series *The Andy Griffith Show* (1960–68). The Taylors lived in nearby Mayberry, a comforting, make-believe world where boys walked barefoot and sheriffs didn't need sidearms. In 2006, the Carolina Hurricanes fought the Edmonton Oilers in a thrilling seven-game series, bringing the Stanley Cup to Raleigh—for Andy, his spectacularly incompetent deputy, Barney Fife, and everyone else to see. And it might have gone something like this:

CREDITS ROLL AS ANDY AND OPIE STROLL BESIDE CREEK WITH FISHING RODS. OPIE SIDEARMS ROCK INTO WATER. THEME MUSIC UP: SPRIGHTLY WHISTLING

FADE IN:

INT. SHERIFF'S OFFICE – LUNCH

OPIE ENTERS, SPORTING CAM WARD CAROLINA HUR-RICANE JERSEY.

OPIE:

Pa! Pa! Johnny Paul got to stay up. Said Edmonton won game six. I don't think I could stand it, Hurricanes lost. We're not going to lose the Stanley Cup again, are we, Pa?

ANDY:

We win, that'd be wonderful. But if'n we don't, we're just going to have to look the other fella square in the eye, stick out a hand, say congratulations.

OPIE:

Pa, I hate losing.

ANDY:

Sometime you have to. Long as you're a good sport, though, you don't ever have to be a loser.

OPIE:

It's easier to be a good sport when you're winning, isn't it, Pa?

EXT. FLOYD'S BARBER SHOP—AFTER LUNCH

ANDY IS READING A NEWSPAPER, SITTING ON BENCH, FLANKED BY DEPUTY BARNEY FIFE AND BARBER FLOYD LAWSON.

BARNEY:

Are you nuts? Stick out your hand to Edmonton, Chris Pronger will cut it off.

ANDY:

Barney!

BARNEY:

Boy, I hope we beat them Edmonton Oilers. I hate them. Hate 'em…hate 'em.

ANDY:

Well, what's got into you?

BARNEY:

Have y'ever seen such poor sports in all your life?

FLOYD:

Canadians are mean.

ANDY:

Floyd, you never been north a' Durham.

FLOYD:

Bad tippers, too. Take Turkey Tyson.

ANDY:

He's not Canadian.

FLOYD:

His wife is. And she's mean. That's why he's a bad tipper.

BARNEY:

Ugly, too—same as all them Tyson girls. Fly a quail through the living room, whole family would point.

FLOYD:

Oh, that's good. They'd all point.

ANDY:

Barney, I'm surprised at you.

BARNEY:

Don't be knave, Andy. We got trouble on our hands. Them Edmonton Oilers are coming into Mayberry. They win, you're gonna have a foreign element running hog-wild through Mayberry.

FLOYD:

Canadians.

BARNEY:

Running hog-wild!

ANDY:

I believe I'm looking at a couple spoilsports.

FOLDS PAPER, GETS UP, WALKS AWAY.

BARNEY:

You're being knave, Andy. KNAVE!

FLOYD:

Oh, I bet that Chris Pronger, I bet he's a bad tipper.

EXT. OUTSIDE COURTHOUSE—AFTER SCHOOL

OPIE, JOHNNY PAUL AND BOYS PLAY HOCKEY ON STREET AS ANDY PASSES IN SQUAD CAR, WAVING AT BOYS. DISCARDED WINDBREAKERS SERVE AS GOALPOSTS.

OPIE:

Car!

INT. COURTHOUSE

ANDY ENTERS, SEES BARNEY ADDRESS GOMER AND GOOBER, TOWN MECHANICS, STANDING AT ATTENTION, BROOMS OVER SHOULDERS.

Shakiest gun in law enforcement: Barney Fife

BARNEY:

Now men, there are two kinds of police officers: The quick and the dead.

ANDY:

Barney, what's going on?

BARNEY:

Nipping a civic insurrection in the bud.

ANDY:

A what?

GOMER:

Hey, Andy.

ANDY:

Hey, Gomer.

GOOBER:

Hey, Andy.

ANDY:

Goober.

BARNEY:

We're facing clear evidence of peril, Andy.

ANDY:

We're facing the Edmonton Oilers, is what we're facing.

BARNEY:

Tell him, Gomer.

GOMER (recites):

You Say Mar-Cannon, he's the feller in nets for the Oilers, from Fin-lund. Ales Hem-ska, pronounced Alice. Boy, I bet he gets a lot a ribbing. That's in Your-up, too, Andy . . .

ANDY:

Barney, where you going with this?

BARNEY:

Andy, we can't wait for the smoking gun that could come in the form of a mushroom cloud.

GOMER:

Shaz-a-yum!

ANDY:

They's hockey players, Barney, not terrorists.

BARNEY:

Nip it in the bud, Andy. Read any military historian on the subject of war and you will find that every one of them is in favor of bud-nipping.

ANDY:

Barney . . .

BARNEY:

Gomer here will drive us to the game tomorrow night. Then . . .

SNAPS FINGERS.

GOMER (recites):

I drives you all to Raleigh while Goober stays here, guarding locations of…vital homeland s'curity.

ANDY:

Homeland security?

GOOBER:

Barney says he's gonna buy us a soda cracker pie from Foley's. Ain't that right, Barn?

BARNEY:

Skip it, Goober.

GOMER:

Then what I's supposed to do is come back. Patrol the perimeter—sawmill, bank, Wally's Garage, Bluebird Diner, make sure Juanita is OK . . .

ELABORATE WINK.

BARNEY:

What's the code word to come pick us up?

GOMER:

Catfood Hunter.

BARNEY:

CATFISH! Catfish Hunter. Can you remember that?

GOMER:

Sorry, Barn.

BARNEY:

And if I don't say Catfish Hunter?

GOMER:

Then I know you been captured!

ANDY:

Barney, have you lost your mind?

LEAVES COURTHOUSE.

BARNEY:

You're being knave again, Andy. KNAVE!

GOOBER:

I love soda cracker pie.

EXT. RURAL HIGHWAY – EARLY EVENING

IN A SQUAD CAR, A SMILING GOMER IS DRIV-ING. ANDY IS BESIDE HIM. BARNEY, OPIE AND AUNT BEA ARE IN THE BACKSEAT.

INT. SQUAD CAR

OPIE:

Who's your favorite Hurricane, Barney? Mine's Eric Staal.

BARNEY:

Well, I…

OPIE (pulling on sweater):

'Course, they wunt be anywhere without Cam Ward. He's the goalie, Aunt Bea.

AUNT BEA:

Isn't that wonderful?

BARNEY:

Now Aunt Bea, in hockey, goaltending is your navy…

OPIE:

Then there's Rod Brind'Amour. He's their leader…

BARNEY:

And your air force…

OPIE:

Who do you think is more valuable, Barney: Rod Brind'Amour or Eric Staal?

BARNEY:

Well…

OPIE (rolling down window):

OOH-EE! LET'S GO, HURRICANES!

INT. RBC CENTER (GAME SEVEN, CAROLINA VS. EDMONTON)

ANDY, BARNEY, OPIE AND AUNT BEA ARE IN SEATS BY THE GLASS. FURIOUS ACTION SEQUENCE ON THE ICE AS CAROLINA THROWS THE PUCK AROUND IN EDMONTON'S END.

BARNEY:

Shoot! Shoot!

AARON WARD LEANS INTO A SLAPSHOT FROM THE POINT, WHICH DISAPPEARS BETWEEN JUSSI MARKKANEN'S PADS. THE CROWD EX-PLODES. EVEN AUNT BEA IS EXCITED. BARNEY HIGH-FIVES OPIE BESIDE HIM. THEN TURNS TO HIS BEEFY NEIGHBOR, HIGH-FIVING BEER ONTO HIS SHIRT.

MORE ACTION: HURRICANES FLY AROUND THE OILERS' END, EXCHANGING CRISP PASSES.

BARNEY:

Shoot! Shoot!

AUNT BEA:

Shoot the puck! Shoot it!

ANDY LOOKS AT AUNT BEA WITH A QUIZZICAL SMILE. CUT TO ACTION ON ICE: FRANTISEK KABERLE BANGS IN A SLAPSHOT FROM THE POINT. ANOTHER GOAL. BARNEY GIVES OPIE ANOTHER HIGH FIVE, THEN SMILES AT STILL-WET NEIGHBOR, WHO GLARES AT HIM.

OPIE:

Two-nothing, Pa, we're gonna win.

ANDY:

Now, Ope. Game's not over.

AUNT BEA:

I never dreamed physical sensation could be so stimulating.

MORE ACTION: EDMONTON STORMS CARO-LINA'S NET, KNOCKING CAM WARD DOWN. FERNANDO PISANI SCORES ON THE REBOUND. NOW IT'S 2–1 CAROLINA.

AUNT BEA:

Oh no.

BARNEY (screaming):

Penalty! That's a penalty!

ANDY:

I believe it's gonna count.

BARNEY:

They ought to throw that Chris Pronger out of the game.

ANDY:

He weren't even on the ice, Barney.

BARNEY:

Was so. [Makes karate moves.] Just give me five minutes with that bully. I'd teach him a lesson.

THIRD-PERIOD ACTION: THE HURRICANES' CAM WARD MAKES A BRILLIANT SAVE ON A PISANI REBOUND. BARNEY LOOKS STRICKEN. AUNT BEA IS HIDING HER EYES. BARNEY IS JUMP-ING UP AND DOWN. THERE'S A FACEOFF, WITH JUST OVER A MINUTE LEFT, IN THE CARO-LINA END. ERIC STAAL PASSES TO JUSTIN WILLIAMS, WHO GOES IN ALL ALONE ON AN

EMPTY EDMONTON NET. HE SCORES. CARO-LINA WINS THE STANLEY CUP.

AUNT BEA IS BANGING ON THE GLASS. ANDY SMILES AT THE SIGHT OF HER, THEN TURNS TO HIS BOY.

OPIE:

We won, Pa. We won.

ANDY:

We surely did. Enjoy it. Give Edmonton credit, too. They're a real fine team. Real fine.

ANDY THEN TURNS TO BARNEY, WHO HAS FAINTED IN HIS SEAT.

EXT. RBC CENTER—LATER

THE BEAMING TAYLORS AND BARNEY FIFE STROLL PARKING LOT, AMIDST GREAT CEL-EBRATION.

BARNEY:

That sure was something, wasn't it?

ANDY:

Yeah.

BARNEY:

Opie, that's the biggest sports thrill this town has seen since Mayberry Union High beat Mount Pilot—regional football championship, back in the day.

ANDY:

Yeah.

BARNEY:

Your father was quarterback. I was his favorite receiver.

ANDY:

I remember you being mostly on the bench. Didn't Orville Hendrick start that game?

BARNEY:

Who'd you like better—him or me?

ANDY:

Well…

BARNEY:

We was best friends, Andy. I was your favorite receiver.

ANDY:

I expect you're right. Best phone Gomer, tell him come pick us up.

BARNEY:

No problem-o.

TAKES CELL PHONE FROM POCKET.

BARNEY:

Hi, Sarah… yeah, I know, 3–1. Get me the Court House.

INT. COURTHOUSE

GOMER AND GOOBER ARE SITTING AROUND ANDY'S DESK, HAVING WATCHED THE GAME ON TV. GOOBER SHOVELS BACK SODA CRACKER PIE. GOMER REACHES FOR THE PHONE.

GOMER:

Suh-prize, suh-prize! We won, we won!

BARNEY:

We sure did, Gomer. Now come pick us up.

GOMER:

Sure, Barn...what's the secret password?

BARNEY:

Ah...

GOMER:

Barney, are you all right?

BARNEY:

Ah, Gaylord Perry.

GOMER:

Goober, they got Barney...

GOMER DROPS THE PHONE, GRABS HIS HAT AND RACES OUT OF THE OFFICE. GOOBER, STILL CHEWING SODA CRACKER PIE, PICKS UP THE PHONE.

GOOBER (mouth full of dry crackers):

...

BARNEY:

Gomer! Gomer! Is it Hoyt Wilhelm?

GOOBER:

...

BARNEY:

Oh, for heaven's sakes. I'm okay. I just forgot the password, is what happened. GOMER?

GOOBER:

...

EXT. EMPTY RBC ARENA—LATER

THE TAYLORS AND BARNEY ARE SITTING ON A BENCH. OPIE IS STILL HAPPY. THE OTHERS AREN'T.

ANDY (to Barney):

You beat everything, you know that?

AUNT BEA (looking up):

Oh, Andy, I think I can see a bat in the air.

BARNEY (reaching for his gun):

Where?

ANDY GLARES AT HIS DEPUTY.

BARNEY:

Bats get in your hair, you'll go crazy. It's a fact, Andy.

JUST THEN, A BIG BUS PULLS UP BESIDE THEM. DRIVER OPENS DOOR AUTOMATICALLY. IT'S THE SPECTATOR BARNEY SPILLED BEER ON. HE GLARES AT BARNEY. THEN:

DRIVER:

Everything okay, Sheriff?

ANDY:

We're waiting for a taxicab, is all.

DRIVER:

Way this city is celebrating, you won't get one of those for hours. Where you going?

ANDY:

Mayberry.

DRIVER:

That's on the way to the airport. Hop in.

INT. EDMONTON OILERS' TEAM BUS

OPIE AND AUNT BEA QUICKLY FIND SEATS NEAR THE FRONT. THE PLAYERS ARE SILENT, STARING OFF INTO SPACE. ANDY FINDS A SEAT NEXT TO COACH CRAIG MCTAVISH, WHO MAKES ROOM.

ANDY:

Much obliged.

BARNEY:

Andy, Andy...

BARNEY IS BY HIMSELF NOW. AND PETRIFIED.

OFF-CAMERA VOICE:

Sit down.

BARNEY JUMPS INTO A NEARBY OPEN SEAT. HE LOOKS UP. HE'S SITTING BESIDE BIG CHRIS PRONGER.

LONG PAUSE.

BARNEY:

Can I please have your autograph, sir?

FADE TO END CREDITS. THEME MUSIC UP: MORE HAPPY WHISTLING. ANDY AND OPIE RETURN FROM THE CREEK WITH A STRING OF BASS. CUT TO COMMERCIAL PITCH FOR AROMA-ROAST SANKA COFFEE.

Glen Wesley hoists the Stanley Cup.

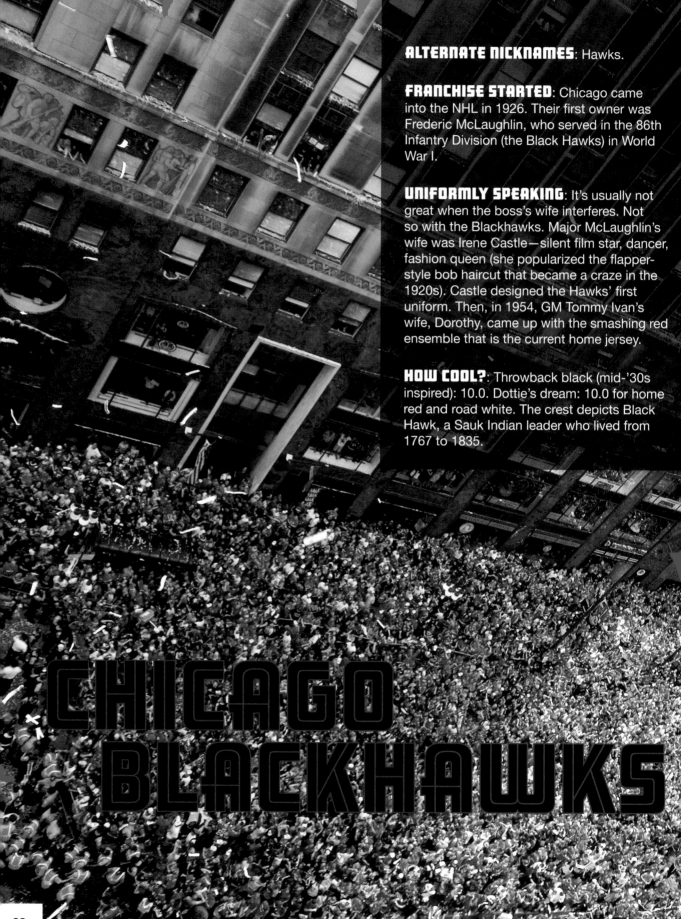

ALTERNATE NICKNAMES: Hawks.

FRANCHISE STARTED: Chicago came into the NHL in 1926. Their first owner was Frederic McLaughlin, who served in the 86th Infantry Division (the Black Hawks) in World War I.

UNIFORMLY SPEAKING: It's usually not great when the boss's wife interferes. Not so with the Blackhawks. Major McLaughlin's wife was Irene Castle—silent film star, dancer, fashion queen (she popularized the flapper-style bob haircut that became a craze in the 1920s). Castle designed the Hawks' first uniform. Then, in 1954, GM Tommy Ivan's wife, Dorothy, came up with the smashing red ensemble that is the current home jersey.

HOW COOL?: Throwback black (mid-'30s inspired): 10.0. Dottie's dream: 10.0 for home red and road white. The crest depicts Black Hawk, a Sauk Indian leader who lived from 1767 to 1835.

CHICAGO BLACKHAWKS

THE AGONY: Dollar Bill Wirtz, owner of the Blackhawks from 1966–2007, let four generations of great players, from Bobby Hull to Jeremy Roenick, escape to greener (in terms of money) pastures. And had police chase peanut vendors from the area immediately around the Chicago Stadium. His lawyers argued that peanut shells would draw insects and therefore posed a health hazard.

THE ECSTASY: 1961 and 2010, baby: The Hawks win the Stanley Cup.

FANATIC: Two million Chicagoans played hockey hookey on Friday June 10, 2010, to celebrate the Blackhawks winning their first Stanley Cup in 49 years. (See photo.)

Average ticket + parking
+ hot dog + beer:

$93.64
(4th highest in the NHL)

Toddlin' Teams

Chicago is the Second City, where civic attractions inevitably come in pairs, from mayors Daley (Richard J., Richard M.) and TV medical series (*ER, Chicago Hope*) to fast-food innovations (deep-dish pizza, Chicago-style hot dogs[1]) and civic valedictorians (Carl Sandburg, Saul Bellow).

In sports, the twosomes continue: Michael and Scotty's basketball Bulls won six championships. Baseball's most famous saying? "Let's play two," by Chicago Cubs shortstop Ernie Banks.

Finally, in hockey, Chicago's team, the Blackhawks won two championships in the past half century, both powered by twin-engine motors—Bobby Hull and Stan Mikita in 1961, Jonathan Toews and Patrick Kane in 2010.

Hullabaloo

The first thing you have to know about Chicago's team in the 1960s is that it operated in the NHL's so-called Golden Era, the six-team grouping that existed, so the story goes, in fruitful harmony from 1943–67. That's a stretcher, as Mark Twain would say. More proof that history is written by the winners—in this case, Montreal, Toronto and Detroit, who won all but one Cup in that quarter-century span, while New York, Boston and Chicago competed for bronze. The Hawks were widely held to be the farm team of Detroit owner James Norris, who

also had a controlling interest in Chicago. Hawks made the playoffs twice from 1945–58, finishing last nine times.

Then Bobby Hull arrived—Mickey Mantle on skates. An Adonis with a pitchman's dimpled smile and an autograph pen that never ran out of ink. In every NHL city, but especially Chicago, Bobby would sign programs for hours after games. He couldn't do enough. And what Bobby couldn't do, Glenn Hall, an acrobatic, rubbery-legged goalie, and Stan Mikita, a brilliant tactician who rated as hockey's best passer, could. Hull was 22, Mikita 20 when the Hawks won the

Bobby Bare: Hockey's Adonis, Robert Marvin Hull.

---

[1] There are more hot dog stands in Chicago than all other fast-food franchises combined. Burger King? No way—the hot dog is Chicago's bunned monarch.

Stanley Cup in 1961. The farm system was flush with eager teenagers—and future stars—like Phil Esposito and Kenny Hodge.

Windy City hockey fans felt like they'd died and gone to Montreal. Chicago Stadium, the Madhouse on Madison, was the most exciting sports venue in North America through the '60s, and certainly the loudest, courtesy of a fabled 3,663-pipe organ that produced the noise level of 25 brass bands.

The Hawks were often disappointing after '61. No more Stanley Cups. They should have won in 1967 and '71. But for a disastrous trade that sent Esposito, Hodge and Fred Stanfield to Boston, there could have been more still. The Scooter Line, a trio led by Mikita with horseshoe-bald Doug Mohns and whippet Kenny Wharram, operated on some magic telepathy—picture the Sedins as triplets! Then there was Hull, circling behind the net, legs crossing over, exploding up the left side, unleashing a slapshot goalies could only flinch at.

Another goal!

With that, a great noise shook the stadium. Just as the organ reached full cry, a foghorn blared, creating a din like two ships passing in a canyon.

It was almost like being in love. Bobby Hull's Hawks didn't win enough Stanley Cups, true. But all his goals, the many hours spent smiling and signing autographs, did something more important. Hull, Mikita, Glenn Hall and hunched-over, charging defenseman "Moooooose" Vasko made Chicago a big-league hockey city.

The Remarriage

Chicago fans didn't abandon the Blackhawks. On the contrary, the

Hawks pretty much asked them to leave. The team got through to the mid-'90s with some success. They had exciting players—whirling Denis Savard; Jeremy Roenick; and Chris Chelios, Chicago-born, though he played with a nasty edge, as if raised in a suburb of Hades. But they were all traded or chased away, like Bobby Hull, because of money.

The team was run by dour GM Bob

"Honey, meet your Uncle Dennis."

Pulford, about whom St. Louis scout Bob Plager said, "If Pully is drinking in a bar at 5 p.m., the bartender asks him to leave so they can have happy hour."

Hawks made one playoff appearance between 1996 and 2009 and were named the worst franchise in sports by ESPN in 2004. Owner Bill Wirtz dealt with bad fortune in classic bad management style: by firing the messengers. Chicago sacked their popular TV announcer, Pat Foley, as well as Wayne Messmer, the guy who sang the national anthem, turning every pregame into the Fourth of July. Finally, the Hawks punished their fans, canceling home TV broadcasts. Average attendance in 2006–07 was 12,727—leaving nearly 8,000 empty seats in the United Center on the average night. The franchise's worst moment came that season, when Wirtz died. The Hawks asked fans to observe a moment of silence. They booed.

Wirtz's son Rocky took over in 2007 and acted quickly, hiring a new president, John McDonough, an innovative marketer who had done great things with the baseball Cubs. McDonough put the Hawks back on TV and welcomed home Hull and Mikita as ambassadors. In 2009, the Hawks played outdoors at Wrigley Field, creating a sensation and boosting average attendance to 22,247.

Chicago and hockey were back in love. The team made the playoffs in 2009 and won the Cup a season later, drawing two million to a downtown parade. Wirtz and McDonough deserve credit, as do GM Stan Bowman and his father, senior advisor Scotty (who named his boy after the Stanley Cup). But really, the championship team was assembled by another twosome: previous GMs Dale Tallon and Mike Smith.

There are two things you can't trade for or sign as a free agent in the NHL: big, mobile first-line defenders and number one centers. Smith is the guy who landed the league's best defensive pairing, Brent Seabrook and Duncan Keith. He also got power forward Dustin Byfuglien—murder on skates.Tallon was better still, drafting Jonathan Toews and Patrick Kane and acquiring Patrick Sharp, Kris Versteeg, Brian Campbell, John Madden and Marian Hossa.

The keys were Toews and Kane, who arrived in Chicago and became roommates and instant best friends in 2007. Like Hull, Kane was a 5′10″ nightly highlight reel. He even came with a superstar's double-digit number: 88. Toews was a scout's dream: a big, fast, mature two-way center. The Hawks gave him a virtuous captain's numeral: the same 19 worn by Sakic, Yzerman and Bryan Trottier.

Kane was like Hull in other ways. Bobby was a youthful terror who staged contests to see who could fire slapshots out of Chicago Stadium through a second-level exit ramp. Brother Dennis, a Hawk teammate, describes how, when Chicago was playing an exhibition game in southern Ontario, where Bobby had starred in junior, a young girl approached him, blurting, "My mom says you're my father."

Bobby quickly gestured to his brother. "Honey, meet your Uncle Dennis."

In the summer of 2009, Kane got into a fight with a cabbie in Buffalo, his hometown; subsequently, pictures of him shirtless in the back of a limousine with two girls were all over the Internet. But the Second City gave him a second chance, figuring, hey, he's 20 years old, a big, floppy puppy who sometimes gets too much beer in his water dish.

Besides, how much trouble could he get into with Toews as a roommate? Named captain in 2008, Jonathan has the intensely focused look of a committed young priest, or maybe Eliot Ness, the Prohibition agent assigned to keep down the roar of the Roaring

Twenties in Chicago. When Toews was a seven-year-old in Winnipeg, his mother, Andree, noticed he was unusually quiet during a drive to the rink. She felt his forehead—he was running a fever. "We're turning around. You're not playing hockey," she said.

"No. I'm going to play," Toews said, putting his skate down.

He's never changed. The summer of 2009, old Winnipeg friend Kyle Shewchuk asked if Jonathan wanted to hang out. "He looked at me and said, 'I can't come out tonight,'" Shewchuk reported. "'This upcoming year is my year. I know big things are going to happen. There's the Olympics, my team is awesome. I have to take it easy this summer.'"

Jonathan's mother thinks her son's rooming with Kane is a good idea.

"I always call them the odd couple…. They're a good balance for each other. If they were both like Jonathan, they'd be so serious. If they were both like Patrick, they'd be wild. Patrick is good for Jonathan; he makes him

laugh. They're fun together. They're buddies."

The buddies helped their respective countries to the Olympic final in early 2010, where Jonathan won gold, was a tournament All-Star and was named Best Forward. Then came the NHL playoffs. The Great Man theory doesn't work in hockey—teams win. Duncan Keith was the best Blackhawk in 2009–10. And there were heroes galore in the postseason, starting with big Dustin Byfuglien, who took the bite out of the San Jose Sharks, at one point scoring seven times in as many games. Patrick Sharp had big goals. Antti Niemi, the goalie with the name out of a Beatles' song, was incredible.

But for teams to win, their best players have to be just that. And Toews and Kane, just 22 and 21, were Chicago's top scorers in the postseason. In the final, Philadelphia contained them for five games, but in the sixth, the youngsters were fearless and resolute. Playing in the NHL's most intimidating rink, Toews won 16 of 23 faceoffs and set up Byfuglien's opening goal.

Standing in the shadows of Hull and Mikita: Patrick Kane and Jonathan Toews against Detroit.

It was tied three-all going into overtime, when Chicago's Brian Campbell collected a clearout at the opposition blue line and chipped a short pass to Kane. He gave Philadelphia's Kimmo Timonen a head fake worthy of old Chicago Bears' running back, Walter Peyton, then darted wide, snapping a quick shot that caught Philadelphia's goalie, Michael Leighton, leaning awkwardly. The skimming puck sailed between Leighton's legs, across the goal line, disappearing under the white leather support that holds down the net.

Where was the puck? The Philadelphia crowd grew silent. Kane raced away, throwing off his gear, helmet and gloves first, like a kid released from school, racing to the beach for a holiday swim. The Chicago Blackhawks had won their first Stanley Cup in 49 years.

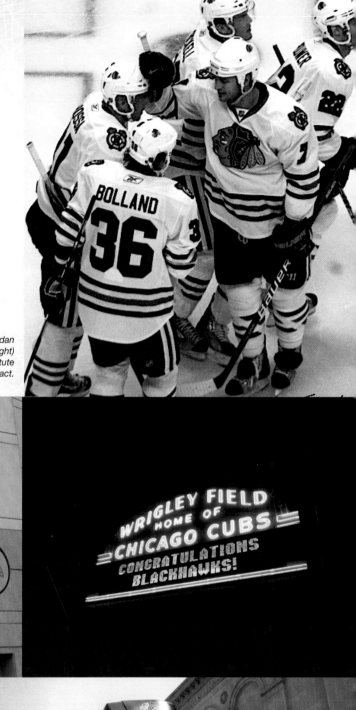

(top) Team celebration; (middle left) Red Bull Energy Dunk: Michael Jordan gets way up for Chicago Blackhawks 2010 Stanley Cup drive; (middle right) Wrigley tribute; (bottom) Even the lions in front of the Chicago Art Institute get into the playoff act.

COLORADO AVALANCHE

ALTERNATE NICKNAMES: Avs, the 'Lanche.

FRANCHISE STARTED: The World Hockey Association granted a franchise to the San Francisco Sharks in 1972. The financing didn't work out, so the team migrated to French Canada, calling itself the Quebec Nordiques. The club prospered there, joining the NHL in 1980, pestering provincial rival Montreal for 14 seasons before escalating costs (and the sinking Quebec franc) forced a move to Denver in 1995.

UNIFORMLY SPEAKING: The buyer, Charlie Lyons, decided to call the team the Colorado Rocky Extreme. Sounds like an ice cream, everyone complained. So the club threw eight names out and asked fans to choose. Cougars, Black Bears and Avalanche, the eventual winner, were popular choices. The Avs' wine sweater with a snow-capped mountain/letter *A* crest is . . . well, maybe Black Bears would've allowed for a better look.

HOW COOL?: Burgundy home: 6.8. White away: 6.9.

Joe Sakic winds up for a slaphot before the game.

THE AGONY: The Quebec Nordiques select Eric Lindros first overall in the 1991 draft. But Lindros, who is thought to be the heir to both Wayne Gretzky and Paul Bunyan, refuses to sign.

THE ECSTASY: Quebec trades Lindros to Philadelphia for Peter Forsberg, along with several other useful players and $15 million (enough to keep young star Joe Sakic in the fold). Forsberg and Sakic lead the Avalanche to Stanley Cup wins in 1996 (just after leaving Quebec!) and 2001.

FANATIC: Avs goalie Patrick Roy, winner of the Conn Smythe Trophy (playoff MVP) in both of Colorado's Cup triumphs, had boxes of VHS tapes sent to him on the road. Not film of the next team he was facing, but copies of his favorite TV show, the granny-friendly mystery series, *Murder, She Wrote*.

Peter Forsberg retired fourth in career assists-per-game, behind Wayne Gretzky, Mario Lemieux and Bobby Orr.

Average ticket + parking + hot dog + beer:

$61.37

(26th highest in the NHL)

Star Wars: The Next Generation

Vegas, please, what are the odds of one of a franchise's great stars having a son who is, upon arrival, a top player for the same club? While you're at it, what are the chances of another kid pinning the autographed sweater of his idol up on a bedroom wall and then, a few years later, while still a teenager, growing into that uniform, emerging instantly as the star of his favorite team?

Furthermore, what are the odds of both next-generation stars landing on the same club?

The answer would be … well, it's never happened before. Won't ever again. Yet that's what's going on in Denver, where Colorado's top centers are Matt Duchene and Paul Stastny. The former hopped into the Avalanche lineup at 18 in 2009, taking the spot of vacated idol Joe Sakic. The latter is the son of Peter Stastny, the franchise's first superstar—a pivot man with more points than anyone not named Wayne Gretzky in the '80s.

Paul Stastny wears the same number as his father: 26. Duchene is 9, a digit removed from hero Sakic's 19.

Both are from hockey families. Three of Duchene's uncles played Division I college hockey in the U.S. One, Newell Brown, is a coach in Anaheim. Two of Stastny's uncles, Anton and Marian, skated alongside his father in the NHL. Paul's brother Yan is also a pro with big-league experience.[1]

There is one major difference: the Stastny and Sakic family histories are tales of danger and heroism out of a Le Carré novel—The Nordique Who Came in From the Cold, Peter Stastny, crossed armed borders with a hockey stick instead of a rifle. The Sakic story is almost the same. Duchene, on the other hand, grew up in a shinny wonderland where the proprietor of every other store on Main Street was a friendly, successful NHLer.

In 1980, Peter Stastny was the best player on the Czech national team. He was also a patriot who railed against injustice in his communist homeland. Can't be both, the party warned, advising Stastny that another outburst would end his career. "To hear this, it was like someone poured icy water on your naked body," Stastny said. Playing in Austria that summer, he and his pregnant wife, along with brother Anton, slipped out of a hotel in the middle of the night, their hearts racing, and were met at an airport by Quebec Nordiques officials who gave them temporary identities to evade Czech security. Days later, after a few well-placed bribes, the trio were in the New World.[2]

Peter knew three languages: Slovak, Czech and Russian. His first year in North America, he picked up two more, English and French, along with the NHL's rookie-of-the-

year award. He was a six-time league All-Star. His family loved Quebec City. Son Paul was born there in 1985. Another youngster came into Peter's life three years later, when teenage Joe Sakic joined the Nordiques and almost right away, at Peter's request, landed on the team's power play.

Stastny saw himself in the young man—his quiet determination and fearlessness. Probably, he hoped Paul would grow up to be like him. After all, they came from similar backgrounds. Joe's father, Marijan Sakic, was born in communist Yugoslavia, a stonemason's apprentice who spent 14-hour days pushing around boulders. One night, at age 15, he slipped across the border into Austria. Soon,

Matt Duchene against the King.

---

[1] Yan Stastny played for Edmonton, Boston and St. Louis in the NHL and joined CSKA Moscow in the KHL in 2010.

[2] Peter and Anton later spent $30,000 in bribes to bring brother Marian to Quebec. They would all play on the same line.

he was in Canada, working construction in British Columbia, where Joe was born in 1969.

"No, I wasn't afraid crossing the border," Marijan Sakic said later. "I didn't believe [the guards] would kill a boy."

Hockey is a nomadic life. Stastny would be traded to New Jersey, then St. Louis, taking Paul with him. Before leaving Quebec City in 1990, though, Peter advised the team to make Sakic captain, and told his protégé, "You have the talent to lead this team from the bottom to the top. This is your team now."

In 1995, it was the Nordiques that were traded, moving to Denver. There, Stastny's hopes for Sakic and son Paul came true. The Avalanche won Stanley Cups in 1996 and 2001. Six seasons later, Paul Stastny joined his father's old team. "You know what was fun?" Stastny told reporters. "When Paul came to Colorado, Joe asked specifically to play with him on the power play."

Joe Sakic's unknown protégé, Matt Duchene, thrilled to Colorado's Cup wins as he watched them on TV in Haliburton, Ontario. Colorado was his team. He grew up with Sakic's and Patrick Roy's jerseys on his bedroom wall.

Two hours from Toronto, Haliburton (population: 5,526) is the small-town capital of Canadian hockey. Hockey is what you do in winter, while swimming, waterskiing and more hockey fill the summer months. Matt shot pucks in his backyard rink in June, wearing beekeeper's headgear to keep away the black flies.

Growing up in Haliburton was like living in a hockey theme park. Matt's best friend, Cody Hodgson, led Team Canada to gold in the 2009 world juniors. When the boys went to town for hockey, they got skates sharpened at ex-NHLer Glen Sharpley's Source for Sports before visiting the arena, which was decorated with murals of Ron Stackhouse, a local high school teacher who once recorded six assists in a game for

Pittsburgh, and Bernie Nicholls, a 70-goal man for the Los Angeles Kings in the 1988–89 season.

Afterward, the kids could go to McKeck's for something to eat. The owner and proprietor was Walt McKechnie, a 19-season man in the NHL.

Early press reports on Duchene made mention of his freakish hockey knowledge. He knew which sticks NHLers used[3] and designed hockey gear. Geek stuff. But if you saw him play junior with the Brampton Battalion, you knew he was more than a hockey-factory robot. Matt played with the same joy and sense of purpose that distinguished Joe Sakic. What's more, he was the rare player with his own GPS system. He knew where to go and how to get there.

No one was sure where he'd go in the 2009

NHL lottery. Duchene knew where he wanted to be: he wore an Avalanche burgundy tie on draft day in Montreal. His first year, Duchene scored 24 goals and put his team in the playoffs with a shootout goal over Roberto Luongo. Last season, he appeared in the All-Star game.

Paul Stastny made the U.S. team in the 2010 Olympics. His father at different times represented Czechoslovakia, Canada and Slovakia. Peter Stastny left Slovakia, where he is a member of European parliament, to see his son receive a silver medal in Vancouver.

After Duchene's first year in Colorado, McKeck's restaurant named a dish after him, Matt's Chicken Quesadillas ("an Avalanche of flavor"). And throughout Haliburton—indeed, all over the hockey world—kids began pinning his jersey up on their bedroom walls.

---

[3] Sportscaster James Duthie gave Duchene a quiz on draft day. To the question "What sticks do Milan Hejduk, Paul Stastny and Joe Sakic use?" He promptly replied, "Easton Synergy toe hook, Sher-Wood wooden straight curve, and Easton SC2, curve similar to mine."

Hockey Canada: Haliburton, Ontario.

ALTERNATE NICKNAME: None.

FRANCHISE STARTED: 2000.

UNIFORMLY SPEAKING: The NHL's most star-spangled uniform since the old New York/Brooklyn Americans (1925–42). The Blue Jackets' crest has Ohio's flag wrapped around a big star. The color scheme is Old Glory red, white and blue. The blue home jersey is as stirring as the Fourth of July. Their third uniform features a Civil War cannon.

HOW COOL?: Home: 8.2. Cannon crest: 7.8.

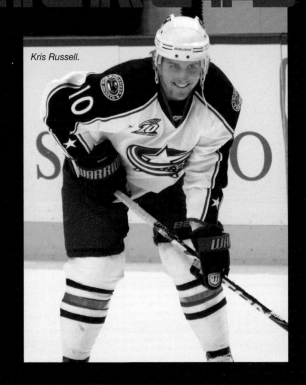

Kris Russell.

Blasting equipment: Blue Jacket beer, with patriotic team crest (right) and the club's handmade 1857 Napoleon canon (far right), which is shot off whenever Columbus scores.

THE AGONY: Missing the playoffs for their first nine years.

THE ECSTASY: Well, relief, anyway. The Blue Jackets finally make the postseason in 2008–09.

FANATIC: At 15, future Blue Jacket star Rick Nash performs 1,500 sit-ups and 500 push-ups during workouts.

Patriot Games

Civil War generals Ulysses S. Grant and William Tecumseh Sherman came from Ohio. Before battles, President Lincoln predicted, "If there are many Ohio soldiers to be engaged, it is probable we will win."

All of which helps explain why Ohio's NHL club has a Civil War fixation. Blue Jacket goals are greeted with cannon blasts. Before the puck is dropped, the team shows a clip from the film *Glory* in which an officer asks, "If this man should fall, who will lift the flag and carry on?" Suddenly, Blue Jackets pop up, shouting, "I will. I will."

Actually, the team isn't quite so recklessly patriotic. After Columbus lost four straight in its cannon-crested duds in 2010, they stopped wearing them. And the Blue Jackets have yet to muster a Sherman-like march, having not claimed victory in a single playoff match.

Still, Columbus won its most significant patriot game. In the summer of 2009—hours before July 4, in fact—the Blue Jackets inked their captain, star and only reason for hope, Rick Nash, to an eight-year, $62-million extension.

Leaf Nation groaned, "For God's sake, why?" Nash grew up just outside Toronto, in Brampton. He was introduced to shinny the old-fashioned way—playing with Dad, older brother James and Uncle Al on a frozen pond lit by car headlights. He scored 115 points in 34 games as a Toronto bantam. The Leafs watched him win the NHL's top scorer award, collecting 41 goals as a 19-year-old, and kept their payroll as trim as a maiden to lure him home as a free agent in 2010. In T.O., he'd be watched by millions three times a week on TV—a national hero and the international face of the sport if he could lead Leafs to the Stanley Cup.

Hello, world; good-bye, Columbus.

Instead, he stayed in Columbus, playing on a team handcuffed by a low payroll, the Stanley Cup an improbable dream.

Why? Why? Why?

Well, first off, players must react to hearing that the troubled Leafs need them to help win a Stanley Cup with all the enthusiasm with which movers respond to the news the piano goes on the third floor. Also, Nash, in signing with the team that has treated him well, was demonstrating the loyalty fans hope for in their sporting heroes.

But it's more than that. Hockey is no longer Stanley Cup or bust—the only way for a great player to prove his worth. Gone are the days when a Garry Unger or Harry Howell, great players on perennial playoff wallflowers, watched the Stanley Cup with stomachs sick from stewing competitive juices.

Miss the playoffs today, and the world beckons. With Columbus out of the Stanley Cup, Nash has played in three world championship tournaments, scoring 21 goals and adding 18

assists in 27 games, helping Canada win silver medals in Vienna (2005) and Halifax (2008). Want to know how imposing a forward Nash can be? YouTube the play, in the 2007 championship game in Moscow, where number 61 took a pass at the blue line against the Finns, flying past defender Pekka Saravo, who finally tackled him. Twisting and falling, Nash, in mid-pirouette, still somehow controlled his arms, stickhandling the puck past the Finnish goalie.

The incredible goal gave Canada the tournament. Named tournament MVP, Nash was on top of the hockey world. Three years later, of course, he helped Canada win an Olympic gold medal in 2010.

More consolation prizes: in 2008, Nash received an ESPN Espy play-of-

Nash has played in three world championship tournaments, scoring 39 points in 27 games

the-year nomination for an incredible one-on-three Fred Astaire goal-scoring move around two Phoenix defenders and the goaltender. That spring, the 24-year-old passed from flesh-and-blood player to electronic superhero. While the Stanley Cup wrapped up in Pittsburgh and Detroit, Rick donned a padded stretch suit and skates marked with reflective balls for a motion-capture session on a tiled polymer rink in Novato, California. Skating, stickhandling and scoring, Nash replicated a highlight reel of his own goals as they flashed on a nearby screen.

As he raced, the reflective balls on his uniform and skates were lit up by dozens of infrared lights and, in turn, captured by high-speed cameras and calculated by computers into fluid animation for the NHL 2K9 computer game.

Between takes, an assistant sprayed silicone on the polymer to rejuvenate the "ice."

By the following Christmas, hundreds of thousands of kids climbed into Rick Nash's avatar and pretended to be their own hockey hero.

DALLAS STARS

Left: The great Gump Worsley, 5'7", 155 pounds and one of the Minnesota North Stars first stars.

Below: Jason Arnott appears to be suffering sympathetic labor pains while wearing Dallas's controversial fallopian tube jersey.

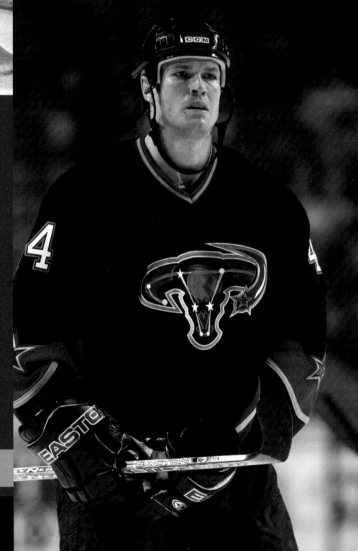

ALTERNATE NICKNAME: None.

FRANCHISE STARTED: As an expansion team in Minnesota in 1967, called the North Stars. In 1991, prepping for a move, Minnesota dropped North from its name. A buyer materialized in 1993, and the club migrated to the Lone Star State—with the benefit that they didn't even have to change their logo.

UNIFORMLY SPEAKING: The North Stars wore green and gold; just before the move to Dallas the look evolved to a dull black (home) and white (away) look, except for that crazy interlude (2003–06) when their alternate jerseys had a fallopian tube crest.

HOW COOL?: In Utero: 6.0. Puck black: 6.0.

THE AGONY: Inglourious basterd Sean Avery's Dallas sojourn (2008), during which, for $3.5 million, he scored three goals, insulted fans and made an insensitive comment about an ex-girlfriend that got him suspended. He walked out of NHL headquarters in novelty sunglasses.

THE ECSTASY: Brett Hull's Texas two-step inside the crease while scoring the goal that won Dallas the Stanley Cup in 1999. (See Buffalo Sabres: The Agony.)

FANATIC: Stars broadcaster Daryl "Razor" Reaugh, who works as hard to find aphorisms as captain Brenden Morrow toils in front of the net. And if Morrow were to score on a rebound, Razor'd say, "The early bird may get the worm, but it's the second mouse that gets the cheese."

Steve Ott.

Average ticket + parking
+ hot dog + beer:
$59.68
(28th highest in the NHL)

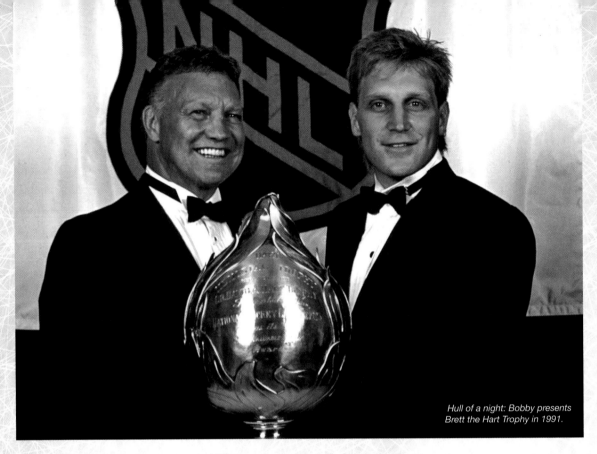

Hull of a night: Bobby presents Brett the Hart Trophy in 1991.

Oedipus Tex

He is the son of a famous man, evidently less talented than his father—lazy, maybe, but with a wastrel's easy charm and an undeniable affinity for the family business that made him, when he buckled down, a right-wing Texas hero and twice champion of the world, thereby eclipsing the old man.

That's right, President George W. Bush. But also, come to think of it, Brett A. Hull.

Few sons had had bigger, more pointed shoes to fill than these two.

Asked how he felt about his son's rise to power, President George H.W. Bush said, "You remember when your kid came home with two A's—and you thought [he] was going to fail. That's exactly what it's like."

Bobby Hull, hockey's greatest star in the '60s, with a build like Popeye halfway through a can of spinach, described Brett's play as "slovenly."

George W.'s nickname growing up was Shrub. Brett's? Huggy Bear.

Shrub was an average student. No junior team drafted Huggy.

Neither was supposed to inherit the business: Bobby Hull Jr., Brett's older brother, made it in junior hockey. Jeb Bush, Dad's favorite, and George W. were up for election in 1994. W won Texas. Jeb lost Florida. When George phoned his father with the good news, he was hurt by the response. "Dad's only heard that Jeb lost," he commented. "Not that I've won."

W's relationship with his father was marked by Oedipal competition and Freudian stress. Brett also longed for his father's approval…and career. After succeeding in Tier II junior in B.C., he won a scholarship to the University of Minnesota-Duluth, where he asked for number 9, his dad's numeral. It was retired. During a stopover in Chicago, he tried to phone his old man, whom he hadn't spoken to in years (his parents had had a messy divorce). But Dad's phone number was also retired—as in unlisted.

Both George W. and Brett had a moment of truth where they changed personal habits. W quit drinking in 1986 and became born again. Brett stopped eating (so much) in 1989 and became 195 pounds again.

George W. was more of a right winger than his father—a social and fiscal conservative. Brett also lined up to the right of his father, who played left wing.

W and Brett were unorthodox decision makers who relied on experts. "I'm not a textbook player, I'm a gut player," W said. "I'm hard to check because I never have the puck," Hull admitted. "I let everyone else do the work while I get into the openings…. It's an instinctive game, and I just go on my instincts."

Both were blessed with what W's dad called "the vision thing."

"I shoot the puck quickly and don't aim," is how Brett explained his goal scoring. Dad Bobby made famous the slapshot. Brett perfected the one-timer. Other players used the shot, but

Brett shaved a fraction of a second off his release by dropping to one knee before accepting a pass, putting him three-quarters of the way through the shooting motion by the time the puck arrived.[1] He scored 86 goals for the St. Louis Blues in 1990–91. Only one other player, Wayne Gretzky, has scored more goals in a season.

W was governor of Texas from 1995 until 1999. Brett played for the Dallas Stars from 1998 until 2001.

Both were accused of cheating. Brett won a Stanley Cup for Dallas in 1999 by scoring a goal with his foot in the crease. W became president of the United States in 2000 after a controversial recount in Florida.

Unlike his father, W was a two-term president, winning again in 2004. And unlike dad Bobby, who won a single league championship, Brett was a two-time Stanley Cup champ.

_____
[1] Today, Steve Stamkos uses the same shot to deadly effect for the Tampa Bay Lightning.

In addition, to winning in Dallas, he later hoisted the trophy with Detroit in 2002.

W and Brett both played with a little strut. W appeared on an aircraft carrier, dressed in a flight suit, to herald the end of the Iraq War. A sign behind him read, "Mission Accomplished."

While with St. Louis, Brett once jumped onto the ice in the last minute of a tie game in Los Angeles. There was already a right winger on the ice. The referee told the Blues to lose a player. Hull barked at Rich Sutter to get off the ice. When the puck was dropped, Brett raced up the ice and fired the game-winning goal over Kelly Hrudey's shoulder.

Sauntering back to the bench, Brett advised his teammates with a smirk, "As if we're going to play overtime in L.A."

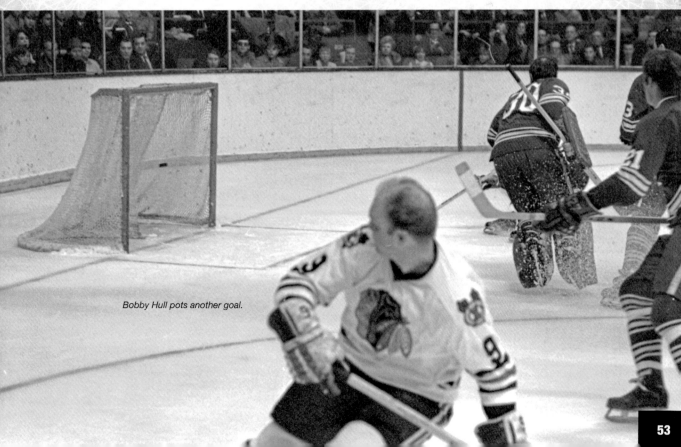

Bobby Hull pots another goal.

53

DETROIT RED WINGS

ALTERNATE NICKNAMES: Wings, Winged Wheels and, when the tires are flat, Dead Things.

FRANCHISE STARTED: In 1926, Detroit acquired an NHL franchise, purchasing and relocating the 1924–25 Stanley Cup champion, Victoria Cougars. The club played its first season across the river in Windsor, Ontario.

UNIFORMLY SPEAKING: Detroit's hockey team was called the Cougars; after that, the Falcons. Wheat baron James Norris, who once skated for the Montreal AAA—an amateur team whose emblem was a winged wheel—bought the club in 1933, telling coach Jack Adams, "We'll call the team the Wings. In fact, we'll call it the Red Wings. Our emblem will be the winged wheel—that's appropriate here in Detroit."

HOW COOL?: Norris's making nice with the auto industry results in an altogether thrilling uniform. Home: 10.0. Away: 10.0.

Old Man Winter, Gordie Howe.

Hockey floater: Wings 1997 Stanley Cup parade.

THE AGONY: From 1967—82, Detroit made the playoffs twice, earning the nickname Dead Things.

THE ECSTASY: The Howe–Lindsay Wings captured the Cup four times in the 1950s. The team won four more times between 1997 and 2008.

FANATIC: During the 1952 playoffs, Detroit fishmonger Jerry Cusimano threw an octopus onto the ice, to represent the number of victories the Wings would need to win the Stanley Cup. The team swept both playoff series that year—a game for every tentacle. Now, mollusks are tossed out in postseason for good luck, turning Joe Louis Arena into an Octopus's Garden. The record for most octopi thrown in a game: 54. The biggest ever weighed 30 pounds.

Playoff performer: Spirit of Detroit statue in 2009 postseason.

Average ticket + parking + hot dog + beer:

$80.38

(8th highest in the NHL)

Winged Wheels

"Detroit, Detroit, got a hell of a hockey team
Got a left-handed way of making a man sign up on that automotive dream"

Paul Simon, *"Papa Hobo"* (1971)

Detroit's first hockey dynasty lasted from 1948 to 1955, when the club finished first seven straight seasons, winning four Stanley Cups. The next grand epoch arrived in 1993 and continues to this day—an incredible run that has seen Detroit reach the Stanley Cup final six times, succeeding four times, granting the Motor City a new nickname: Hockeytown.

The focal point of the first Red Wing dynasty was Jack Adams, an eccentric overachiever who drove his players to the NHL summit—no other NHL club has ever topped the standings seven years in a row—then pushed his masterwork off a cliff, destroying everything.

Adams was born in Staal Territory (what is now Thunder Bay, Ontario) and liked to tell reporters he'd grown up playing hockey in weather so cold that his extremities—nose, ears and crotch—turned to ice. All of which might explain why Jack Adams could be such a cold prick. But perhaps we're too harsh. Adams arrived in pro hockey at a rough, unprofitable time. He made $800 his first season, helping the Toronto Arenas to the Stanley Cup in 1918. And he learned that the sport was a cutthroat business from playing in Montreal's old Jubilee Rink, where he was once sliced from eyebrow to Adam's apple. There were no team doctors then—just a trainer with a bucket of ice water at the end of the bench.

Adams was brought to a hospital after the game. There, the supervising nurse, who happened to be his sister, implored him, "Stop this hockey nonsense before it kills you, Jack."

Too late! Jack Adams was already addicted to hockey—to the exhilaration of flying combat and the satisfying copper taste of exhaustion that comes afterward. He retired from playing to coach the Detroit Cougars in 1927 and suffered with the team through the Great Depression. Detroit built 5,337,000 cars in 1929. By 1931, production was down to 1,332,000. The hockey team was broke. In response, the Wings sponsored food and clothing drives, letting fans into the Olympia free in exchange for charitable donations.

The club was saved by grain millionaire James Norris, who courted the failing auto industry, changing the name of his investment to Red Wings and dropping a winged wheel onto the front of the sweaters, in 1932. "We'll

Detroit monuments: Steve Yzerman billboard on the Cadillac Building.

grow strong together," Norris proclaimed.

Adams liked the "strong" part. Flush with Norris's money, he developed a fat, rich farm system. Ever the cutthroat, Adams wasn't above kidnapping children. Wings scout Bob Kinnear nabbed Terry Sawchuk from East Kildonan, Manitoba, at age 14. Fred Pinckney lured 15-year-old Gordie Howe out of Saskatoon. Carson Cooper, a former NHL star, stole Red Kelly and Ted Lindsay from St. Mike's College, blocks from Maple Leaf Gardens. "The boys were so young when they came to the Wings," Adams said, "that when I came home from a trip, they would rush up to me, yelling, 'Daddy, Daddy.'"

He was a demanding, overweening patriarch. From

Their top trio, the vaunted Production Line of Ted Lindsay, Sid Abel and Gordie Howe, finished 1-2-3 in scoring and combined for 256 penalty minutes, more than any other NHL unit.

scouts, he wanted big, fast players. It helped if they were mean. And he wanted his heavyweight speedsters playing dump-and-chase hockey. Throw the puck into the other guy's end and get there first, or a close second, rubbing defensemen into the boards, securing odd-man advantages.

"If you passed it more than twice, you might never play another game with Detroit," forward Johnny Wilson told writer Rich Kincaide. "Jack put the pressure on you all the time. Shoot the puck in,

chase the puck. Make quick passes, drive the net."

In time, Adams developed a team that suited his oversized personality. Detroit's rival in the 1950s was Montreal, a club that, going into the decade, didn't measure up to the Wings. In the 1949–50 season, Montreal forwards were, on average, 5′9″, 166.1 pounds; the Red Wings' forwards: 5′11″, 180 pounds.

And these Winged Wheels had chains on their winter tires. Their top trio, the vaunted Production Line

of Ted Lindsay, Sid Abel and Gordie Howe, finished 1-2-3 in scoring and combined for 256 penalty minutes, more than any other NHL unit. Diminutive, fiery Lindsay and powerful, uncertain Howe were inseparable—best friends who each provided the other with a vital, missing ingredient. Terrible Teddy gave Howe swagger, while Big Gordie granted Lindsay overwhelming strength.

The two players embellished Adams's dump-and-chase game. They stayed after practice, working long hours to memorize the boards. There were certain spots in Detroit's home rink where the puck bounced back at funny angles. Skating in from center, one winger would bank a shot into the corner, searching for the magic corner pocket that spit the puck back out between the circles, where the other winger suddenly materialized, startling defenders who hadn't taken geometry class at the Olympia.

With the Production Line leading the chase, Detroit won Stanley Cups in 1950, 1952, 1954 and 1955. The team owned two of the best goalies in the world—Terry Sawchuk held down the job in Detroit, while understudy Glenn Hall cooled his skates in Edmonton, with Detroit's top farm team. Big, young Vic Stasiuk and bigger, faster, younger Johnny Bucyk couldn't break into the lineup as one of Detroit's starting nine forwards. Bucyk and his fellow future Hall of Famer Norm Ullman were, like Hall, starring on the minor-league Edmonton Flyers, Western Hockey League champs in 1953 and 1955.

General manager Adams had built the best team in hockey. But then the general lost his army, turning from patriarch to prosecutor. But it was more than that—creepier. Adams became a mad inventor who wanted to experience the life of his creations.

"The last three days, tell me what you've eaten, how much sleep you've got and what you've done," Gordie Howe remembers Adams asking one day. Howe dutifully retraced the previous 72 hours. Adams nodded and made observations, at one point ordering Gordie to stop swimming. Depletes the air in your muscles, leaving your arms like flat tires, Adams said.

The Detroit Strangler: Jack Adams and Terry Sawchuk

Actor Al Waxman, who played Adams with chilly precision in the 1995 hockey drama *Net Worth*, had a theory about what went wrong with the Red Wing executive.

"Adams and his wife had a happy marriage but no children," Waxman told writer Gare Joyce. "So he made the team his family. The players were his boys, his sons. He stood beside Ted Lindsay when he took his U.S. citizenship. He was godfather to his players' kids. He went to their weddings, approved their marriages, but resented their mates. He was protective of his players. He called Howe 'The Big Fellah,' but wouldn't let Howe get married until he was 25. This man had immense love, but with love came a proprietorship. The players were both children and chattel."

And when the children grew up and challenged Dad, Adams ordered them out of the house. After one Stanley Cup win, Ted Lindsay asked Adams why the players' league-dictated $3,000 championship bonus came to only $2,235. Adams stopped talking to him.

Other Wings were also upset with their bonuses. To hell with them all, Adams figured.

In the summer of 1955, he sent Sawchuk, the best goalie in hockey, along with future star Vic Stasiuk, to Boston. Then he threw away the Wings'

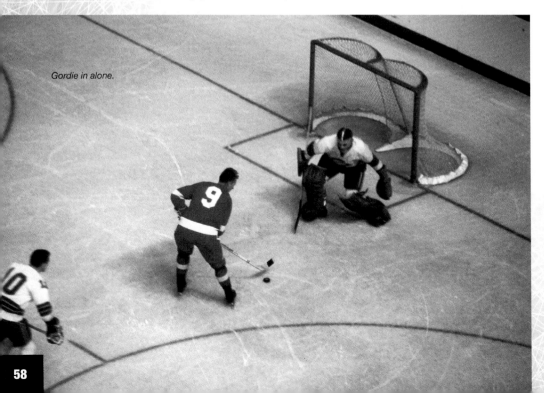

Gordie in alone.

58

checking line, demoting Marty Pavelich and trading Glen Skov and Tony Leswick, along with Johnny Wilson and Benny Woit, to Chicago. Two summers later, he finally got rid of Lindsay, along with Glenn Hall (who had told Adams off in the dressing room one day). The two were dispatched to Chicago.

Losing Hall meant Adams had to trade his best young minor leaguer, Johnny Bucyk, to Boston to reacquire Sawchuk. Then, in 1960, Red Kelly, who embarrassed Adams by advising a Toronto reporter, Trent Frayne, that he'd played through the previous playoffs on a broken ankle, was traded to the Toronto Maple Leafs.

> ## He went to their weddings, approved their marriages, but resented their mates.

For all of that—for future Hall of Famers Sawchuk, Hall, Kelly, Lindsay and Bucyk, along with a number of skilled character players, the cohesive mortar that had made Detroit a great team, players like Pavelich and Leswick—Adams got 10 cents on the dollar.

They were a last-place team by the 1958–59 season and struggled to make the playoffs for another four years, whereupon Adams was fired. He couldn't quit the sport that made him, however. Nor could he stop reliving Detroit memories. Months later, he and Tommy Ivan, his coach in the Red Wings' magic years, reunited to create the Central Hockey League. It would be too much to say hockey killed Jack Adams, as his sister predicted. But he did die at his desk, thinking hockey, in 1968.

The key contributors who ushered in Detroit's return to glory wouldn't impress Jack Adams. Both were on the small side and looked to be mild as May. When the hockey player, a first-round 1983 draft pick, arrived, coach Nick Polano scratched his head. "He was a little skinny kid [about 165 pounds] and I thought, 'How can this kid help us?'...Our first game was in Winnipeg. I had him on the third line. He went around [defenseman] Bobby Dollas like he wasn't even there and beat the goalie."

Polano quickly moved the little center to the first line, where he stayed for parts of three decades.

Detroit vs. Philadelphia in the 1970s.

Winged Wheelers

Unemployment in Detroit is well above the national average—some say close to 30 percent. Chrysler and General Motors slipped into Chapter 11 bankruptcy protection in 2009. "While they're living it up on Wall Street in that New York City town, here in the real world, they're shutting Detroit down," country singer John Rich recently lamented.

Say it ain't so. Detroit cars have played a starring role in the American dream for more than 100 years. The pursuit of happiness has always required bucket seats. A question, then, for Detroit car and hockey lovers: If Ted Lindsay were a car, what kind of car would he be? How about Darren McCarty? Nik Lidstrom? I posed those very questions to car-loving writer friends Bill Anderson (a Windsor boy) and Andrew Meeson. Their answers:

Sloping lines: Gordie Howe and a late '40s Cadillac.

Gordie Howe

BILL: The 1949 Cadillac. The 1948 model had the first real tailfin (based on the lines of the P-38 Lightning aircraft). The styling was stunning for its time, but the '49 took that design and dropped a V8 into it. The result was a luxury car with unparalleled smooth performance and drop-dead gorgeous lines. The boat-tail roadster versions were the most beautiful postwar fastbacks ever built.

Ted Lindsay

BILL: I think a good match for Ted Lindsay would be the Plymouth Fury, based on the name alone—plus, Richard Petty famously drove Plymouths in his heyday. A '58 Plymouth was also the car in Stephen King's 1982 novel *Christine*, so how do you like that—a car as nasty as Lindsay?

ANDREW: The Oldsmobile 88 (a.k.a. the Rocket 88), introduced in 1949, was powered by the V8 Rocket engine. Considered the fastest passenger car in America. Cleaned up on the stock car circuit. Ike Turner named a song after it (officially recognized as the first rock 'n' roll song).

Red Kelly

ANDREW: The Chevrolet Bel Air. Unlike the chrome-laden monstrosities of Buick, Pontiac or Cadillac, the Bel Air had a crisp, clean design. From 1955, it had an optional small-block Chev V8 that was so reliable it was produced for several decades. With a wide variety of body styles and interiors, the Bel Air nameplate was sold from the mid-1950s until 1975.

The Bruise Brothers (Bob Probert and Joey Kocur)

BILL: The Pontiac Firebird and Chevy Camaro, maybe? Hard-edged, throwback muscle cars favored by hosers and townies everywhere. I swear they are still making them on some junk planet in outer space and dropping them here at night in every town with less than 5,000 people and no jobs.

Steve Yzerman

BILL: Just as Yzerman successfully transformed himself in mid-career into a great two-way player, Cadillac rebranded itself, going from a country-club land yacht to an edgy luxury coupe, perfect for the prosperous Boomer who wanted to flaunt it while avoiding the "mid-life crisis" look of a red Mustang convertible. A brilliant ad, quoting Led Zep's "Rock and Roll," that ran during the 2002 Super Bowl resulted in a 16 percent sales increase.

Nik Lidstrom

ANDREW: Like Lidstrom, a two-country hybrid (Sweden and the United States), the Ford Fusion shares a platform with the Japanese-designed Mazda 6. An economical family sedan that gets solid gas mileage and boasts European-style handling. Quietly effective both for hauling the family and for carving through S-bends. It's one of the main reasons Ford is in better shape than its Detroit brethren.

Darren McCarty

ANDREW: The Impala SS. General Motors resurrected the Impala nameplate in 1994 and gave it a high-performance variant—the SS. Though the name harked back to the Impala SS of the early 1960s, this Impala was a big brute of a family car, but the SS version had a 5.7 L small-block V8 similar to the Corvette's, in a much less show-offish package. Not subtle, but it was effective, so much so that police departments picked up on it for their cruisers.

And lest we forget,

Howie Young

ANDREW: Great skater with terrible personal problems. The only Wing to fly alongside superstars Gordie Howe and Frank Sinatra (appearing in the Chairman of the Board's film *None But the Brave*, in which he had one line: "Damned mosquitoes."). Automotive disappointment, thy name is Edsel.

Bart Crashley

BILL: With a name like that, it's gotta be the "unsafe at any speed" Corvair.

The bespectacled executive who turned Detroit around never played anything more serious than ball hockey. Even then, back in Scarborough, outside Toronto, the future GM was probably a late pick when teams got divvied up—the guy who had to jump into snowbanks after lost balls.

And he'd do it, too. Both Jimmy Devellano, the executive, and Steve Yzerman, his star player, love hockey the way some men need the army.

Jimmy D, as he likes to be known (his lone bit of flash), quit school in ninth grade, becoming a government clerk. Nights, he coached and watched hockey. When the NHL expanded in 1967, Jimmy volunteered to scout the Toronto area for the St. Louis Blues—for free! He even paid his way to league functions, where he made a point of shaking everyone's hand. That last part is significant. Networking would make him hockey's most successful CEO.

Eventually, Jimmy D moved to St. Louis before joining Bill Torrey in New York, where, as director of scouting, he helped create an Islanders dynasty. In 1982, he was hired by Mike Ilitch, Red Wings' owner and inventor of a wondrous slab of Americana, two-for-one pizzas sold in coffin-shaped boxes—Little Caesars. It wouldn't be easy working for a self-made millionaire who had to win. But Ilich's will (and wallet!) along with Jimmy D's Rolodex made the Red Wings world champions.

The pizza dough was crucial. When Devellano arrived, the Red Wings were weak everywhere. Yzerman was a godsend, but to anchor the defense, the Wings needed a seen-everything workhorse to settle the team. Devellano wanted Brad Park, a free agent winding down his career in Boston. Park had a post-playing career job lined up in Beantown though. He needed the pot sweetened, his future provided for. Ilitch threw in two Little Caesars franchises to sign the Hall of Famer.

With Yzerman and Park, Detroit was better. Still, like Park, fans needed an incentive to return to the Olympia. So Ilitch raffled off a free Detroit car every game: Here's a brand-new 1983 Chevrolet Camaro, thanks for coming. Live it your way, from today's Chevrolet!

Devellano continued to excel at drafting. Some harvests were spectacular. In the 1989 draft, held in Minnesota, Detroit picked off useful players the first two rounds—Mike Silinger and Bob Boughner—then took out their world atlas, grabbing two superstars in a row, Nick Lidstrom (Sweden, third round) and Sergei Federov (USSR, fourth). Much later, in the 11th round, when other teams were busying themselves with dinner reservations, the Wings gambled on Vladamir Konstantinov, a hard rock defender on Red Army.

For most other clubs, the prospect of signing Fedorov and Konstantinov would be wishful thinking. Not for Detroit. The son of Macedonian immigrants, with four years in the U.S. Marines, Mike Ilitch (born Michael Ilievski) knew how to cut corners as well as deals.

Nineteen-year-old Fedorov ducked out of a Seattle hotel during a tournament, following

Wings vice president (and Ilitch's son-in-law) Jim Lites to an airport. A Little Caesars plane took him to Detroit, where a pen, contract and fancy new Corvette awaited. Konstantinov was trickier. Lites hired a Russian mobster to bribe five Soviet doctors, at $10,000 per misdiagnosis, to sign affidavits suggesting the defenseman was mortally ill, his stomach lousy with cancer. Foreseeing a tide of medical bills, the Red Army released Konstantinov, freeing him to join Detroit.

The Wings made another important hire in 1989, as GM Ken Holland (Devellano's protégé and successor) hired a Swedish fly-fishing guide, Hakan Andersson, to scout. In 1994, the Wings gave Andersson a 10th-round fantasy pick that he used to select Tomas Holmstrom, who turned out to be a dependable winger and a colossal power-play irritant—a sturdy Swedish spruce who stands in front of the net, oblivious to chopping sticks.

The Wings made Andersson their European scout, and he's kept them in Cup contention, providing a successful team that never had high draft choices with lottery pick–caliber All-Stars—Pavel Datsyuk late in the sixth round in 1998; Henrik Zetterberg, seventh round, 1999; and Johan Franzen, third round, 2004.

Deep drafts ensured that the Red Wings put a compelling team on the ice. But for all the team's depth and Steve Yzerman's heroics, including a six-season span in which the center averaged 55 goals, Detroit failed to win a Stanley Cup. Mike Ilitch wasn't happy. The propellers on his executive jet were twitching. Devellano heard that his boss was flying in a new coach, Iron Mike Keenan, about whom Brett Hull would complain, "He's the kind of guy who will stab you in the back right to your face."

Here is where Jimmy D showed he was tough in a way that bullying Jack Adams never was. Adams phoned owner Jim Norris from the dressing room minutes after every game, like a kid reporting home from school. And he never contradicted his boss. With his team at the crossroads and a hurricane blowing in his face, Devellano, now Detroit's director of hockey operations, told Ilitch something he didn't want to hear: Keenan was the wrong man. Though a talented coach, Iron Mike could wreak havoc on the organization, scaring everyone away. And if he did that, then didn't work out, where would the Wings be?

"So, Jimmy, what do you want me to do about a new coach?"

Devellano already had a man—two in fact—in the

back of his Rolodex: Al Arbour and Scotty Bowman, coaches he'd worked with in New York and St. Louis (and more important, winners of a combined 10 Stanley Cups).

"Go get one of them," Ilitch commanded.

"Which one?"

"I don't care. Either one."

The son of a Montreal blacksmith who never missed a day of work and a mother who threw cards into a fire after losing at euchre, William Scott Bowman was no skate in the park. He could be abrasive and resembled Mussolini behind the bench—arms folded, chin thrust out. But Bowman cared only about winning and didn't hold a grudge. As a junior, he'd had his career ruined by Jean-Guy Talbot, who lopped off a piece of Scotty's skull with a high stick.

Seventeen years later, as coach of St. Louis, Bowman grabbed Talbot off waivers, giving him a job for three seasons.

Scotty was a genius behind the bench. No one was better at finding an edge. Coaching Montreal to five Cups in the '70s, he had a trick to free up Guy Lafleur's line. When an opponent shadowed the superstar right winger, Bowman had Guy jump after the opposition center. Suddenly, two men were on

Lafleur, and Pete Mahovlich or Steve Shutt was fancy free.

Bowman knew what was wrong with Detroit. They were trying to score and hoping to win. It had to be the other way around. To change the team, Bowman needed to take apart and reassemble the game of one player, Detroit's biggest star: Steve Yzerman, a 58-goal scorer the season previous. The coach called the captain into his office in 1993 and told Yzerman he wanted him to be a two-way player.

Natural-born scorers don't want to hear about defense—or see their names slide down the scoring list. It's like a movie idol being told he no longer gets to kiss the girl, that from now on he's a character actor. Dany Heatley quit the Ottawa Senators when told he had to work harder in his own end. Yzerman, however, thrived on challenges. In 1988, he had ripped up his right knee. After a summer of intense rehab, he returned to rack up 65 goals and 90 assists, his best campaign ever.

Steve Yzerman heard every word Bowman said.

"Yzerman transformed himself from one of the great offensive players of the game to one of the greatest two-way players in the game," Ken Holland told *Sports Illustrated*. "And if you're [a teammate] sitting in that locker room seeing a guy with his skills chipping the puck out of the defensive zone, blocking shots, staying high in the slot to prevent odd-man rushes, winning faceoffs, playing hurt, hitting the bike and the workout room after the game is over, you're going to worry about those things too…. He set the tone for our franchise."

With Yzerman leading a quartet of superb two-way centers that included Sergei Fedorov, Igor Larionov and Kris Draper, the Stanley Cup finally returned to Detroit. Bowman's Wings dispensed with the hated Colorado Avalanche, then breezed by Philadelphia in four games to win the trophy in 1997, ending a 42-year drought. The next spring, Yzerman led all playoff scorers, winning the Conn Smythe Trophy, bringing the team another championship.

In 2002, playing on a surgically repaired knee, Yzerman stood up in the dressing room with the Wings down two games at Vancouver, opening playoff round. He made a speech—rare for him. "We have to win…we can win," he said. The team won four straight, then pushed aside St. Louis and Colorado (another murderous seven-game series), before defeating Carolina for their third Stanley Cup in six years. Yzerman was again the playoff scoring leader.

They're a machine now, Winged Wheels in perpetual motion, everything—money, management and manpower—in sync, traveling deep into the playoffs every spring. In 2008, the Detroit Red Wings, led by captain Nik Lidstrom and coach Mike Babcock, won another Stanley Cup. By then, vice president Stevie Y and senior vice president Jimmy D were upstairs in the team's luxury suite, enjoying the ride in leather-upholstered comfort.

The Hockey News *called Niklas Lidstrom the "best European-trained player ever in the NHL."*

EDMONTON OILERS

ALTERNATE NICKNAMES: The Oil, Greasers.

FRANCHISE STARTED: As a charter member of the World Hockey Association in 1972 (as the Alberta Oilers), jumping to the NHL in 1979.

UNIFORMLY SPEAKING: Oil was discovered near Edmonton in 1947. Gulf Oil, with its blue-and-orange color scheme, once had a sponsorship deal with the Oilers. The team retained the company's blue-flame look.

HOW COOL?: Alberta's NHL teams accepted *Miami Vice*'s "no muted earth tones" fashion dictum. Lots of bright sun/water colors—oranges, reds and blues. Still, how often does anyone reach in the closet for a sweater from the '80s? Home: 6.8. Away: 6.2.

Uniformly white fence in Oiler country.

THE AGONY: Edmonton defender, Steve Smith banks a puck into his own net off goalie-teammate Grant Fuhr in the third period of a tie seventh game in the 1986 playoffs. The flub gives rival Calgary Flames the win, ruining Edmonton's chances at accomplishing an historic run of five straight Stanley Cups. The Oilers won championships in 1984 and 1985, then 1987 and 1988.

THE ECSTASY: Stanley Cup wins in 1984, 1985, 1987, 1988 and 1990.

FANATICS:

Wayne takes faceoff against Calgary.

Oiler fans in Fanzoni during 2006 parade. The Oiler logo was created by former part owner (and comic book entrepreneur) Todd McFarlane. The oil-drop logo was used by Edmonton on their third jersey at the time.

Average ticket + parking + hot dog + beer:

$88.05

(6th highest in the NHL)

A Material Boy: a superstar and his loot—Wayne didn't need the disposable razors.

Lil Wayne

In the mid-'80s, Edmonton Oilers rookie Shaun Van Allen was knocked cold in a mid-ice collision. A trainer booted out to check on him, then returned to the bench. "The guy doesn't know who he is," he told coach Glen Sather.

"Tell him he's Wayne Gretzky," Sather said.

It's a joke the Oiler faithful have replayed for years, with diminishing returns. Every season, the team drafts high, and young players knock themselves out, but the Oilers go nowhere. Fans grow frustrated, watching players with no identity. Some find they're shouting at their TVs: "Please, please be Wayne Gretzky. Be Glenn Anderson. Paul Coffey. Mark Messier. Grant Fuhr. Jari Kurri. Kevin Lowe."

So, good luck, Taylor Hall, Jordan Eberle and Magnus Paajarvi. Practice your beautiful skating, blue Oilers, before it fails. But there will never, ever again be a professional hockey team as bold and thrilling as the '80s Oilers. No player in any major sport has been MVP eight straight years— Gretzky was a one-off. Besides, with a salary cap, who could afford a second line like Messier, Anderson (50-goal men both) and "The Grate One," Esa Tikkanen? So, Sherman, let's give Edmonton a vacation from last place and set the WABAC machine to Alberta during the 1981 Christmas season. Let's examine one week—two games—in the life of Wayne Gretzky and his blue-flame Oilers.

No, wait. First, let's stop off in Brantford, Ontario, a decade earlier to discover the origin of the Great Gretzky. That story usually begins with his hockey inventor father, Walter, but it's important to understand that Gretzky would have been Great anyway. In his early teens, the left-hander pitched a no-hitter in an Ontario baseball tournament, deploying a baffling array of knuckleballs, slow-bending curves and expertly located not-so-fast fastballs. And get this: Prior to the next game, he warmed up throwing right-handed.

What Walter did was give Wayne a Jedi-worthy education in hockey. Lessons started when the youngster first skated at his grandparents' farm at the age of two. Soon, Lil Wayne cruised Walter's backyard rink, a neighborhood wonder with lights, boards and perfect ice (achieved by leaving sprinklers on overnight—no tide lines). Wayne played all day with kids from the street. He also received private tutorials from Obi-Walter. A course was set up—bleach bottles evenly spaced, like buttons on a shirt. Wayne raced through, perfecting a speedy sideways swoop. Walter also had Wayne feather passes over dropped

sticks. Taught him pool players' secrets about bank shots off the boards.

> ## "Know where the puck is going, not where it is," was Walter's Jedi maxim.

"Know where the puck is going, not where it is," was Walter's Jedi maxim. Apprentice Wayne also had homework: Saturdays, he watched *Hockey Night in Canada* with a notepad. Without looking down, the little boy traced the puck's progress, memorizing game patterns. "Know where the puck is going…"

Wayne played in a league, too—defense and forward, on the ice for all but a few shifts, scoring 378 goals for the Nadrofsky Steelers in 1970–71. He was 11. Other Branford parents, jealous as Cinderella's sisters, booed him. Whatta buncha, we groaned, learning about the spoilsports.

Looking back, Walter and Wayne probably were a pain in the ass. If you were in Brantford, with a son who wasn't seeing the puck because a coach (Wayne's uncle Bob) wanted to win by a touchdown, giving his nephew a skate up on the

NHL, you'd have booed, too. Ah, but talent does what it can; genius what it must. Walter, if he did over-encourage his son, was only pushing Wayne in a direction he was already racing. Probably, it was like the sight of someone walking a puppy straining on a leash—difficult to decide who's walking who.

In 1974, Walter named a Toronto couple as Wayne's legal guardians so he could play Junior B. Wayne was 14, the youngest Vaughan National, skating against 20-year-olds. Still, Wayne couldn't get enough hockey. He met Paul Coffey playing ball hockey that same year. Next season, Wayne was called up to major junior by the Peterborough Petes. After that, he was a Soo Greyhound, then played on the Canadian team at the world junior championship, where he was the best player on the ice, collecting 17 points in six games. Months later, the whirlwind continued—forget about 12th grade, Wayne was in Edmonton, the newest star in the WHA.

The last week of 1981 was hoser heaven in Edmonton. Bob and Doug McKenzie's comedy record, *The Great White North*, was #1 on the charts on Christmas day. *Get Lucky*, by the Alberta band Loverboy, was #2. That's how Edmontonians felt—lucky. The Eskimos, with Warren Moon at

quarterback, were in the middle of a run that would see them win five Grey Cups in as many years. The Oilers had been welcomed into the NHL in 1979 and were good—really good—within two seasons. In the spring of 1981, in the playoffs, Gretzky, Mark Messier, Coffey and Andy Moog—four kids who still were young enough to play junior—helped Edmonton knock off hockey royalty, Guy Lafleur's Montreal Canadiens.

Seven months later, the boys were at it again. And Gretzky was on a roll. By Christmas, he'd scored 41 goals in 37 games. Fifty in 50, the magic Rocket Richard record[1] was possible, experts agreed. Wayne figured it was in the bag. At 20, he was piling up goals faster than anyone in NHL history.

"I think I'm going to get four tonight," Wayne told Paul Coffey the morning of the Oilers' December 27 game against the Los Angeles Kings. He had a feeling.

In the first period, Gretzky whipped a rebound home

[1] Maurice Richard was the first NHLer to score 50 goals, doing so in the 50-game 1944–45 season. Mike Bossy scored 50 in the first 50 games of 1980–81. Wayne Gretzky would get 50 in under 50 three times (1981–82, 1983–84 and 1984–85). Mario Lemieux matched the feat in 1988–89, and Brett Hull accomplished it in back-to-back years (1990–91 and '91–92).

before defenders spotted him. Next came a pair of shorthanded goals. Wayne appeared out of nowhere for an easy tip-in and then later melted through defender Jay Wells as if he wasn't there. Another marker came on a break-away, in alone. The fourth was a balletic wraparound. He now had 45 goals in 38 games.

Why couldn't the Kings find 99, the biggest number in hockey? Coach Parker MacDonald let his team off the hook. Covering Gretzky, he said afterward, was like "trying to throw a blanket over a ghost."

Who knows what Wayne got up to over the Christmas holidays? Perhaps the 20-year-old did another commercial. He was everywhere in those days: magazine covers, TV ads, on bus shelters and billboards.

At night, Gretzky was with teammates. He hated being alone. Even when they weren't playing hockey, the Oilers were playing, hitting bars and restaurants like Earls and Yiannis Taverna. Maybe they went to a film. To show what kind of hockey town Edmonton was at the time, *Slap Shot*, the 1977 Paul Newman hockey movie, was still playing at the Plaza I and the West Mall 5.

Gretzky and Paul Coffey were on their way to breakfast on December 30 when Wayne sniffed the winter air and said, "I think I'm going to get five tonight."

"Yeah, whatever," Coffey replied. It was a crazy thing to say. The Philadelphia Flyers were in town. Bobby Clarke—Darth Vader with Shirley Temple curls—would be shadowing Wayne.

It didn't matter. Watching film of that historic contest at half-speed, you begin to understand Gretzky's remarkable anticipation. In the first period, Coffey fires the puck in from the blue line. Goalie Pete Peeters and his defense edge to the right of the net, following the shot, as Wayne eases into the left edge of the crease. Know where the puck is going, not where it is. The puck caroms off the back boards onto 99's stick and is in the net before the Flyers turn around. Goal number 46. The Northlands Coliseum explodes.

After that, Wayne unexpectedly turns to a seldom-used weapon—the slapshot. Wayne's doesn't look or sound right. Never quite disappears into a blur or thunders off the boards like Paul Coffey's blasts. Still, in close, it's a viable weapon. Wayne isn't strong, but he has unfailing timing. An ability to see a play unfolding, to understand when to shoot. Minutes later, Gretzky

carries the puck in along the right boards, heading to the middle. Again, Peeters and the Philly defense move with him—to their right. Oiler teammate Dave Semenko races to the net, shopping for a rebound. At the precise moment that Semenko enter Peeters's vision, Gretzky, without looking up, chimes a slapshot off the left post, catching the distracted goalie moving the wrong way. Perfect shot. Forty-seven. Bedlam.

Next, he's dancing down the left side. Peeters moves out, taking the left side of the net away. That's where the previous goals had gone. Gretzky again surprises him, blasting a slapshot into an open sliver under his right armpit. Forty-eight. Pandemonium.

Now he's back on the right boards, speeding in his familiar hunched-forward posture. Skating right at defenseman Bob Hoffmeyer. Just before colliding, he flies left at an unexpectedly sharp angle—the bleach-bottle swoop. He's winding up even as he's cutting and golfs a shot past Peeters's hand, again just inside the post. Forty-nine.

Ten seconds left. Six–five, Edmonton. Peeters is pulled for an extra attacker. Someone chips the puck off the boards. Gretzky gets it at center. Bill Barber, the only Flyer remaining, skates backward, trying to steer him off. Just past the Philadelphia blue line, Gretzky

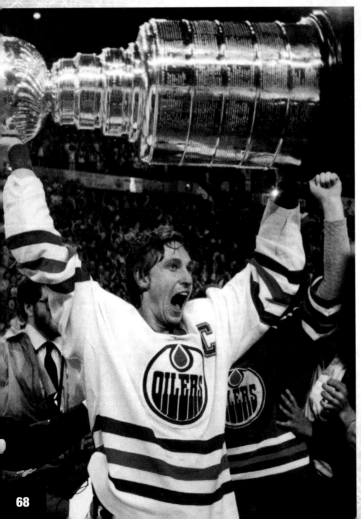

He's got the whole world in his hands. Wayne Gretzky in 1984.

swerves. Shoots. Barber dives. The puck one-hops the middle of the net.[2]

Fifty. Nirvana.

Finally, someone tackles Gretzky and escorts him into the corner of the rink. It's teammate Mark Messier. Seconds later, the Oiler team is on top of him, celebrating the shattering of Richard's record. The Northlands Coliseum is throbbing. Nineteen eighty-one is almost over. December 31 is 90 minutes away, but no one in the rink will be going to a New Year's Eve party this good.

Life passes in years, hockey in seasons. Wayne Gretzky's best season is debatable. But if you inspect his career chronologically in an effort to establish his hockey prime, it would have to be 1981, his 20th year. (This task is made easy because Wayne's birthday is January 5.) In the last half of the 1980–81 season and first portion of 1981–82, Gretzky scored 95 goals and 142 assists, for 237 points. The Christmas week of 1981 was his absolute peak: nine goals and two assists in two games.

[2] Gretzky scored 11 empty-net goals during the 1980–81 season.

BORN UNDER A BAD SIGN

Why were the Gretzky Oilers so good? How come the Oilers of 2009–11 finished with a clear view of the field? Any number of reasons, you could argue. A wide disparity in talent. Injuries. Birthdays.

That's right, birthdays. According to Canadian author Malcolm Gladwell's book, **Outliers**, the date of your birth is a factor in athletic success. As he explained to ESPN:

> *In Canada, the eligibility cutoff for age-class hockey programs is January 1…. Coaches start streaming the best hockey players into elite programs, where they practice more and play more games and get better coaching, as early as eight or nine. But who tends to be the "best" at age eight? The oldest, of course…who can be as much as almost a year older than kids born at the other end of the cut-off date. When you are eight years old, 10 or 11 extra months means a lot. So those kids get special attention. That's why there are more players in the NHL born in January and February and March than any other months.*

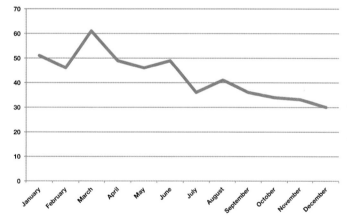

No, that's not your dwindling financial portfolio. It's from an 2008 ESPN tally of birth months for NHL players born from 1980 to 1990.

Do Gladwell's findings explain the Oilers' past glories and current woes? Kinda. The 1981–82 Oilers, the team discussed in this chapter, had 22 players born in the first half of the year. Its two best players, Wayne Gretzky and Mark Messier, were born in January. (Any bets Walter Gretzky knew about this birthday thing before Malcolm Gladwell?) Eleven players were born in the last half of the year.

It's just the other way around in 2009–10, when 13 are born in the first six and 17 are born in the last six months. Nine are born in September—Dustin Penner, Shawn Horcoff, Ryan Potulny, Mike Comrie, Zach Stortini, Ethan Moreau, Colin McDonald and Dean Arsenie.

That's too late! Which may help explain why the 2009–10 Oilers played as if they were born under a bad sign. They were.

ALTERNATE NICKNAME: None.

FRANCHISE STARTED: In the 1993 expansion.

UNIFORMLY SPEAKING: They're called the Florida Panthers. And that's what on the front of their jersey—a big ol' swamp cougar. Sure looked great back in the beginning, when goalie John Vanbiesbrouck played here, wearing a mask that was who-put-something-in-my-drink freaky. The current sober blue top with its splashy orange panther crest is tame by comparison. And mixed-up. Like someone wearing a clown's tie with a dress suit.

HOW COOL?: Home: 6.2. Away: 5.8.

THE AGONY: Trading All-Star goalie Roberto Luongo in 2006 for Todd Bertuzzi, who would score all of one goal for the Panthers.

THE ECSTASY: Pavel Bure is the NHL's top goal scorer in 1999–2000 (58 goals) and 2000–01 (59).

FANATIC: On December 2, 2010, Florida Panthers gave out free yarmulkes as part of their Hanukkah celebration.

Put Your Cat Clothes On: former Panther Cory Stillman (left) and Stanley C. Panther (right)

Average ticket + parking + hot dog + beer:
$79.12
(13th highest in the NHL)

Year of the Rat

It seemed so much fun at first. Three years into their existence, the Florida Panthers were as hot as their tropical uniforms. Forty-one home games in the 1995–96 season, 41 sellouts. They had an interesting coach, young Doug MacLean (hailing from P.E.I., he'd pronounce it "inneresting"), a rugged-the-way-Americans-like-'em scoring leader, Scott Mellanby, who happened to be the son of *Hockey Night in Canada* producer Ralph Mellanby. They even had a storyline that got them on ESPN's SportsCenter.

What happened was that a rat raced across the Panthers' dressing-room floor before the opening game of the season. Mellanby reacted as any forward would upon seeing a small black blur coming his way: he one-timed the rodent against the wall. He scored two goals that night. Counting the dead dressing-room visitor, that made "a rat trick," Vanbiesbrouck joked. The story caught on. Sixteen plastic rats hit the ice in the Panthers' third game.

It got better: in the Year of the Rat, the Panthers went to the Stanley Cup final, losing to Colorado. In just their third season! And in playoffs, with cameras rolling, fans threw thousands of rats—a whole plague's worth— onto the Miami Arena ice.

But all that happened long ago. The Panthers go into the 2011–12 season as the first NHL team to miss the playoffs 10 seasons in a row. Versus, the NHL's primary TV outlet in the U.S., didn't have a single Florida game on its schedule in 2010–11. The team had only one sellout in 2009–10, so they "downgraded" their arena capacity, stretching a tarp over 2,000 seats in the upper rows—let's face it, an embarrassing move. Like a bald guy always wearing a hat.

Come to think of it, there has always been an air of—is shiftiness too strong a word?—to the NHL's most southern club. Miami was awarded the team and that's where the team first played.

Five years later, the Panthers were skating a half-hour away in Sunrise, a town of 90,000 that was to be called Sunset, except developers figured that might bum retirees out.

Even the club's name is a bit of a con. In 1993, Florida sponsored a name-our-team contest—a routine PR move that allows an expansion team free publicity while securing a customer target list. The only problem was that then-owner Wayne Huizenga, billionaire Blockbuster developer and master of the buy-build-and-sell, had already chosen "Panthers," hoping to promote the cause of Florida's endangered swamp cats. Down to 100 or so in Florida, panthers are solitary creatures and need wide-open spaces to maneuver.

Hey, maybe they should relocate a couple to the upper reaches of Sunrise's BankAtlantic Center. Do panthers eat rats?

St. Patrick banishes rats from his crease in the 1996 Stanley Cup finals.

LOS ANGELES KINGS

ALTERNATE NICKNAMES: None.

FRANCHISE STARTED: L.A.'s first hockey royalty was the minor-league Monarchs, who won a Pacific Coast Hockey League championship in 1947. The Kings ascended to city's hockey throne in 1967, joining the NHL in its great expansion year.

UNIFORMLY SPEAKING: The Kings' first jersey (1967–88) was purple and gold with—oops!— a queen's crown (see below). Wayne Gretzky's outfit (1988–98) was a Hollywood exec's wheels— black pearl and buran silver. The current jersey is a hybrid of the first two: black and blue with a king's crown.

HOW COOL?: Mr. Mustard: 6.4. Joel Silver: 7.0. Blue-black hybrid: 7.1.

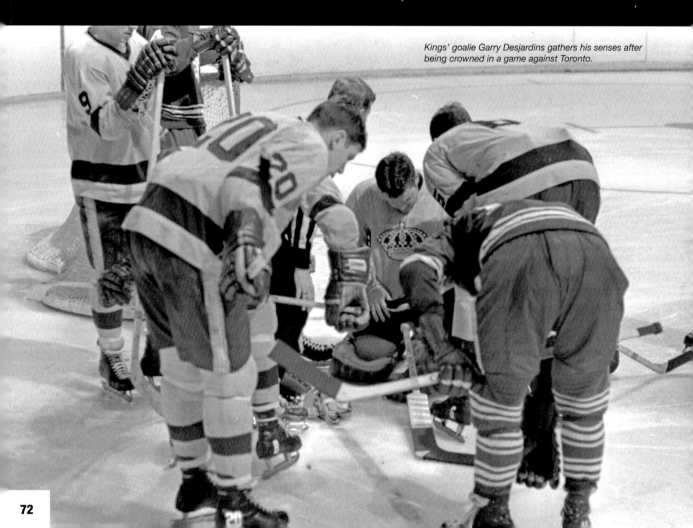

Kings' goalie Garry Desjardins gathers his senses after being crowned in a game against Toronto.

THE AGONY: Gretzky's Kings were on the verge of a Stanley Cup crown in 1993, about to sweep the Canadiens in the first two games of the final, played in Montreal, when Marty McSorley was called late for having an illegal stick. Montreal tied the score on the ensuing power play, won in overtime and never looked back.

THE ECSTASY: Gretzky's L.A. legacy is at hand. Kids born in California during 99's reign were taken in the first round of the NHL draft in 2010: Beau Bennett (by Pittsburgh) and Emerson Etem (Anaheim).

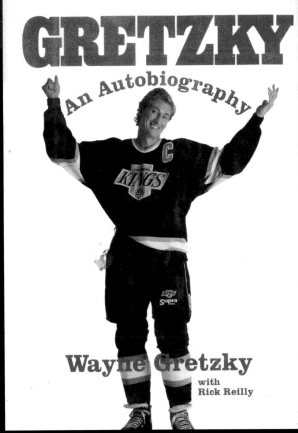

Wayne Gretzky's 1990 autobiography.

FANATIC: Kings broadcaster Bob Miller likes to tell the tale of how a slapshot sailed over the glass in the L.A. Forum, snatching the wig off an inattentive fan.

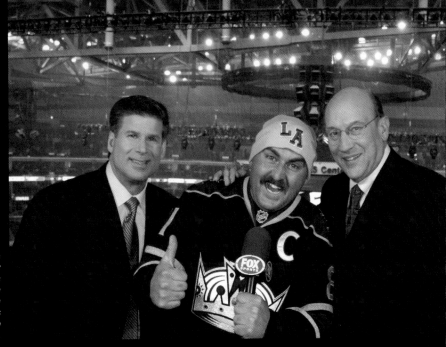

"AYYY!" Los Angeles super-fan, publicity hound, Ramidogg, gives the Fonzi sign upon finding himself between Kings' TV announcers Jim Fox (left) and Bob Miller (right).

Average ticket + parking + hot dog + beer:
$78.03
(14th highest in the NHL)

"Long ago and far away"

The Kings' first owner, Jack Kent Cooke, was a cheapskate who wanted to squeeze as much advertising revenue as possible out of game broadcasts, advising announcer Bob Miller to integrate sponsors' names and products into the action.

"How?" Miller wondered.

"There's Marcel Dionne scooting down the ice like a Datsun," Cooke offered.

"No," Miller said.

The angry owner told Miller and color man Dan Avey that they were fired unless they came up with sponsor-friendly phrases. "You could say, 'Kings score 10 seconds after the start of the game,' and I'd go, 'Dat-soon?'" Avey later joked. Miller came up with a painless compromise: "Let's look at the Datsun scoreboard."

Miller still does the Kings' games. He and color man Jim Fox are congenial hosts who go about their business with an unruffled professionalism that befits a team operating in the capital of show business. Despite their good work, however, their broadcasts, indeed the work of too many hockey TV crews, maintain a rinky-dink aura.

In my lifetime, TV has perfected and ruined pro sports for average fans. Broadcast revenues helped the Maple Leafs go from a company Conn Smythe sold for $2.3 million in 1961 to a $1.7-billion entertainment empire. The New York Yankees George Steinbrenner bought in 1973 for $10 million are worth $1.6 billion.

There is a consumer dividend: Televised sport spectacles are often urgent and compelling as the latest Hollywood blockbuster, which they resemble in style and content—emphatic narratives with a limitless appetite for stylish action scenes. At the same time, the $40 tickets I had at Maple Leaf Gardens in 1986 are now $250. The $18 dugout seats I loved in Yankee Stadium during the early '90s go for $2,500.

For most fans, stadiums are nothing more than studios, and games are something they watch on television. The sports complex of the future, Dallas's Cowboys Stadium, built in 2009, boasts the world's largest high-def screen, a 180-foot, 600-ton Jumbotron.

Finally, you can go to a game and watch it on TV.

Alas, the broadcasters' race for a

Drew Doughty steps out of a castle onto the Staples Center ice.

TV has perfected and ruined pro sports for average fans.

bigger, more immersive TV spectacle has bypassed hockey, where cameras remain locked in pre-Gretzky settings, where too much action is covered by a panning center-ice camera that, like a car's windshield wipers, goes left-right, left-right, where game coverage, like the fairy-tale castle opening of the L.A. Kings games, seems curiously "long ago and far away."

Here are one fan's notes—nine observations, two rants and a concluding argument—that came from watching two 2011 NHL double bills.

The Cable Guys

St. Louis at Los Angeles, Fox West, January 13
Toronto at Carolina, Sportsnet, January 24

1) I can't see the blue crowns on the epaulets of L.A.'s inky home outfits on Fox's high-center-ice master shot. How is it possible I'm watching black-and-white programming on a 42-inch high-def television? Why is that, switching from football or basketball to hockey on American cable, I always feel like I've been kicked out of good expensive seats and stuck up in the nosebleed section?

2) Fox's acoustics are perfect, capturing the *rsssk-rsssk* of chopping skates. A player loses his stick, and it's as if a pipe dropped in my TV room.

3) American TV often has trouble with hockey's two intermissions. Fox does the same thing in both breaks: The hosts spoon-feed dull questions to athletes. On an old *Saturday Night Live*, Bill Murray played a sports hero, answering an interviewer's every query with "I was just fortunate." It worked. Still does.

4) Jim Fox describes two Kings as rink rats. Bob Miller cracks, "Yeah, well, they're still single." A nice human moment. The best announcers understand that sports telecasts provide companionship as well as competition.

5) Seconds into the Leafs–Hurricanes game, announcer Joe Bowen shouts, "What a hit…Holy Mackinaw!" No sport is more dependent on century-old catchphrases than hockey. Pittsburgh's Mike Lange sometimes yells, "Buy Sam a drink and get his dog one, too" after goals.

6) Neither Fox nor Sportsnet run an out-of-town score crawl or show highlights from other games. As if they're afraid you'll leave for a better game. Old-fashioned protectionism isn't viable in today's media. Kids watch TV with one eye while surfing on their laptops. Networks would be best advised to offer full-service sports entertainment—sit down, enjoy, we'll give you highlights, scores, do everything but shell your peanuts.

7) The NHL should move its goal-review war room to New York. In the Toronto–Carolina game, a puck appears to go in. Off to Toronto we go for a summary judgment. And wait. And wait. Why did the Canadian cross the road? To get to the middle. Ten minutes later, the war room decides it's still not sure. No conclusive evidence—no goal. An irritable Judge Judy type would've had the gavel down in 30 seconds.

8) "Okay, what was that round, black thing that went into the net?" Doug McLean asks Nick Kypreos during the intermission that follows. Host Daren Millard looks on as a fight breaks out. The Sportsnet crew are hockey's premier analysts—impassioned without being grave, concise, funny, sporting and always good company.

9) The Sportsnet contest was spirited entertainment, but after a weekend of watching NFL playoffs from field level, I sometimes couldn't help feeling I was watching a great hockey game from so-so seats. Why, 60 years after the sport came to TV, do we still use the same basic camera angles that were in use when Foster Hewitt called games?

The 93-Percent Solution

Time magazine reported in 2009 that only 7 percent of all NFL fans have ever attended a game. Is pro hockey any different? The NHL has spent so much time trying to improve its game to draw spectators. Perhaps it's the spectacle more than the game that needs work.

Don Cherry and his frequently loyal sidekick, Ron MacLean.

Network

Washington at Toronto, January 22,
Hockey Night in Canada, CBC
Philadelphia at Chicago, January 23,
NBC

1) During the intermissions of both telecasts, there are arguments over New Year's Heritage Game, in which Washington's Dave Steckel blindsided Sidney Crosby, giving him a career-threatening concussion. NBC's Mike Milbury tells America that hockey is a man's game; soccer moms can go make muffins. The NFL protects its quarterbacks as if they're national monuments; hockey treats superstars like contestants in *Survivor: Winter Warriors*—good luck and don't cry on your way out of the arena. Maybe it's a Great White North thing. Margaret Atwood could be talking about the NHL when she wrote, "The central symbol for Canada…is undoubtedly Survival…for early explorers and settlers, it meant bare survival in the face of 'hostile' elements."

2) HNiC is brilliant at packaging highlights—deft, in-close montages. "Coach's Corner," during the first intermission, feels as comfortable as an old pair of slippers. When the tires are humming and the motor purrs, this is still the best hockey show on TV. NBC's game, by comparison, is a travesty. Sound mix is bad. You can hardly hear broadcasters Mike Emrick and Eddie Olczyk. The cramped, tricked-out intermission studio looks like a booth at an electronics trade fair. Milbury and Pierre McGuire get into a shapeless squabble in their segment. It's not as if Americans can't do hockey. MSG in New York is as good as any Canadian cable sports network. NBC should be ashamed, and hockey should be embarrassed, by their U.S. free TV showcase.

MINNESOTA WILD

ALTERNATE NICKNAME: None.

FRANCHISE STARTED: The Minnesota North Stars, a 1967 expansion team, left for Dallas in 1993; then came a seven-year ache. Minnesota's second NHL era began in 2000.

UNIFORMLY SPEAKING: The runners-up in the name-the-team contest could've been interesting: the Blue Ox or the White Bears. Instead, Minny went with Wild and a trippy logo: evergreen trees, rust-colored sky, harvest moon. Look again, and it's the face of a snarling cougar. There's a problem though: the logo turns into a golf divot when the player behind it is moving.

Minnesota Wild and crazy guys.

HOW COOL?: Rust home jersey: 6.5. White away: 5.9.

THE AGONY: We knew Bob Dylan dug hockey from his autobiography, *Chronicles*—"The things I did growing up were things I thought everybody did—march in parades, bike races, play ice hockey." So you'd think he'd give a shout-out to a fellow Minnesotan when he named his All-Star team. Nope. Here's Bob with fellow singer, Kinky Friedman[1]:

Kinky: "Bob, who's your favorite performer?"

Bob: "I've always liked Garry Unger from St. Louis. Bobby Clarke. Dan Maloney. Butch Goring…."

Kinky: "I've never heard of those guys."

Bob: "They're hockey players; when you said 'performers,' I thought you were talking about hockey players."

THE ECSTASY:

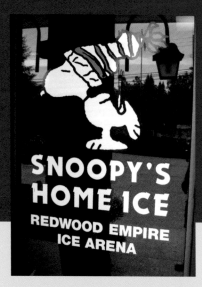

SNOOPY'S HOME ICE
REDWOOD EMPIRE ICE ARENA

FANATIC: In 1975, Minnesota's Charles Schulz, creator of *Peanuts*, began Snoopy's Senior World Hockey Tournament in Santa Rosa, California. In 2007, Duluth, Minnesota's 85-year-old Mark Sertich scored five goals in a game.

[1] From the book *Big Man: Real Life & Tall Tales*, by Clarence Clemons and Don Reo.

Average ticket + parking + hot dog + beer:

$83.13
(10th highest in the NHL)

Requiem for a Heavyweight

This is written five days after Derek Boogaard was found dead in his Minnesota apartment. We don't yet know why. We know he was recovering from a concussion received in a December 9 fight against Matt Carkner of the Ottawa Senators. And that the hockey player had fought 206 times since joining the Regina Pats as a teenager. Peers voted him the most intimidating fighter in hockey. When his contract with the Minnesota Wild expired in the summer of 2010, the New York Rangers signed the 28-year-old giant to a four-year contract worth

The Boogieman throws a delighted shiver through the crowd.

close to $7 million. General Manager Glen Sather explained the deal by saying the player with two excited vowels in his name was "the biggest and the toughest" player in the game.

"I'm not afraid to do what I do," Boogaard confirmed. "New York knows what type of player I am."

We know that after fight 206 the toughest player in the game was afraid to go outside. That he remained worried sick in his New York apartment for three weeks. That he wore sunglasses when he finally emerged, regardless of the weather. That sunlight was too much for Derek Boogaard on even a cloudy day.

We know that he was a good guy off the ice. When Ranger teammate Marian Gaborik received a concussion, Derek phoned daily. "I want you to call me and we'll do something for at least an hour just so you get out of your apartment," Boogaard told his friend, explaining that he didn't want the Slovak to go through what he had.

We know that with two weeks left in the Rangers 2010–11 season, Boogaard left the team to enter the NHL/NHLPA Substance Abuse & Behavioral Health Program. And that he had done so before in Minnesota.

And we know that the NHL was a lifelong dream that never quite came true for Derek Boogaard.

Len Boogaard drove all day to see his son's 2005 Minnesota Wild debut. He hoped the NHL would be different for his boy. "Derek was used in one role playing junior," he told a reporter. An enforcer—a goon. "An absolute gimmick," Wild GM Doug Risebrough

fumed, "like he wasn't even a human being."

Derek Boogaard grew up in the cold, the penalty boxes of prairie arenas, listening to parents grumble about his roughneck play. Every other winter, it was another town, as his RCMP-officer dad rotated from Saskatoon to Stroud, Herbert and Regina. But the complaints stayed the same. Discouraged, Derek hung up his skates

> ## Derek Boogaard grew up in the cold, the penalty boxes of prairie arenas, listening to parents grumble about his roughneck play.

at 15, only to become tangled in a magic beanstalk—a half-year, 10-inch growth spurt. Returning to hockey closer to seven feet than six, he won some fights and turned junior, collecting three goals, 653 penalty minutes and an inevitable nickname: The Boogieman.

The taunts continued. Derek was traded from Regina to Prince George, British Columbia, far from home. We know he didn't fit in. That he lived with four families his first year. Teammates ridiculed him.

"A lot of the stuff I got was deserved, but some of it wasn't," he told a Prince George paper.

Still, there is no getting around it, when Derek Boogaard made the NHL he was there to do one thing. Warren Zevon's song "Hit Somebody" set the scene for his arrival:

There were Swedes to the left of him
Russians to the right
A Czech at the blue line looking for a fight
Brains over brawn—that might work for you
But what's a Canadian farm boy to do?

The 6′7″, 270-pound forward kept throwing them: 62 fights in five Wild seasons, with more KOs or TKOs (eight) than goals (two). He became a tradable stock on Internet fight clubs like dropyourgloves.com; did commercials for a Bloomington store, pretending to toss a clerk around; opened a Saskatchewan hockey fight school for kids.

Boogaard was again ridiculed for the fight school. How could he profit from showing 12-year-olds how to hurt opponents on the ice? But we should ask ourselves: Why would an athlete who signed a $7 million contract return home to charge kids $40 for daylong sessions? Dog walkers made a better profit. No, it's more likely that the hockey fighter genuinely wanted to be there for kids who were prepared to fight like hell just so they could pursue the dream of playing professional hockey. Kids like Derek Boogaard.

"We're not teaching kids how to fight and how to hurt people," the fighter said. "We're teaching kids how to protect themselves so they don't get hurt."

A History of Violence

Fight schools? Internet chat rooms? Here's a decade-by-decade chronicle of how hockey fighting became a cult phenomenon, and a sport within a sport.

Forties:

Fighting happened occasionally, spontaneously, and to every class of player. The Leafs' Bill "Wild Man" Ezinicki, the NHL's readiest pugilist and a first-line winger, had seven fights in 1947–48: two in his temperament division, against Bill "The Beast" Judza and Emile "Butch" Bouchard, but also with stars Rocket Richard and Gordie Howe.

Fifties:

More of the same: Bruins bruiser Fern Flaman led the NHL in penalty minutes (150) in 1954–55, fighting stars (Bill Mosienko and Doug Harvey) and ruffians (Marcel Bonin and Glen Skov) alike. Detroit had the most brawls: 22 in 70 games.

Sixties:

More fights: Montreal leads with 38 in 1964–65. John Ferguson is a new breed: a hired gun who draws first. He shoots down Ted Green 12 seconds into his first NHL shift! What could Teddy have done to make him so mad? In 1964–65, Fergy singles out bad guys—the Reggie Flemings and

Eric Nesterenkos. The era of fighting as a premeditated scare tactic is at hand.

Seventies:

Halloween! The Big, Bad Bruins and Bigger, Badder Flyers dominate the early part of the decade, winning four Cups. The Flyers combine for 103 fights in 1974–75. In 1977, the NHL adopts the third-man-in rule, ejecting players who jump into brawls. The result: fewer bench-clearing brouhahas and more dramatic one-on-one duels, to be repeated endlessly on TV sportscasts. It's no coincidence the movie *Slap Shot* also comes out that year.

Eighties:

More fighting still! NHL scorers, like presidents and movie stars, now need bodyguards. Gretzky has his own security firm: Semenko & McSorley. In the 1955 Stanley Cup playoffs, there was a fight every 10 games. In the 1985 postseason: a whopping one and a half per game.

Nineties:

In 1992, the NHL creates the instigator rule, giving an extra two minutes to whomever starts a brawl. Fewer fights result, especially in the playoffs. In the 1995 postseason, the league is down to a fight every 0.22 games.

Oughts:

To get around the instigator rule, brawlers arrange play dates. Georges Laraque wore a mic for a 2007 game, in which he challenges Raitis Ivanans. "Want to?" Georges asks as they meet for a faceoff. "Square off?" is the next question, followed by "Good luck, man." Where fights were once manifestations of escalating tensions and involved everyone, they're now artificial diversions performed almost exclusively by players who are incidental to the action. And look at the crowd by the glass after fights, how they're laughing at the fighters "like they're not even human," to quote Doug Risebrough (see photo, page 77). Meanwhile, on the Internet, hockey pugilists exist as costumed superheroes—gladiators fighting in a Roman Colosseum fantasy league.

Toronto Maple Leafs' Jim Harrison in a tussle along the boards.

MONTREAL CANADIENS

ALTERNATE NICKNAMES: Habs, Flying French-men, *Le Bleu-Blanc-et-Rouge, Le Tricolore, La Sainte-Flanelle, Le CH, Le Grand Club, Les Glorieux*.

FRANCHISE STARTED: The Montreal Wanderers were the pride of English Montreal, winning four Stanley Cups (1906–08 and 1910). Inevitably, a French club followed—les Canadiens, charter members of the National Hockey Association in 1909.

UNIFORMLY SPEAKING: In their first decade, the Canadiens didn't know what to wear. Star Newsy Lalonde sported a blue fleur-de-lis jersey in 1909. The next season, Montreal's sweaters were red with a green maple leaf. Two years later, there was a barber-pole look. Then came the crucial 1912–17 metamorphosis and the CH (*Club de Hockey*) crest…*Et voilà*, when the team joined the NHL in 1917, Montreal adopted the classic, per-fectly balanced *Tricolore* they've pretty well been wearing ever since.

HOW COOL?: Home red: 11.0. White away: 10.0.

Wall of fame: Le Blond Demon, Guy Lafleur.

THE AGONY: The World's Fair is staged in Montreal during Canada's Centennial year. The Habs had won the Cup in 1965 and '66, and '68–69. A win in '67 would've meant five in a row. *Zut alors!* A valiant, gristly old stew of a Leafs team upset them in the finals. Henri Richard is so embarrassed, he seldom ventures outside to enjoy Expo that summer.

THE ECSTASY: All the times God dropped everything to assist in a Habs Cup win. In the 1960 final, George Armstrong of the Maple Leafs shoots the puck past Jacques Plante, right through the net. No goal. In overtime of game six in 1966, Henri Richard and the puck slide into Detroit goalie Roger Crozier. The Cup-winning puck somehow ends up behind Crozier. In game seven of the 1971 final, the Habs are down and seemingly out to Chicago when Jacques Lemaire golfs a slapper from center that travels over goalie Tony Esposito's shoulder, refracting just under the crossbar. The Canadiens rally to win. In '79, Boston is three minutes away from eliminating Montreal when a mysterious force pushes Stan Jonathan onto the ice, even though six Bruins are there already. Guy Lafleur scores on the too-many-men power play. Habs win again. Montreal is down a game and a goal to L.A. with two minutes left in 1993, when King Marty McSorley's stick sprouts an illegal bend in the blade. (No, Uri Geller wasn't in the house.) The Habs score on the resulting power play and go on to win the game and the series.

FANATIC: Actor Viggo Mortensen wears a Montreal jersey under his robe while shooting *Lord of the Rings*. It helps him feel like a hero.

Actor Viggo Morensen reveals his true colors at the Toronto International Film Festival.

Average ticket + parking + hot dog + beer:
$119.49
(2nd highest in the NHL)

What If the Flying Frenchmen Flew Forever?

Rocket Richard with coach and former linemate, Toe Blake.

This is where the fight starts. "What?" Leaf fans fume. "You're telling me Montreal controlled, like, 700 teams in Quebec? Cripes, how many more could there have been?" That's why, in the 1940s and '50s, Montreal had the Richards and Geoffrion, Plante, Beliveau, Moore, Harvey, Bouchard and everyone else skating right from Quebec junior onto the Canadiens.

And the rest the league…what did it get? Camille "The Eel" Henry in New York, a 130-pound power-play specialist with back problems.[1]

Is it possible both sides missed the point? Montreal didn't have to connive to draft or sign French-Canadian players. They volunteered. Keep in mind, this was an era when French-Canadians were discriminated against, being called frogs on the ice.[2]

Between 1940 and 1960, the Flying Frenchmen won eight Stanley Cups, more than anyone. And how many MVP trophies did French players win?

Two: Maurice Richard in 1943 and Jean Beliveau in 1956. In 1944–45,

There is an argument among hockeyists—a donnybrook, if not an outright brouhaha—over whether Montreal received a special indulgence from the NHL that allowed them a competitive home advantage. At one extreme, sour Leaf fans, you have those who argue that until 1970, the Canadiens could order anything they wanted à la carte off the Quebec Junior Menu.

"Let's see, I'll have Plante and Beliveau and…oh, the Dickie Moore looks good."

Their opponents, often from Quebec, rightly point out that it was only for a few years during the Great Depression and much later, from 1963–69, that

there was a formal understanding that Montreal could claim two French-Canadian juniors a year before the rest of the league could make its choices. And all they really got out of the deal was Michel Plasse, Reggie Houle and Marc Tardif—good players, but hardly a there-you-have-it explanation as to why the Canadiens won 24 Cups.

The reason Montreal did so well shopping at home, another theory goes, is that GM Frank Selke engineered hockey's first industrial farm system—750 teams, most in Quebec, but also some in Winnipeg and Regina, with a few minor-league teams in the States.

---

[1] There was another French player whom the Canadiens failed to protect in the '40s. At a Quebec City tournament, Detroit Red Wings brass were astonished to find future Hall of Fame defender Marcel Pronovost was available, and they acquired him for their junior team.

[2] NHL referee Red Storey told CBC Radio in the '60s that the league asked officials to take it easy on teams visiting Montreal during the Habs' glory years in the late '50s. "Our instructions were to be careful what penalties we gave to the visiting team. Make sure it was a good one, otherwise we ruined a good game."

Rocket astonished hockey, scoring 50 goals in as many games, but the Hart Trophy went to Prairie linemate Elmer Lach. In 1954–55, the top of the NHL scoring race at season's end looked like this:

		G	A	PTS
1	**Bernie Geoffrion**	38	47	75
2	**Maurice Richard**	38	36	74
3	**Jean Beliveau**	37	36	73

So, who got the MVP? Toronto's Teeder Kennedy, who counted 10 goals while leading Toronto to a .500 record. But the great Leaf captain was calling it quits, so in lieu of a gold watch, the league gave him its big silver trophy.

In the middle of last century, French-Canadian players were drawn to Montreal like iron filings to a magnet. Lord knows, you've probably read enough about what Maurice Richard

and the Montreal Canadiens *mean* to Quebec. But here is a poem about the Rocket you may not have encountered:

Maurice Richard

When he shoots, North America roars,
When he scores, the deaf can hear the cheers,
When they send him to the penalty box, the switchboards light up,
When he passes, the new guys dream.
He's the wind on skates,
He's all of Quebec on its feet.
He scares the rest—he's life in action.
— Félix Leclerc

Still, it's true that Montreal diligently tended its farm system. Frank Selke's successor, Sam Pollock's first big job with the Canadiens was riding fence through Montreal's pastures of plenty, making sure rustlers didn't get a Ranger or Bruin brand on prize players. In 1963, the NHL began to

dismantle its sponsorship system of amateur teams. To compensate the Canadiens, who would be the big losers in the transition, Montreal was allowed the option of the first two picks every season, a policy that lasted until 1969.

Despite the advent of the universal draft, Pollock did connive to keep great French players skating for Les Glorieux. Before the 1971 lottery, the GM courted the league's weak sisters, swindling some, securing four of the top 20 picks. Guy Lafleur, Marcel Dionne, Richard Martin and Jocelyn Guevremont were available. Could Montreal get Lafleur and Dionne? One could only dream. If not, Martin was a tolerable consolation prize. All three would be Hall of Famers—Flying Frenchmen with the wind in their skates. Then, trouble: It looked as though none of the Habs' draft picks might land in the top two. No Dionne or Lafleur! So Pollock improved a weak team (Los Angeles) that was in the way. It was nothing short of stock manipulation. And so Montreal got their man: Guy Lafleur.[3]

Next season, Pollock came calling on the Islanders' GM Bill Torrey with chocolates and nylon stockings, trying to get the expansion team's pick—and the rights to Denis Potvin. It didn't happen. Potvin went to the Islanders in '72. Meanwhile, Buffalo had nabbed Gilbert Perreault with the first pick in 1970. Dionne (Detroit) and Martin (Buffalo) escaped. *C'était fini.* Great French players were suddenly everywhere.

But what if Montreal had retained its territorial rights? What if the Flying Frenchmen had flown forever? On the next pages, a plausible chronology (a doomsday scenario for Toronto fans) of what might have happened.

---

[3] Montreal also got a pretty good defenseman with the 20th pick that year: Larry Robinson.

An electric performer: Boom Boom Geoffrion.

POUR TOUJOURS,

The Seventies

GOALIES: Ken Dryden, Dan Bouchard*,

DEFENSE: Denis Potvin* and Larry Robinson, Guy Lapointe and Serge Savard, Jocelyn Guevremont* and Andre "Moose" Dupont*.

FORWARD LINES: Steve Shutt, Marcel Dionne* and Guy Lafleur; Rick Martin,* Gilbert Perreault* and Rene Robert*; Don Marcotte,* Jacques Lemaire and Jean Pronovost*; Bob Gainey, Doug Risebrough and Mario Tremblay.

BENCH: Pete Mahovlich, Murray Wilson, Jimmy Roberts.

POWER PLAY: Potvin and Robert (point); Shutt, Dionne and Lafleur (forwards).

PENALTY KILLING: Robinson and Savard (defense); Gainey and Roberts, then Lemaire and Risebrough (forwards).

GENDARMES (Law Enforcement): Guevremont and Dupont on defense, with Mahovlich, Robinson and Tremblay patrolling the northern perimeter.

ON THE ICE: Taking advantage of the second great renaissance of Quebec forwards (after the Beliveau-Geoffrion crop in the '50s) and the addition of Denis Potvin on the blue line, the Flying Frenchmen create endless havoc with their speed and finesse, finishing teams off with a merciless power play. The real Montreal Canadiens of 1976–79 were perhaps the best hockey team ever, winning four Cups in a row. This bunch would've added one more to the front end and two more on the other side.

CULTURAL IMPACT: Guy Lafleur's disco record goes platinum.

The Eighties

GOALIES: Patrick Roy and Brian Hayward.

DEFENSE: Raymond Bourque* and Kevin Lowe,* Larry Robinson and Denis Potvin,* Chris Chelios and Steve Duchesne*.

FORWARD LINES: Michel Goulet,* Mario Lemieux* and Mike Bossy*; Luc Robitaille*, Denis Savard* and Kevin Dineen*; Ryan Walter, Guy Carbonneau and Stephane Richer; Bob Gainey, Brian Skrudland and Claude Lemieux.

BENCH: Mike McPhee, Shayne Corson and Chris Nilan.

POWER PLAY: Potvin and Bourque (point); Mario Lemieux, Savard and Bossy (forwards).

PENALTY KILLERS: Robinson and Lowe (defense); Gainey and Carbonneau, then Goulet and McPhee (forwards).

GENDARMES (Law Enforcement): Robinson and Chelios on defense, with Claude Lemieux, Corson and Nilan walking the beat up front.

Montreal Canadien hero, Mario Lemieux.

ON THE ICE: The emergence of Mario Lemieux and Patrick Roy as dominant players make the Canadiens a colossus. And fire a decade-long feud with Edmonton's great team. The rivalry would be comparable to the epic '50s struggle between Howe's Wings and Richard's Canadiens, only better: Gretzky vs. Lemieux, Bossy vs. Kurri, Roy vs. Fuhr, Coffey vs. Bourque.

CULTURAL IMPACT: Although Quebec flirts with independence this decade, it is Toronto, going through the worst of the Harold Ballard years, that secedes from Canada. "They'd rather quit than fight," comments Al Strachan on Hockey Night in Canada.

---

*Quebec ringers added to the 1985–86 Montreal lineup from other teams.

*Quebec ringers added to the 1974–75 Montreal lineup from other teams.

LES CANADIENS!

The Nineties

GOALIES: Patrick Roy and Martin Brodeur*.

DEFENSE: Ray Bourque* and Patrice Brisebois; Mathieu Schneider and Eric Desjardins; Steve Duchesne* and Lyle Odelin.

FORWARD LINES: Luc Robitaille,* Mario Lemieux* and Stephane Richer*; Kirk Muller, Vincent Damphousse and Claude Lemieux*; Brian Bellows, Pierre Turgeon and Mike Keane; John LeClair, Stephane Lebeau and Scott Mellanby*.

BENCH: Guy Carbonneau, Gilbert Dionne, Todd Ewen.

POWER PLAY: Bourque and Schneider (point), Mario Lemieux, Turgeon and Richer (forwards).

PENALTY KILLING: Bourque and Desjardins (defense), with Keane and Carbonneau, then Muller and Mellanby (forwards).

GENDARMES (Law Enforcement): Odelein and Desjardins (defense) with Ewan, LeClair and Claude Lemieux looking mean up front.

ON THE ICE: The real Habs took the Cup in 1993 and would've won more with the aforementioned crew, especially if coach Jacques Demers, a players' guy, coaxed maximum efforts out of the, shall we say, mercurial Richer, Turgeon and Claude Lemieux. Other challenges: Mario's health and the *Kramer vs. Kramer* dynamic between goalies Roy and Brodeur.

CULTURAL IMPACT: The back pages of French-language Quebec dailies are alive with the debate over who should play goal: Roy or Brodeur. It's a '90s variation on such questions as Beatles or Rolling Stones? Sinatra or Elvis?

The Oughts (2000–10)

GOALIES: Martin Brodeur* and Robert Luongo*.

DEFENSE: Sheldon Souray and Eric Desjardins,* Andre Markov and Patrice Brisebois, Mathieu Dandenault* and Francois Beauchemin*.

FORWARD LINES: Alexandre Burrows*, Vincent Lecavalier* and Martin St. Louis*; Simon Gagne,* Saku Koivu and Danny Briere*; Vincent Damphousse,* Mike Ribeiro* and Alexei Kovalev*; Chad Kilger, Yannick Perreault and Michael Ryder.

BENCH: Craig Rivet, J. P. Dumont,* Georges Laraque*.

POWER PLAY: Souray and Kovalev (point); St. Louis, Lecavalier and Briere (forwards).

PENALTY KILLING: Markov and Dandenault (defense), with Koivu and Ribeiro, then Kilger and Rivet (forwards).

GENDARMES (Law Enforcement): Souray and Rivet (defense) with Kilger and Ribeiro watching Laraque's back in enemy territory.

ON THE ICE: Hmm…while this particular club would've handled the Western Conference champions the Calgary Flames in the 2004 Cup final, even a Montreal fan would have to admit that this decade's team does not compare favorably to the All-Star editions from previous decades. The Flying Frenchmen seem to be in descent. Until….

CULTURAL IMPACT: Canada is up in arms after *Maclean's* magazine runs the cover story "Misconduct! How the Montreal Canadiens Keep Stealing the Stanley Cup." The magazine alleges that Canadiens GM Bob Gainey pulled a fast one in employing a 2005 Quebec pick on Sidney Crosby, who, he successfully argued, was *pur laine*—a real Canadien—because dad Troy played goal for Verdun in Quebec junior hockey. The Canadiens, with Crosby as captain and Jaroslav Halak starring in net, won the Stanley Cup for the 30th time in June 2010.

---

*Quebec ringers added to the 1992–93 Montreal lineup from other teams.

*Quebec ringers added to the 2003–04 Montreal lineup from other teams.

85

NASHVILLE PREDATORS

ALTERNATE NICKNAME: Preds.

FRANCHISE STARTED: As an expansion team in 1998.

UNIFORMLY SPEAKING: Nashville arrived in the NHL with a tiger in need of an orthodontist for a crest. Why's that? Because in 1971, bones of a 10,000-year-old smilodon were found on a local construction site. Dusting a nine-inch fang, a worker announced, "Boys, we got a saber-toothed tiger here."

HOW COOL?: The crest is definitely a grabber, but the home jersey itself is kind of blue blah: 6.0. The away white gets lost on the ice: 5.5.

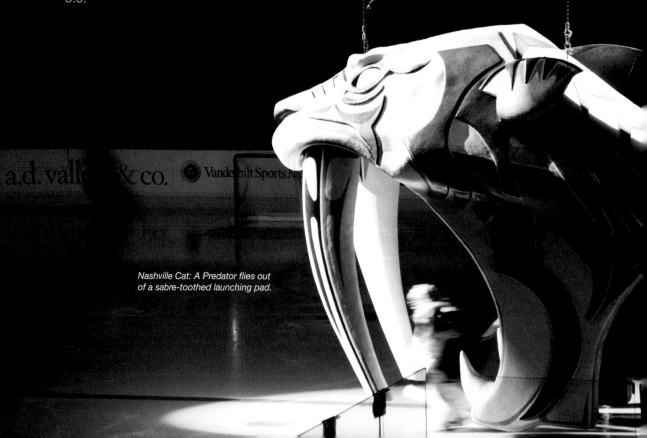

Nashville Cat: A Predator flies out of a sabre-toothed launching pad.

a.d. vall & co.   Vanderbilt Sports

THE AGONY: Losing back-to-back first-round playoff series to the San Jose Sharks in the springs of 2006 and '07.

THE ECSTASY: Predator defenseman Shea Weber's slapshot has been timed at 103.4 miles per hour. Playing for Canada in the 2010 Olympics, he put all of his 6'4", 234-pound frame into a shot that traveled at warp speed, disappearing on its way to the German net. Minutes later, using slow motion, it was determined that the puck actually flew through the netting and Weber was credited with a goal.

Viva Shea!

The only floater in Nashville's lineup.

FANATIC: The Predators' ADHD mascot, Gnash, bungee-jumps from the scoreboard, swinging inches off the ice.

Average ticket + parking + hot dog + beer:

$72.04
(19th highest in the NHL)

Made for Each Other

That's the Nashville skyline: the corner of Fourth and Broadway. Music City's best alt-country venues are in East Nashville, but if you want to honky-tonk, the saloons pictured below are ripe for a swaller an' a holler. Places like the Second Fiddle and Tootsie's Orchid Lounge, where hungry songwriters Willie Nelson and Kris Kristofferson once lay in wait for country stars to drift in from the Grand Ol' Opry across the street.

On winter nights, the best show in town is across the street and down a couple of blocks—a little something the city's hockey team calls "Smashville."

That's where you'll find the Bridgestone Arena, the gleaming glass lair of the Nashville Predators. Though the rink has an impressive big-league swoop, once inside, fans settle into a *Bull Durham*-y, small-town ambience. Before games, you can ride the Zamboni or sit in the penalty box in exchange for a charitable donation. Costumed schoolgirls sweep the ice during stoppages, collecting glassy-eyed catfish that fans smuggle in (and wisely heave onto the ice in the first period, before the cats ripen).

Then there are the leather lungs in section 303, with their cheerfully antiquated fight songs:

We got a rope
We got a tree,
All we need's a referee.

Nashville is a groovy little town. Tom T. Hall[1] once sang that, and it's true. Davidson County rounds off to 600,000 residents, but that still makes Nashville the second-smallest market, after Raleigh, in the NHL. Which helps explain why the Predators have the lowest budget in the league—typically, $40 million, two-thirds of what division rivals Detroit and Chicago spend.

A rival GM can buy all kinds of weaponry with $20 mil—a long-range cannon to improve the power play, or some Moscow dynamo to perk up the second line.

[1]Tom T. Hall and Kris Kristofferson are considered Nashville's most literate songwriters. "We're the only people in Nashville who can describe Dolly Parton without using our hands," is how Hall once explained their status.

Heck, he can have both if he wants.

Despite a low payroll, the Predators put a good team on ice. Even in a three-piece suit, coach Barry Trotz looks like he's just come out of the weight room. And his teams are workaholics. Feet always moving. Cycling endlessly in the corners. In the 2005–06 season, the Preds topped 100 points, but lost to San Jose in the playoffs. Sensing he had a team that could go places (and knowing he had unworkable contracts due), GM David Poile figured the 2006–07 season was Smashville's best-before date.

What the Predators needed, Poile felt, was Peter Forsberg. A relentless attacker, the Swedish center once set up a Stanley Cup–winning goal while playing despite a ruptured spleen! Alas, Forsberg was employed by Philadelphia, who wanted three past and future first-round draft picks for his services. And at age 33, the center had missed stretches of the previous seasons with injuries. The great warrior now had an Achilles everything.

Country music is a treasure trove of folk wisdom. One Top 40 philosopher (and Atlanta Thrashers fan!), Kenny Rogers, contends you have

to know when to hold and when to fold them. NHL hockey was a popular cult entertainment in Nashville. Games against the Red Wings, those northern carpetbaggers who bought up hockey's best free agents,

> **Poile figured Forsberg could win Nashville a Stanley Cup and make the Volunteer State enlist in hockey.**

traveling far into the playoffs, sold out. At the same time, the Predators themselves never won a playoff series. Poile figured Forsberg (Foppa to his friends) could win Nashville a Stanley Cup and make the Volunteer State enlist in hockey. He made the deal.

His first week in town, Forsberg had an opportunity to play the hero. The visiting Montreal Canadiens tied the game at five with seconds left. Saku Koivu put the Canadiens ahead in the shootout. Foppa, the last Predator attacker, was up. If he scored, the game continued.

There was a reason Trotz had Forsberg skating cleanup. Number 21 had scored the most memorable shootout goal ever, at the

1994 Olympics, for Sweden against Canada. With a gold medal on the line, Forsberg, a left-handed shot, raced in at full speed, shifting left, pulling Canadian goalie Corey Hirsch with him. Just as he'd seemingly jumped track, Forsberg went to his backhand, taking the stick with his right hand, stretching that arm as far as it could go, and slipping the puck one-handed into a deserted net.

Sweden honored the goal on a 1995 postage stamp.

Meanwhile, back in what was then the Sommet Center, the Nashville crowd was in full holler when Forsberg grabbed the puck from the Predators' tiger-jaws center-ice logo. Unlike in his Olympic shootout, number 21 moved cautiously. From the blue line in, his head was motionless, as he studied Habs goalie Jaroslav Halak. As the skater neared the net, fans made a noise like a braking train.

Finally, someone went for his gun. Forsberg threw a head shiver, jumping left. Halak fell, his legs spread-eagled. The forward saw an inviting patch of empty net: the top right corner. He went to shoot. Then, was suddenly borne aloft, parallel to the ice, as if a carpet had been pulled—whoa!—right out from under him. He slipped, then fell, spinning clockwise, coming to a stop with his head across the goal line. While the puck wobbled disinterestedly off into the corner.

The Nashville crowd let out a punched-in-the-stomach groan. Foppa had flopped.

It was a bad omen. Forsberg played honorably in Nashville, scoring an overtime goal to defeat the hated Red Wings in the next home game, but the Preds bowed out in the first playoff round. To San Jose. Again.

The Forsberg gamble failed. But grafting a frozen sport onto sub-tropical terrain might be considered a riskier venture. And when Nashville's season ended, there was talk about the Preds following their mascot-crest, the sabre-toothed tiger, into extinction. It didn't happen. Despite the occasional heartache (annual playoff disappoint-ments), fans remain faithful. Which probably shouldn't be a surprise. As Nicholas Dawidoff observed in his book, *In the Country of Country*, rock and roll is about youthful rebellion; country music is about adult disap-pointment.

In a lot of ways, country and hockey are made for each other. Country music is all about Saturday night and Sunday morning. Hank Williams was "Rootie Tootie" at midnight. Come sunup, though, it was "I Saw the Light." Likewise, Nashville's

orneriest Predator ever, Darcy Hordichuk (2005–08) fought like hell on Saturdays; Sunday morning, the Christian was born again, clasping red, raw knuckles in prayer.

There is also the matter of pedigree. Nashville's biggest hockey star, captain Shea Weber, hails from Sicamous, British Columbia, a town of 3,192. His dad worked 9 to 5 in a sawmill. Nash-ville's biggest female country star, Carrie Underwood, grew up in Checotah, Oklahoma, a community of 3,481. And her dad worked in a sawmill.

It wasn't inevitable that Carrie should find a hockey husband. But given the bedrock, small-town values that in-form both country music and hockey, neither was it surprising. And if you followed her romance in the press, it all seemed to happen as simply and straightforwardly as a country song—with a requisite touch of pedal-steel schmaltz.

Karen Fisher, a country music–loving hockey mom in Peterborough, Ontario, saw Underwood's winning performance on *American Idol* on TV in 2005 and thought, "Oh, Mike would love this." So Mom taped the performance and gave it to her son, an Ottawa Senators forward. Mike Fisher liked what he saw and heard, and so, when Underwood played Scotia-bank Place, Ottawa's home

Another Web gem: Shea lets loose with another slapshot.

Carrie Underwood (right) with an unidentified Predator fan.

rink, on March 21, 2008, he went for a look-see.

One of Underwood's band members invited the off-duty Senator back-stage. Sparks flew. With his fashion-model hair, square jaw and athletic physique, Fisher looks like the kind of guy who could wake a princess with a kiss. Just as Underwood resembles Snow White after a morning at the beauty salon. But there was a stronger bond: Both Fisher and Underwood enjoy thrilling, sky-high careers. They're also staunch Christians who believe that a kite needs a strong hand to fly right.

Fisher has a special message on his hockey stick—"Rom. 12:12," refer-ring to St. Paul's letter to the Romans: "Be joyful in hope, patient in afflic-tion, faithful in prayer."

Underwood performed her big hit "Jesus, Take the Wheel" the evening she met Fisher. It was Good Friday—a holy day in the Christian tradition.

Mike and Carrie were married two years later on a "Summer Night in Georgia," according to a *People* magazine cover story. Fisher gave his princess a diamond tiara. Guests found their tables with designated wedding pucks.

In February 2011 the Preds decided they needed Fisher as much as Underwood did, and so GM Poile turned gambler once again, sending a first-round as well as a conditional draft pick to the Ottawa Senators for the hardworking center.

The Fisher–Underwood marriage isn't a country music–hockey one-off. Singer Gretchen Wilson composed the Predators' working-class anthem, "Smashville Bound":

I work a double shift on Monday,
Tuesday I get up before dawn
Wednesday pourin' coffee,
Thursday night I'm tending the bar
Well, when Friday finally rolls around,
I call my hockey tonkin' friends
And we're Smashville bound.

And this is the only rink in the NHL where fans hand out song/cheer sheets. Everyone from Amy Grant to Trisha Yearwood has sung the national anthem. Country acts occasionally perform between periods. Coach Trotz sometimes sings from the Garth Brooks songbook to inspire players. Quoting Brooks's song "The Dance," he suggests that hockey, like love itself, is a high-stakes gamble that must be taken.

"Our lives are better left to chance," the coach says. "I could have missed the pain. But I'd have had to miss the dance."

Riot in Cell Block 303

The shift-disturbers who antagonize opposition players at the Bridgestone Arena are well organized. Section 303 has its own website (www.section303.com) and a 2,000-fan mailing list. At games, the gang that National Public Radio calls "the loudest section in the loudest arena in the NHL" hand out cheer sheets.

Here are some of their greatest hits.

Foggy Goalie Breakdown

It's taunt the goalie time

It's taunt the goalie time

Let's make him cry and whine

It's taunt the goalie time

Let's score another goal.

Let's score another goal.

The goalie is a hole.

Will the Clavicle Be Unbroken?

Let us pray these things three:

Fight thee!

Bite thee!

Smite thee!

And everybody said, "a-men!"

I Can't Help Falling When Shoved by You

One-two-three-four, he just hit the icy floor!

Five-six-seven-eight, where the hell d'you learn to skate?

A scout's dream: 22-foot, 6,000-lb power forward; impossible to move in front of the net. Only known enemy is seagulls. Designed by Devils fan Jon Krawczyk, the sculpture is now located in Newark, New Jersey's Prudential Center's Championship Plaza.

ALTERNATE NICKNAME: Devs.

FRANCHISE STARTED: Born as the Kansas City Mohawks in 1974. The Chicago Blackhawks declared exclusive NHL rights to aboriginal caricatures, so the Mohawks became the Kansas City Scouts (1974–76); after that, the Colorado Rockies (1976–81) before moving to Jersey in 1982.

UNIFORMLY SPEAKING: The original uniform looked like red-and-green Christmas wrapping. Their tree-colored pants disappeared in 1992. The current jersey, in blood red and black, is perfect for a team that plays on Tony Soprano's turf.

HOW COOL?: Very. And we're not just saying that for fear of having the ziti beaten out of us. Home: 8.4. Away: 7.2.

NEW JERSEY DEVILS

THE AGONY: Devil Scott Stevens (1991–2004) had a trick for icing forwards. He'd lie in wait for skaters coming down the other wing. When they slipped past their defender, Stevens left his zone, sliding sideways, catching the head-down winger unaware. *Bada-bing! Down goes Eric Lindros ... Paul Kariya ... Ron Francis ...*

THE ECSTASY: Winning Stanley Cups in 1995, 2000 and 2003.

FANATIC: A 1995 *Seinfeld* episode has Elaine's boyfriend, Puddy, in a devilish mood, taking the whole gang to a playoff game and then screaming his team on. ("Messier, you suck!") The TV incantations worked—the Devils took the Cup a month later.

Puddy Face.

Average ticket + parking + hot dog + beer:
$77.37
(16th highest in the NHL)

Home Games

There is a photo around, easy enough to Google, I'm looking at it now, showing a very young Martin Brodeur making a melodramatic save playing street hockey. Could be a kid anywhere, playing the hero. Certain features make it easy for us to determine the shot's origin, however. It's thoughtfully composed. The photographer knew where to be, what to look for. And the kid is wearing bulky, adult equipment. Finally, the desperate kick save accompanied by the anguished, Jesus-on-the-cross expression—that's Jacques Plante's signature move!

So the photograph was taken somewhere that goaltending is a passed-on tradition—as a profession, religion and art form.

Welcome to Montreal, goaltending capital of the world. Montreal's Martin Brodeur would eventually become New Jersey Devils' Marty Brodeur. (Hockey is the lone occupation where men grow into children's names.) As it turns out, the picture and pads belong to Martin's dad, Denis Brodeur, who won Olympic bronze in net for Canada in 1956, then became a successful photographer. The Brodeurs lived in Saint-Léonard, Montreal's Little Italy. The Brodeurs aren't the only goalies here. The Vancouver Canucks' Roberto Luongo grew up a slapshot away.

It's like that in Quebec. Jacques Plante's sister lived next to

The rivals: Patrick Roy and Martin Brodeur.

Bernie Parent's family in Montreal. Seven Vezina Trophies right there. By 2005, 734 Quebecers had made the NHL—121 of them goalies. Many arrived after Patrick Roy, a netminder who, by virtue of his temperament, wardrobe and skill, changed goaltending into a superheroic activity, becoming hockey's Schwarzenegger.

A lot of Roy's superpowers originated with the costume. He wore oversize everything. And, like Arnold, he vanquished enemies with cruel one-liners. After a Jeremy Roenick taunt, Roy shrugged, "I can't hear what he says because my ears are stuffed with Stanley Cup rings."

He won two with Montreal (1986 and 1993) and another with the Colorado Avalanche (2001). In doing so, Roy transformed his position, spreading pads wide across the ice and fanning his upper body like a cobra, making nets behind him disappear. Significantly, he was a revolutionary hero when Quebec contemplated separating from Canada. Roy certainly did. In 2000, after letting in nine goals against Detroit, instead of apologizing, Patrick got mad at the Canadiens, telling owner Ronald Corey, "This is the last game I play for Montreal," then skating off to Colorado.

Balls? *Balls!*

Roy inspired his province. Before Patrick, two Quebec goalies had been chosen in the first round of the NHL draft in 22 seasons (Michel Plasse, 1968, and Michel "Bunny" Larocque, 1972). After Roy, 11 goalies from *la belle province* went in the first round between 1990 and 1999.[1] Brodeur was the lone successor to threaten Roy's sovereignty (*roi* means "king" in French). Arriving in New Jersey in 1992, Martin led the team to a Stanley Cup in 1995. Still, he remained Roy's sidekick. Their nicknames said it all:

Roy was Saint Patrick, descendent of Morenz, Richard and Lafleur; Brodeur was Marty, heir to Toe Blake and Dickie Moore—wonderful, best-supporting-actor types.

Roy told the world where to get off. Kid brother Marty stayed home and played it safe. In 1995, his fiery agent, Gilles Lupien,[2] wanted Brodeur to test the market. What could he get in New York or Toronto?

In the playoffs, when the scandal broke, he was a wall.

But Brodeur understood what he had in Jersey—the NHL's best GM, Lou Lamoriello, and three marvelously efficient defensemen in Scott Niedermayer, Scott Stevens and Ken Daneyko. Besides, New Jersey was a lot like Montreal, minus the stress. Coaches Jacques Lemaire, Jacques Laperriere, Pat Burns and Larry Robinson started with the Habs. Marty spoke to his goalie coach, Jacques Caron, in French. Playing in New Jersey also meant bus hops to Philly, Long Island and Manhattan for away games. Brodeur would be sleeping in his own bed most nights. You've seen Tony Soprano's lilac-

_____

[1] Martin Brodeur, Jocelyn Thibault, Eric Fichaud, Dan Cloutier, Jean-Sebastien Giguere, Marc Denis, Roberto Luongo, Jean-Francois Damphousse, Patrick DesRochers, Mathieu Chouinard, Maxime Ouellet.

[2] Lupien was more passive on the ice. Mordecai Richler once wrote, "Lupien treats the puck as somebody else might being caught with another man's wife."

calm neighborhood on TV: manicured blue-green lawns, wide streets with quiet, gleaming cars. That's where Marty lived: North Caldwell, New Jersey. Summers, he'd disappear with his wife and kids to a cottage in the Laurentians, near Montreal.

Brodeur, negotiating without an agent, took less to stay in New Jersey. His union filed a grievance. Brodeur agreed to play for Canada in the 1998 Olympics, but Roy made it clear that he wanted to play every game. *Hasta la vista,* baby. The goalies barely talked. Marty said nothing about these slights. The only newspaper angle on him was the wonderful story of how, after every Stanley Cup win, he'd bring the trophy back to Montreal. Cops closed off Rue Mauriac, and he'd host a ball hockey tournament for his old pals. North of the street lamp, one team; south of it, the other. Games to seven. First to four wins takes the Stanley Cup.

If Marty Brodeur was a play-it-safe, stay-at-home recluse, he sure made living in a cocoon seem like a good idea.

Maybe fans figure they know what happened next in Marty Brodeur's life, but no one probably could explain what happened to the goalie in 2002–03. Except, perhaps, 17th-century French author Blaise Pascal, who said, "*Le coeur a ses raisons que la raison ne connaît point.*" ("The heart has its reasons that reason knows not at all.")

Early in 2003, a Montreal crime weekly, *Photo Police*, published a blind item on a nameless Quebec goalie having an affair with his sister-in-law. The hockey player was being sued for $9 million U.S. in alimony by his wife. The other skate was sure to drop. Brodeur came clean to *Le Journal de Montreal*, acknowledging that he and his wife had separated. The past year had been difficult. And yes, he was now with his wife's half-brother's ex-wife, Genevieve.

There is never a good time to blow up a family. Not with four kids. Professionally, the timing couldn't have been worse. Brodeur was in his prime, 29 years old in February 2002, when he started for Canada in the gold medal game against the United States. The World Cup in Montreal lay ahead. His own team, New Jersey, was a playoff favorite. Complicating matters, a labor conflict loomed. Cripes, maybe he'd be out of work: another divorced dad wondering how he was going to make things work.

Home games can be the hardest. Divorce and scandal can scuttle careers. Think of Tiger Woods.

Incredibly, Marty Brodeur's two seasons in hell were the best of his career. He looked imperturbable, shutting down the Americans in Utah, and then winning his first Vezina Trophy in 2002–03 after throwing 11 shutouts. In the playoffs, when the scandal broke, he was a wall. Eight more shutouts, an NHL postseason record. Three came in

the Devils' Stanley Cup final series against Anaheim—in which Brodeur won his third Stanley Cup. In the 2004 World Cup, another win for Canada, Brodeur's goals against average was a microscopic 1.00.

He was now, everyone agreed, the best goalie in the world. And an authentic local figure: knowingly flawed, but redeemed by passionate commitment. He could be the hero of one of Jersey native Bruce Springsteen's songs—"Prove It All Night," maybe. After 2004–05 was lost to a labor dispute, Brodeur came back hungrier than ever, posting 35 shutouts from 2005–10. Soon, he had all the NHL goalie records—most career shutouts, most wins.

He wed Genevieve, had another child. Another old, often fractious marriage improved. Patrick Roy graciously attended the 2009 game where Brodeur tied St. Patrick's record for most NHL wins—551. Afterward, the goalie who had played a robot Terminator his entire career paid Brodeur the supreme compliment. "He's like a machine," Roy said.

Hmm, this might be a problem. Marty looks behind him for a puck entering the net during the 2006 Olympics in Torino.

NEW YORK ISLANDERS

ALTERNATE NICKNAMES: Isles, Fish-sticks.

FRANCHISE STARTED: The Islanders came to the NHL along with the Atlanta Flames in 1972.

UNIFORMLY SPEAKING: Long Island is long: nearly 120 miles long. And seven and a half million people call it home, more than the population of Ireland. The Isles are Long Island's only pro team. Their first logo, an NY with the Y extending into a hockey stick, was created on short notice by a local ad agency. In 1995, the team created a new design that looked like Captain Highliner on a three-day drunk. After a barrage of complaints, the old crest was reinstated in 1997. Actually, the original jersey, maybe because it was thrown together in three days, always looked a little clunky, like a police rep team.

HOW COOL?: Home: 6.0. Away: 6.2.

A short Islander.

Captain Denis Potvin flanked by bearded Butch Goring after an Islander Cup win.

THE AGONY: Erstwhile Long Islander F. Scott Fitzgerald once said, "There are no second acts in American life." For Islander fans, that's all there is. The club finished last in its first two seasons, collecting a boatload of draft picks: Denis Potvin, first pick in 1973 draft, and then the big '74 haul—Clark Gillies, Bryan Trottier and Bob Bourne, three great forwards in a row, topped by a late steal, Stefan Persson. In 1977, the Isles had their moment of truth, with the 15th pick and two players to choose from: Dwight Foster, a good, safe all-around forward, and Michael Bossy, a prolific goal scorer who couldn't check his coat. "I can teach a player to check, but I can't teach a player to score," coach Al Arbour decided.

THE ECSTASY: And so the first act was complete: Bossy joined Trottier and Gillies to form the NHL's top line. Potvin, the last point man to routinely score on a wrist shot, was hockey's most complete rearguard. And come spring, Billy Smith did a passable Terry Sawchuk impersonation. The Islanders' glorious second act began in 1980, when Bob Nystrom chipped a lovely John Tonelli feed into a dramatic, Stanley Cup–winning goal over Philly. After that, three more Cups, all in a row. The Islanders, in their Brooks Brothers blue suits, were the epitome of professionalism, from GM Bill Torrey's classic bow ties to the team's mercifully quick power play, a unit that often put teams to rest with a single shot—usually by Bossy.

THE AGONY, PART 2: Alas, the third act arrived later in the '80s. For two decades now, whenever the Isles have had to choose between a Foster and a Bossy, they've gone with Foster.

FANATIC:

Islander fan wearing a Ranger dress and a gold tinsel wig.

Average ticket + parking + hot dog + beer:

$77.64

(15th highest in the NHL)

The Gangs of New York

Pictured on your right, we see another New York Ranger–Islander fight, hard to tell what year. These guys are always going at it. Every match is an opportunity to get even. Or ahead.

A head on a platter would be even better.

Why is it like this for teams with the same first name—New York? Because brothers fight. Because New Yorkers think they're living in the best city in the world. And they are. Because Long Islanders think New Yorkers are full of themselves. And they're right. Because, as in every family feud, the brothers long ago slipped into a perpetually aggrieved state, eager for any slight that might allow them to exercise their fury.

Here's how one hockey district went all Cain and Abel.

A presumptive offense

In 1972, Long Island wins an NHL franchise. The team, everyone assumes, will be called the Long Island Ducks—that's what the region's Eastern Hockey League team is called. Instead, the suburbanites go with New York Islanders. Ranger fans are furious. Still are. "Hey, when Frank sings 'If I can make it there,' he's not talking about Mineola," they complain.

The diplomatic slip

In the second week of February 1973, during the Isles' first season, the Rangers thump their kid brothers with back-to-back 6–0 wins. Ranger goalie Gilles Villemure laughs, "Just like a tennis match, six-love, six-love. How many times do we play these guys?"

Return serve

Eleven seconds into overtime of the deciding game of the 1975 Rangers–Islanders playoff series: Islander forward J. P. Parise (Zach's dad) tips a pass past goalie Eddie Giacomin. The Rangers are stunned and embarrassed; the Islanders a mite too pleased with themselves. *Rivalry on!*

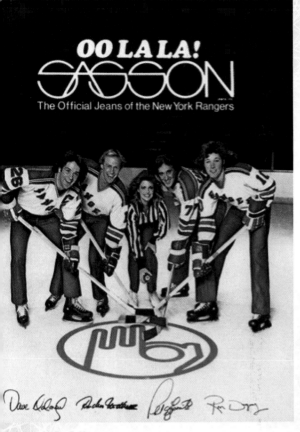

OO LA LA! SASSON
The Official Jeans of the New York Rangers

Cover boys (l-r) Dave Maloney, Anders Hedberg, some girl, Phil Esposito and Ron Duguay.

The Archduke Franz Ferdinand moment

On February 25, 1979, Denis Potvin forcibly escorts Ranger rookie Ulf Nilsson into the boards. Teammates carry Ulf off the ice, his ankle broken. Fans at Madison Square Garden respond with an angry chant: "Potvin sucks, Potvin sucks…" until the shout sounds like a war dance incantation. The rivalry is now a feud.[1]

[1] Jonathan Mahler, author of a book about late-'70s New York, *Ladies and Gentlemen, The Bronx Is Burning*, explains why citizens felt protective of their teams. "Well, it's certainly the case that the city's dire straits—the graffiti-bruised subways, the soaring crime, the burning tenements—somehow raised the intensity of New Yorkers' relationships with their sports teams. Things just felt more personal. Plus, just like the city itself, sporting events felt a little bit out of control. I mean, recall that when Chris Chambliss hit the walk-off home run against the Royals in '76, he wasn't even able to get to home plate because he was mobbed by the mass of humanity that had swarmed onto the field."

Oo la la! The Rangers win.

The Islanders score more goals than any other NHL team in the 1978–79 season, but bow out to the underdog Rangers in the playoffs, victims of big John Davidson's nimble goaltending. Madison Avenue rewards Manhattan's team with a lucrative ad campaign, including TV commercials. Long Islanders hate losing to their windblown-haired big-city rivals.

Boy, it's chili out

On November 13, 1979, the Islanders finally get their corporate perk: Wendy's offers free bowls of chili—*whoopty doo!*—to fans if the team scores five goals against the Rangers. The Islanders are way ahead when the offer is increased to double chilis for 10 goals. The Nassau Coliseum crowd goes crazy when the Islanders bag their quota, defeating the Rangers 10–5.

A square meal

The next time the Islanders visit Madison Square Garden—December 9, 1979—fans throw fish heads at goalie Billy Smith during the national anthem. Later in the game, which the Rangers win, 5–4, fans litter the ice with bowls of chili.

Car wars: Ranger fan attacks former Islander star Denis Potvin.

Isle of Contentment

Spurred on by their upset at the hands of John Davidson the previous season, the Islanders commit to one playoff goalie, Billy Smith, and steamroller the opposition, winning their first Stanley Cup in the spring of 1980. Rubbing sea salt in Ranger fans' wounds, the Islander faithful wave "Oo la la, so soon" signs when the Rangers bow out in the first round.

Adding injury to insult

Little brother Islanders win three more Stanley Cups in a row; gloating fans hit below the belt, serenading Rangers with choruses of "Nineteen forty! Nineteen forty!"—a cruel reference to the last time the Rangers won the Cup. Islanders hit above the belt, too: on December 30, 1981, Clark Gillies knocks the Rangers' Ed Hospodar into 1982 with a right uppercut, breaking his jaw. The feud is getting ugly—real ugly.

The cease-fire

Concerned that fans have been going too far with a taunt that drew attention to Denis Potvin's marital troubles, the Rangers in the mid-'80s stop playing "Let's Go Blue," a University of Michigan fight song that Garden fans spin into anti-Potvin singalongs. At Nassau Coliseum, Isles take the anti-Ranger provocation "The Chicken Dance" out of heavy rotation. Social conversations occasionally break out on the ice: Butch Goring approaches Ranger lady-killer Ron Duguay at the faceoff circle and asks, "What's Cher like?"

A clear violation of the Geneva Convention

The feud reignites on April 5, 1990, in the first game of the playoffs, when the Rangers' James Patrick clobbers Islander star Pat LaFontaine in a brutal, clean mid-ice collision. Afterward, Ranger fans attack LaFontaine's ambulance on the way to Lenox Hill Hospital.

Busted

The New York hockey feud is once again as toxic as Brooklyn's Gowanus Canal. Isles fans wearing sweaters 19 and 40 regularly park in front of Ranger sections and heckle away. Broadcasters are blocked from getting to their booths. One night, Ranger analyst John Davidson is confronted by an older woman who pulls up her sweater to reveal a T-shirt reading "1940."

The frog and the turtle

On April 4, 1998, the Islanders score late in the third to take a 3–0 lead against the Rangers. Coach Mike Milbury calls time out. The Rangers wonder if he's trying to embarrass them. Seconds later, P. J. Stock is whaling away at the Isles' Mariusz Czerkawski. Goalie Tommy Salo steams in to help his sagging teammate—or maybe just to offer corner advice: "Wound him with irony!" Finally, Raging Bull Dan Cloutier, the Ranger goalie, arrives, throwing Salo to the ice, pulling his sweater off and firing 13 overhead rights to the back of the goalie's noggin. Later, he skates to the Islander bench, offering to take on the whole team. You can imagine his throwdown: "C'mon! I'll moidalize ya!"

The Mexican standoff

Two weeks later, on April 15, Stock and Cloutier are walking from the Southgate Hotel to the Garden for the next meeting with the Islanders when three Long Island fans step in front of them, giving them the Sonny Liston penitentiary glare—as if to say, "Let's get ready to rumble." The five stand there, nose to nose, for a New York minute, before the two Rangers remember they're paid to compete against the Islanders, not their fans.

Not her main squeegee

There are lots of fierce rivalries in the world of sport: Boston Red Sox–New York Yankees; Dallas Cowboys–Washington Redskins; any sport involving Edmonton and Calgary; Inter Milan–AC Milan in soccer. But the final word (for now!) on hockey's best/worst family feud is this: In 2007, a skirmish breaks out between Ranger goalie Henrik Lundqvist and a New York Islander Ice Girl. The girl asks Lundqvist to move out of the crease so she can clean it during a TV time-out. He says no. And then, a brouhaha—Lundqvist slashes the girl in her squeegee. She starts yelling. Then the cops (referees) arrive.

*Islander goalie Rick DiPietro and Ranger Al Montoya square off in a
2007 preseason game.*

NEW YORK RANGERS

ALTERNATE NICKNAMES: Blueshirts, Broadway Blueshirts, Broadway Blues.

FRANCHISE STARTED: In 1925, boxing promoter Tex Rickard built the third Madison Square Garden, and installed ice-making equipment. The former Hamilton Tigers became winter tenants, playing as the New York Americans. The Rangers were created as an NHL expansion club a year later.

UNIFORMLY SPEAKING: Rickard planned on calling the team the Giants, but the press dubbed them Tex's Rangers. The name stuck. So has the team's first jersey: a patriotic affair with RANGERS falling down the front like a beauty queen's sash.

HOW COOL?: Home blues: 10.0. Away whites: 9.0.

Broadway Blueshirts: Ranger fans show their colors.

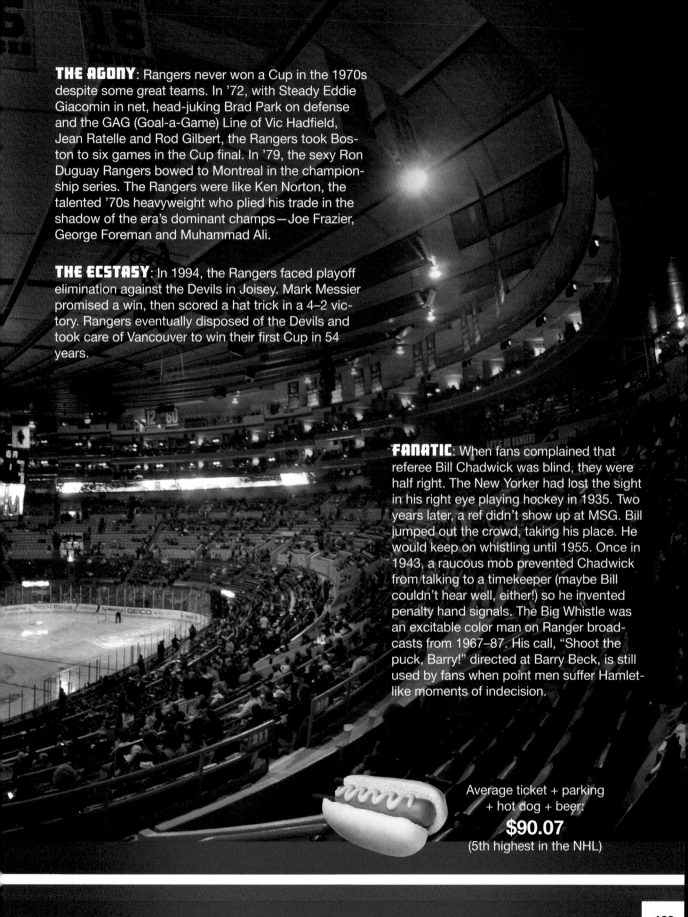

THE AGONY: Rangers never won a Cup in the 1970s despite some great teams. In '72, with Steady Eddie Giacomin in net, head-juking Brad Park on defense and the GAG (Goal-a-Game) Line of Vic Hadfield, Jean Ratelle and Rod Gilbert, the Rangers took Boston to six games in the Cup final. In '79, the sexy Ron Duguay Rangers bowed to Montreal in the championship series. The Rangers were like Ken Norton, the talented '70s heavyweight who plied his trade in the shadow of the era's dominant champs—Joe Frazier, George Foreman and Muhammad Ali.

THE ECSTASY: In 1994, the Rangers faced playoff elimination against the Devils in Joisey. Mark Messier promised a win, then scored a hat trick in a 4–2 victory. Rangers eventually disposed of the Devils and took care of Vancouver to win their first Cup in 54 years.

FANATIC: When fans complained that referee Bill Chadwick was blind, they were half right. The New Yorker had lost the sight in his right eye playing hockey in 1935. Two years later, a ref didn't show up at MSG. Bill jumped out the crowd, taking his place. He would keep on whistling until 1955. Once in 1943, a raucous mob prevented Chadwick from talking to a timekeeper (maybe Bill couldn't hear well, either!) so he invented penalty hand signals. The Big Whistle was an excitable color man on Ranger broadcasts from 1967–87. His call, "Shoot the puck, Barry!" directed at Barry Beck, is still used by fans when point men suffer Hamlet-like moments of indecision.

Average ticket + parking + hot dog + beer:
$90.07
(5th highest in the NHL)

Tie Domi and Bob Probert in 1992.

The Killers

Hockey's most famous fight took place in Madison Square Garden on December 2, 1992, when Tie Domi tussled with Bob Probert. One reason it's famous is the setting. The megaphone is always on when New York teams play. We can still hear Messier promising a Ranger playoff win in '94, an action that echoed Joe Namath's guarantee of a Jets upset over the Baltimore Colts before the 1969 Super Bowl.

On the morning of the Probert–Domi fight, you could read all about it in four newspapers. Goliath Probert, who stood 6′3″ and weighed in at 225 pounds, had been called out by Domi, a grinning, rock-headed David who told reporters he had December 2 circled on his calendar. Goliath was going down. Even the *Times*, normally above such coarse plebeian pleasures, took note of the impending brawl.

Once upon a time, most everyone liked what was called "a good hockey fight." Back in the '60s, in a six-team league, clubs played each other 14 times a season. Brawls had story lines, an accumulation of provocations and misunderstandings that made violence inevitable. Like a cleansing shootout at the end of a feverish crime movie. Sometimes, it was still like that. By the 1990s, however, too many hockey fights felt contrived. Teams fought, even if they only met once a year. Indiscriminate brawling somehow diminished the sport, turning hockey fights into cheap, meaningless socks.

Domi vs. Probert was different. This match had a backstory, as they say in the movies. Both fighters grew up on Ontario's roughest block, Windsor. Goliath's dad was a police detective who let his boys drink at home. Better there than in a car, he probably figured. At 16, Bob was a big, talented hockey player who tried to please and protect everyone. He was also a bad alcoholic.

Growing up, Domi thrilled to Probert's accomplishments. Playing junior, he hoped to be just like him; once in the NHL, he wanted to be Probert, period. Earlier that year, Tie had caught the champ with a right, drawing blood. Afterward, he coasted on one skate, pretending to strap on a championship belt. Probert sat in the penalty box, staring out with dull, spreading hatred.

He got that way sometimes. Coach Jacques Demers once found Probert in the dressing room, a smoke dangling from his mouth. Demers approached his clearly troubled star: "Please, Bob, c'mon. Think what you're doing—to your health, career…" Probert reached for the tool that players use to tailor their hockey sticks, lighting his cigarette with a blowtorch.

Everyone knew what was coming at Madison Square Garden that night. Knowing made the tension both thrilling and unbearable. Domi smiled during the pregame warmup. Fans shouted his name. The grin spread. He chatted with teammates, chopping affectionately at shin pads, as if saying, "I'm okay. Everything's great." In fact, he hadn't slept in 24 hours.

Probert, at the other end, skated in his own orbit. People shouted his name. He never looked up. The hard thing about being Goliath is that there are so many would-be Davids. At 26, Probert had already had 155 pro fights. There'd be 200 more. The week before, he'd fought Kelly Chase in Detroit. Next week, he would twice have to prove himself against Wendel Clark in Toronto.

There was always someone.

When the teams lined up for the faceoff, the Garden began to thunder.

Once upon a time, most everyone liked what was called "a good hockey fight."

Half a minute in, Probert stepped on for a second faceoff. More noise. When the Rangers' number 28 skated onto the ice, the crowd jumped to its feet—not in sections, all at once.

The puck dropped. Domi tried to skate away. Probert pulled him close with his stick. "Might as well get it over with—let's go," he said.

"Let's do it later," David said.

"Let's get it over with," Goliath repeated, shoving the smaller man three times.

Gloves flew off simultaneously, but only one fighter was ready. Domi, a lefty, groped for Probert's left sleeve with his right hand, hoping to free his best weapon. Probert, meanwhile, landed eight uncontested rights—four in a row to the head—before Domi readied himself. David, give him credit, could take a punch. Finally, he got his left working. Now both men were throwing chopping blows. Which tree would go down first?

The Garden chanted "Domi! Domi!" Detroit's captain, and Probert's friend, Steve Yzerman, jumped on top of the bench and was screaming.

David somehow got hold of Goliath's right with his own right hand! Now, they'd have to trade lefts—advantage Domi! But here's where Probert's experience kicked in, all those encounters with gaudy-nicknamed pretenders—Stu "The Grim Reaper" Grimson and "Missing Link" Gaetz.

The Detroit winger knew what was coming and moved easily to his left hand, staying in the fight. He absorbed Domi's best shots, and when the Ranger tired, he pulled his rested right arm free, continuing to pound away. Out of ideas and energy, Domi took eight more to the head and then threw one last blind haymaker. When it missed, Goliath held David still in front of him, readying the smaller man for the coup de grâce, a solid right that sent Domi to the ice in sections. First, his legs forgot their job, wobbling apart, and then over he went, toppling backward with Probert still raining blows on top of him.

Officials pulled them apart. Though bleeding, Domi smiled, waving to the crowd. Probert drifted to the penalty box, listless, head down, hands still balled in fists, looking like a doomed, sleepwalking heavy in a '40s crime movie—Burt Lancaster in *The Killers*. You'd never know he'd won anything. Players did, though. On the Detroit bench, you could see Yzerman shouting at Domi as he gestured to his midsection, pantomiming the fastening of a belt. Goliath was still the champ.

Two mysteries remained after the fight. Why, if Domi had called Probert out, was he unprepared? That one's easy: NHL president Gil Stein had warned Tie that if he started the brawl he promised, it would cost him 20 games. Also, though he'd fought Probert earlier that year, Domi was

more respectful of the game, if not of Probert.

A month earlier, Domi had scored against Buffalo, and then ridden his stick in celebration. Later, in the dressing room, he found Mark Messier. "Tie, trainer's room," the captain said. "Listen, enough's enough," Messier continued when they were alone. "No more of that shit after your fights or goals. If you never show respect for peers, you're never going

Domi smiled, waving to the crowd. Probert drifted to the penalty box, listless, head down…

to have respect in this game."

Why was Probert down? In the next seven days, the Wings would play Minnesota, where Mark Tinordi waited, then it was on to Tampa Bay—Basil McRae was there. After that, back home against Chicago, he and Chris Chelios always tangled, before flying to Toronto—and Wendel Clark.

Then there were Goliath's battles with himself: the struggle not to drink or relax with drugs. Medicines almost every heavyweight champ craves.

Bob Probert spent a relatively short portion of his life making trouble, and the greater part making amends. "He couldn't stand for you to be mad at him," Coach Demers once said. "One

night, a young girl had given him a dozen roses, and he gave them to me for my wife. Another fan gave him a teddy bear, and he gave it to me for my daughter. In 17 years of coaching, I haven't had all angels. I thought I'd seen it all, but I hadn't seen anyone like him…. You see him, even when he's just gotten in trouble, and he has that look that says, 'I'm sorry, help me.'"

Fighting takes its toll. The other Reggie in New York sports lore, Reggie Fleming, scrapped for the Rangers in the late '60s. He did so for every team he played on, for a quarter-century. When he died in July of 2010, at 73, scientists said he suffered from brain damage—dementia associated with head trauma.

The best (and best-loved) fighter in the NHL died the same month, age 45, in a boat near Windsor with his family. A heart attack, they said. What happens when you burn the candle at both ends with a blowtorch.

OTTAWA SENATORS

ALTERNATE NICKNAMES: Sens—and, once upon a time, Ottawa Silver Seven.

FRANCHISE STARTED: The Ottawa Hockey Club began in 1883, became the Senators in 1908, and was a charter member of the NHL in 1917. The club recorded 11 Stanley Cup wins before the Great Depression drove the team to St. Louis in 1934. The Sens returned to the NHL as an expansion franchise in 1992.

UNIFORMLY SPEAKING: Ottawa is the home of the Canadian government. Hence, the name Senators. The original Sens wore a barber-pole jersey. The modern team has a Roman general on its jersey, no doubt pleasing Consiglio Di Nino, the Italian-born Conservative senator from Ontario.

HOW COOL?: Original barber pole outfit: 7:0; Current uniform with Trojan condom logo: 6.8. Track suit warm-up suit alternative with Sens on chest: 4.5

Pizza Deliverance: Ottawa's best ever scoring line.

ALFREDSSON SPEZZA HEATLEY

Enterprising Ottawa grocer organizes Coke cans into Senator logo.

THE AGONY: The Sens draft hockey hunks Alexei Yashin (1992) and Alexandre Daigle (1993), figuring they're landing matinee idols. Instead, they get $16.5-million Hollywood loafers. Yashin signed a $4-million deal he was dissatisfied with upon learning that Daigle—a projected superstar, Guy Lafleur with better hair—had inked a $12.5-million deal. Daigle turned into an amiable floater who tried showbiz before playing in Switzerland. Yashin quit the team for more money—and supermodel Carol Alt.

THE ECSTASY: The combo of Dany Heatley, Jason Spezza and Daniel Alfredsson are the NHL's top-scoring line from 2005–08, delivering fans a berth in the Cup final in 2007, and so much pie (a fast-food chain offers free slices when the Sens score five goals) they're called the Pizza Line.

FANATIC: In 1905, a team from Canada's north, Dawson City, challenges Ottawa for the Stanley Cup, traveling by dogsled, boat and train, and arriving 23 days later. Ottawa outscores its guests 32–4 to retain the Cup.

Average ticket + parking
+ hot dog + beer:
$77.03
(17th highest in the NHL)

Ottawa Senators' kid line.

Signs held by fans read: "Princess Heatley" (with drawing labeled "I'm An All star!"), "$45.M = DIMINISHED ROLE?", and a partial sign reading "Yea..."

Player jersey reads: HEATLEY 15

Rink boards advertising: erCard (MasterCard), pay p (PayPal)

Lone shark: Dany Heatley surrounded by former friends.

In the Night of the Heat

Except at the very end, the Senators were terrible in 2010–11, and the author, an Ottawa native, cannot bear to reflect on their fortunes, except to provide this account of what it might've been like venturing onto the Queensway to join the hate wave to Scotiabank Place on December 2, 2010, for the return of former Senator Dany Heatley. "Heat" infuriated Ottawa by forcing a trade from the team in 2009. The players in our drama are two Senator fans: Earl Gates, a retired firefighter, and nephew Chris, a software millionaire.

We begin with Chris pulling his Lexus in front of Earl's Westboro home. Pearly, as he's known, is waiting on the sidewalk, wearing a disguise: a mask fashioned from a Photoshopped image of Heatley sucking on a baby pacifier that ran in that day's *Ottawa Sun*....

"Peek-a-boo."

"Hop in, Dan. Fifty-goal scorers are always welcome in my car."

"Get my bet down?"

"Senators, Rangers, Vancouver."

"Attaboy. I see the tickets?"

"Glove compartment."

"Holy liftin'—$1,116.21! My first house on Gilchrist was $2,500."

"Cost-of-living adjustment."

"I 'member the Riders—Grey Cup champs. I was a kid. Nothing—zee-row! That's how much my tickets were."

"How's that?"

"Your grandmother, she'd go to IGA for groceries, eh? Use to get Gold Bond stamps free with your bread… pork chops. Put the stamps in a book. Ten books, you had season tickets, bleachers, Lansdowne Park. Bobby Simpson, Russ Jackson, Moe 'the Toe' Racine…"

"Had to buy groceries, though."

"Had to eat, too. Hey, what's goin' on with my seat here?"

"It's heated."

"Thought I was wetting my pants."

"So, who's going to win tonight, Pearly?"

"Senators, baby. What I bet. Got my bet down, right?

"Asked me already. I did indeed. Made one myself, too."

"At-a-be, here's another bet: Chris Neal drops Heatley before first period's over."

"They're friends."

"I was listening to Lowell Green on a radio. You know Heatley was born in Germany?"

"How are things at the Flat Earth Society?"

"Hey, look at that car. Get the window up."

Another car races past. Teenagers in the backseat holler into the cold:

"HEATLEY SUCKS! HEATLEY SUCKS!"

"C'mon, honk the horn. At-a-be, guys!"

"Heatley scores tonight, I'll cheer. He did a good job for us: back-to-back 50-goal seasons, represented Canada when asked—what are you doing?"

"Checking if you're wearing a San Jose jersey."

"Relax."

"How can you support Heatley? Sells out his team—first Atlanta, then us. Screws us again by not going to Edmonton—we had a good deal. He's a traitor. Case closed."

"What was your first job, Pearly Gates?"

"Health and Welfare, Tunney's Pasture—Lab of Hygiene."

"Sounds wonderful."

"Had to soak cruddy beakers in boiling green water, stick them in an autoclave after that. Bunch a scientists working on some disease."

"And?"

"Guy I worked with, Rolly Bedard, he didn't have a hair on his arm from the green lava, eh? I had nightmares I was going to turn into a albino."

"So?"

"So I quit. Worked at Kelly's Funeral Home couple years."

"Didn't dig that, though?"

"Mister Rich Little."

"Then you joined the department. How are you any different than Heatley?"

"What?"

"You quit your first two jobs—weren't happy."

"Cripes, Kate, he's making $7.6 mil a season. I made $2,500, Health and Welfare."

"And you bought a house for less than that. Times change...what..."

A Heatley effigy hanging from a hockey stick bounces sparks off the pavement alongside the Lexus as another car speeds past.

"Hey, I can walk into any station downtown, guys will ask me in, cup a coffee. 'Have a seat there, Pearl.' Heatley, he going to be welcome anywhere, he retires?"

"Good question."

" 'Can't play a sport, be one,' Ernie Calcutt use to say."

"Wise words."

"I don't know, Christopher. After Sens game, first thing I look for inna paper next morning is attendance. We're goin' down, buddy boy. I know what's coming: my first team was Hull-Ottawa Canadiens—Scotty Bowman, coach. Football Rough Riders, they left, too. Baseball Lynx—all gone."

"Ottawa is a government town. Conquering armies, Liberals and Conservatives, come and go. There's a hostage mentality. People don't feel possessive about institutions."

"Open a window. I gotta let one fly."

"Lord."

"Better a vacancy than a poor tenant. So tell me, smart guy, we finish last, who we get first pick?"

"Everyone is talking about Sean Couturier, kid from Quebec."

"Not another French kid. After all we went through with Daigle."

"How can you say that? Your team used to be Montreal."

"Sure, the French are great if you throw a bunch together. What we need is someone like that Jonathan Toews— Prairie kid with hair on his butt."

"Toews is French."

"Get out."

"Mother's French. He went to a French school in Winnipeg growing up."

"Where are we? Why aren't we moving?"

"Traffic is terrible after work, hockey nights, you know that. Senator fans and commuters returning to Carleton Place."

"Why are we playing way the hell out here anyway? Cripes, your grandfather, eh, he had a truck. Orange Day, he and a couple dogans use to go to The Alex on Bank Street—parades all ended up there. They'd steal the horses off the wagons, let them loose out here in a fields."

"We come from a fine family."

"Geez, I hope the Senators win tonight."

"Me too, Pearl."

"It's killing me, being a Ottawa fan. Geez, you'd think politicians were running the team. All the malarkey—letting that stepladder on defense go."

"Zdeno Chara."

"Longer reach than the Catholic Church."

"Great player."

> **"Cripes, Kate, he's making $7.6 mil a season. I made $2,500, Health and Welfare."**

"And please, Lord, before I die, how about we get a goalie with a little starch in his shorts?"

"Be a help."

"Get in behind that fat broad in the van. We can scoot along behind her, like Ronnie Stewart following Kaye Vaughan on a sweep."

Eventually, our heroes' Lexus inches into Scotiabank Place's massive parking lot, directed by hand-waving attendants.

"Cripes, we're going to be in Smiths Falls before you know it."

"Almost there, Pearl. Just another hour."

After parking, Pearly and Chris jump sprightly from their car, instantly invigorated by the milling hockey crowd.

" 'Camptown ladies sing this song, doo-dah, doo-dah.' "

"Sing it, Pearly."

"Great night to win 50 bucks. How much you bet?"

"Hundred."

" 'Gonna run all night. Gonna run all day.' "

Pearly and Chris slip into a fast-flowing river of grinning fans, many of whom shout, "HEATLEY SUCKS! HEATLEY SUCKS!" There are Ottawa Sun Heatley baby masks everywhere. Some ticket holders, younger fans, are carrying handmade signs—"Million Dollar Baby," "Traitor." Anytime a San Jose sweater appears, there is booing—mostly, but not always, good-natured.

"This is great. Just like a Leafs game."

"That's not a good omen."

"Shut your mouth."

Once the river hits the open doors of the east entrance of Scotiabank Place, the line slows to a slow shuffle and the chant grows louder: "HEATLEY SUCKS! HEATLEY SUCKS!"

"Man, we're going to kill them tonight."

"Hope so."

"Hey, Chris, what three teams you pick to click tonight?"

"Vancouver, New York and San Jose."

"What? It's too loud. Can't hear you."

"HEATLEY SUCKS! HEATLEY SUCKS!"

"I said Vancouver, New York and San Jose."

"Wait a minute, Christopher. You telling me you're not hoping for Ottawa?"

"HEATLEY SUCKS! HEATLEY SUCKS!"

"No, I'm hoping for Ottawa. But I picked San Jose."

"What kind of fan are you?"

"The kind who can afford 1,100-dollar seats. Let's go, Pearly, you're blocking the way."

As it turns out, the San Jose Sharks win 4–0. Ottawa plays badly. Dany Heatley draws a penalty that leads to a goal and adds an assist, playing energetically and well most every shift. Later, it is revealed that, like Ottawa fans, he wanted a victory so much that he offered teammates a substantial bounty.

"Million Dollar Baby," "Traitor."

PHILADELPHIA FLYERS

Misty & Jon
April 23, 2011

ALTERNATE NICKNAME: Broad Street Bullies.

FRANCHISE STARTED: One of the six expansion clubs in 1967.

UNIFORMLY SPEAKING: A member of the original ownership group was a Texas Longhorns fan. Hence, the orange jerseys. There was a contest for the name. Philadelphia was almost the Liberty Bells. But a nine-year old, Alex Stockard, came up with Fliers. Changed to Flyers.

HOW COOL?: The orange sweaters looked funny at first. But Philly has grown into its pumpkin-and-witch wardrobe. Home: 8.7. Away: 7.4.

Taking a Flyer on romance.

A sign of the times: Flyers have been in a perpetual search for goaltending since Ron Hextall in the early '90s.

THE AGONY: The New York Islanders knock the Flyers out of the 1980 playoffs (in overtime) on a goal scored with a high stick (Denis Potvin) and a clearly offside marker (Butch Goring).

THE ECSTASY: Winning Stanley Cups in 1974 and 1975. In the 2010 playoffs, French Flys Simon Gagne, Danny Briere and Claude Giroux help the team reach the final.

FANATIC: (See photo.)

Average ticket + parking + hot dog + beer:

$84.99

(9th highest in the NHL)

Spectrum of Evil?

One day during the mid-'70s reign of the Philadelphia Flyers, coach Freddy "The Fog" Shero walked into the Philadelphia Spectrum dressing room with a sloshing pail of water, placing it square on a training table. Saying nothing, he wandered off, leaving his team sharing a single thought:

Huh?

Seconds later, players were back to regular programming—fooling around. Young men from rural Canada, the Flyers insulated themselves from big-league pressure with jokes. In airports, Orest Kindrachuk, 21, or Don Saleski, 23, crawled up baggage carousels. Teammates soon found clothes coming at them in scattered clouds. Bobby Clarke, 23, dropped his dentures into a teammate's rum and Coke at bars.

They did everything together. "If we got off the plane and the first guy went to the bathroom, we all went to the bathroom," Kindrachuk said.

Shero's job was to connect these cast-off jokers. The Flyers came into the league in 1967. Most of the players had been declared surplus by other clubs.

"Ricky, over here," Shero said, suddenly in the dressing room again. Shero was The Fog because he appeared and was gone, like breath on

Ve have vays of making you balk...Dave "The Hammer" Schultz snarls on the cover of Philadelphia Magazine.

a mirror. Ricky was Rick MacLeish. Number 19 was also the rare Flyer who really could fly. He was nicknamed The Hawk because of how he swooped. Shero didn't like swooping. "Take the shortest route to the puck

carrier and arrive in ill humor," was one of his mottos.

"Roll up your sleeve, Rick," Shero said. "I want you to put your hand in that bucket of water. Now pull it out. See that hole that's left?"

"There ain't no hole there, Freddy."

"Well, Ricky, that's how much we're going to miss you when you're gone."

MacLeish got the message: no more swooping, and more ill humor.

Hockey purists called the Flyers the Goon Show. One of the team's many enforcers, Dave "The Hammer" Schultz, sat in the penalty box for the equivalent of more than nine hours in the '74–75 NHL season and playoffs—555 minutes. Teams insisted that the Flyers motor into the arena—no stopping outside to mingle with fans. At Christmas 1973, seven windmilling Flyers waded into a Vancouver crowd. Four had to appear in court before the team's next visit, a bloody battle that Philadelphia won, 10–5.

After that game, Flyers defenseman Andre "Moose" Dupont crowed, "That was lot of fun. We don't go to jail, we beat up their chicken forwards, we score 10 goal, and we win. Now the Moose drinks beer."

And so the legend of the Broad Street Bullies[1] passed into popular culture. In a 1993 episode of *The Simpsons* co-written by Conan O'Brien, Devil Flanders boasts of creating Blackbeard the Pirate and "the starting lineup of the 1976 Philadelphia Flyers."

Although he no doubt admired their crackling-flame colors, the devil didn't invent the world champion Flyers. Freddy Shero did. And he did so not by preaching intimidation, but by creating a nurturing environment that allowed players to find a purpose in (and refuge from) life inside the confines of a team. "We know that hockey is where we live, where we can best meet and overcome pain and wrong and death," he wrote on the team message board one day. "Life is just a place where we spend time between games."

Born to Russian immigrants in Winnipeg, Frederick Alexander Shero (né Shirach) grew up in a large, Depression-era family. Four of 12 siblings died in childbirth. Freddy excelled in sports, quarterbacking Isaac Newton High School to a football championship. Later, he was lightweight and middleweight boxing champion of the Canadian Navy and turned down an offer to turn pro, returning to hockey and the Univer-

Freddy Shero and unidentified admirer.

sity of Manitoba, where he studied Russian literature and history.

He made the NHL as a defenseman (1947–50), and boasted that he was the first New York Ranger to hold a library card. A back injury forced him into the itinerant life of a minor-league coach—20 moves in two decades. Purposeful eccentricity, startling people, became his standard means of persuasion. Coaching in Shawinigan Falls, Quebec, he stopped into a drugstore. "Can I help you?" an attractive salesgirl asked. "I love you," Shero replied. They married 90 days later.

Shero believed coaching was a lifelong pursuit. "A teacher can never truly teach unless he is still learning," he said. Tolstoy and Dostoyevsky weren't the only Russian thinkers Freddy studied. He memorized Russian sports guru Anatoli Firsov's hockey bible long before anyone in North America heard of Vladislav Tretiak or Valery Kharlamov.

> "When you have bacon and eggs for breakfast, the chicken makes a contribution, but the pig makes a commitment."

In time, Shirach/Shero married Russian and Canadian hockey. He believed teams should play in five-man units and in short shifts. He believed in a system—that players lost games and teams won them. But he also believed a good coach carried a bottle opener for beer. And the former boxer believed in fighting—although it may be truer to say he believed in not being afraid to fight. "Success is falling down nine times and getting up 10," was another favorite aphorism.

Although he believed in a system, Shero felt that routine inhibited learning. Flyer hockey practices veered into other sports. Pucks were replaced with hard-to-control tennis balls to improve coordination and soften hands. If he saw skaters going through the motions, Shero cancelled practice and put on a badminton tournament. Sometimes, Flyer forwards became rickshaw drivers, pushing goalie Bernie Parent around on a folded chair. This to promote lower-body strength (and to acknowledge, perhaps, that the superlative goalie often carried the team in games).

Shero never forgot that hockey was a game. The coach staged a five-dollar contest at the end of practice to perfect the wraparound play, where forwards wheel from behind the net

---

[1] The Spectrum was located at the south end of Broad Street. The team currently plays in the nearby Wells Fargo Center.

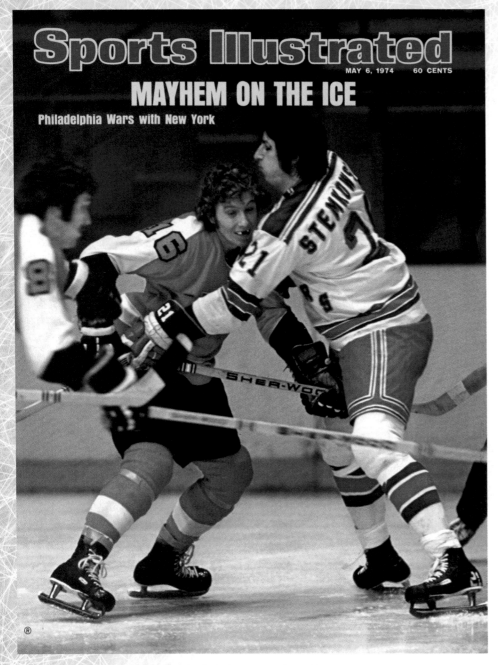

Sports Illustrated

MAY 6, 1974   60 CENTS

MAYHEM ON THE ICE

Philadelphia Wars with New York

Flyers' captain, Bobby Clarke gives Pete Stemkowski an atomic wedgie.

Saskatchewan (population 868), was suddenly the most hated player in hockey's top league. In Boston, a fan yelled out, "Hey, Schultz, there's a town up here named after you … Maah-blehead."

Once, Philadelphia sportswriter Bill Fleischman saw Schultz reading the self-help book *I'm OK, You're OK* on the road. "You okay?" the reporter asked. Schultz shrugged. He wasn't sure. Once he put on the Flyers jersey, though, it was always Hammer time. "Shero loves what I do," he told more than one reporter. Schultz, like the rest of the Flyers, found comfort in being a Shero disciple.

"Success is not the result of spontaneous combustion. You must first set yourself on fire," the coach once wrote in a high religious mood.

Perhaps you're a middle-aged hockey fan, reading this with a frown, thinking, "Hey, I saw the Flyers. They weren't disciples, they were delinquents. That loud arena they played in was the Spectrum of Evil." Well, that's partly true, yes. But don't get carried away, for there is hard statistical evidence to suggest that Shero's Flyers were more than Blackbeard's marauders. That when it mattered most, the team was a tightly disciplined crew—as cool and deliberate as Jack Nicklaus putting for a tournament win.

and try to jam a puck past a nervously shifting goalie.

Crucially, the coach also made players who did grunt work feel valuable. "When you have bacon and eggs for breakfast, the chicken makes a contribution, but the pig makes a commitment," he said. Shero

understood the sacrifice being made by his heavy artillery, the fringe players/fighters with unattractive nicknames who softened up opponents, allowing more offensively talented teammates—Clarke, Bill Barber and Reggie Leach to waltz in and score winning goals.

Schultz, Dupont and Mad Dog Kelly loved Shero, mainly because he made them feel wanted—big leaguers at last.

It wasn't easy being Dave Schultz. A point-a-game forward with the Swift Current Broncos in junior, the young man from Waldheim,

In the third period of their three defining wins—game six of the 1974 final against Boston, game six of the 1975 final against Buffalo, and the 1976 challenge match with the Soviet Red Army team—Philadelphia allowed a combined total of 14 shots on net, none of which got past Parent. *Fourteen!* Against great teams! And get this: in the same 60 minutes, the Flyers took only one two-minute penalty.

All of the victories revealed Shero's maverick thinking. Conventional wisdom had it that to defeat the Bruins you had to keep Orr away from the puck. Shero figured it was too hard to chase both Bobby and the puck, so he decided to throw the puck in Orr's corner and make hockey's best puck handler handle the puck, attacking him with extreme prejudice for every second of his league-leading 40-minute-a-game workouts.

While most NHL coaches pit line against line, Shero matched *lines* against line, throwing nine forwards, in three 30-second shifts, up against Boston's top unit (Phil Esposito, Ken Hodge and Wayne Cashman) and Buffalo's French Connection (Gilbert Perreault, René Robert and Rick Martin). What he wanted to do was use his entire team to tire out the other team's superstars.

Against the Russians, Shero introduced an early variation of the trap play, crowding the center-ice zone. Central Red Army lazily orbited their end, like a plane circling an airport. The Flyers also banged the hell out of the Russians, but truth be told, they treated them no worse than they did the Penguins or Canucks. Red Army left the ice in protest at one point, and offered little resistance upon returning, directing only 16 shots on Parent.

What was noteworthy about so many of the team's big wins was how often pugilists and checkers materialized, as if out of a fog, to score decisive goals. The Bruins had beaten the Flyers in the first game of the 1974 final and were leading the second match by one with a minute to go, when Moose Dupont appeared in the slot to redirect a corner pass from MacLeish into the net. (Clarke later scored in overtime.) Hammer Schultz had the big goal in their third-game win. Defenseman Joe Watson, who never scored, beat Tretiak in the Flyer–Red Army encounter.

The decisive game of the 1975 Cup final was score-less when Reggie Leach dumped the puck behind the net. Bob Kelly spun from behind the net in a furious half-circle, jamming the puck without looking between Roger Crozier's legs for the Cup winner. If it looked as if he'd been practicing the play for years, that's only because he had.

"Hey, Freddy," Kelly said on the bench, "you owe me five bucks."

"Win today, we will walk together forever," Fred Shero wrote on the team's blackboard prior to the Flyers beating Boston to win the Stanley Cup. Maybe Shero's greatest accomplishment was that he convinced his club, an only modestly talented group, that they could become immortal.

That they have. Shero created the template for every subsequent Halloween-orange Flyer team—all built for trouble and mean as a toothache. Later came Ron Hextall, a goalie who racked up more than 100 minutes in penalties in three straight seasons (1986–89). In the '90s, there was the scarifying Legion of Doom—Eric Lindros,

Mikael Renberg and John LeClair. Current Flyers Dan Carcillo and Scotty Hartnell both play with throwback haircuts and mid-'70s Flyers fury.

So far, no Flyer team has walked the walk like Shero's club. Those fearless Flyers might not have been the devil incarnate, as per *The Simpsons*, but they weren't afraid of consorting with evil. During the famous fog bowl of the '75 Cup final, a vaporous cloud materialized above the overheated Buffalo Memorial Auditorium ice. The game was stopped several times. To accentuate the *Hounds of the Baskervilles* mood, a bat swooped down from the Aud roof. Sabres forward Jim Lorentz knocked it out of the air, sending the creature flapping to the ice. At which point, Rick MacLeish removed his hockey glove and picked the flying mammal up with his bare hand.

"Ricky," teammate Joe Watson shouted, "you can get rabies from that thing."

MacLeish shrugged. "What are rabies?" he said.

Orange Order of Ruffians

The Flyers have always led the NHL in nasty nicknames. Bob Kelly had two: Mad Dog and Hound Dog. Later, there was Ken "The Rat" Linesman, who was more irritating than a July rash. Even the Flyers' Swedes were roughnecks. Hence, Ulf "Robocop" Samuelsson. More Transylvania than Pennsylvania, Dan Carcillo is Philadelphia's latest Mr. Evil. Of course, the fighter who had the audacity to beat up a made guy (goal scorer Marian Gaborik) has a nickname: Car Bomb!

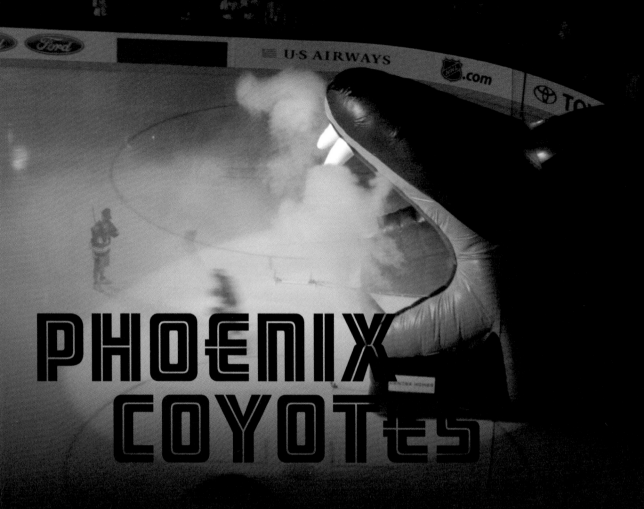

PHOENIX COYOTES

ALTERNATE NICKNAMES: Desert Dogs, Dogs, occasionally Yotes.

FRANCHISE STARTED: As the Winnipeg Jets of the World Hockey Association, beginning in 1972. The Jets flew to the NHL in 1979, before landing in Arizona in 1996.

UNIFORMLY SPEAKING: Jerseys are the same red as the sun-baked sandstone formations in nearby Sedona. Hockey traditionalists might call them Montreal maroon, as they favor the colors of English Montreal's NHL franchise from 1924–38. The howling-coyote-head logo appeared in time for the 2003–04 season, coinciding with the arrival of howling creditors.

HOW COOL?: The singing coyote is fabulous. You can almost imagine it belting out the road anthem of the southwest: "Flagstaff, Arizona, don't forget Wynona. Kingman, Barstow and San Bernardino…Get your kicks on Route 66."[1] Sedona red home: 8.9. Away: 7.7.

---

[1] From the Bobby Troup song "Route 66," made famous by Nat "King" Cole and, later, the Rolling Stones.

Peter Mueller.

Grate Dane: A sewer near the Phoenix Coyotes' home rink in Glendale, Arizona.

THE AGONY: A tie. Winnipeg Jet Bobby Hull getting the wig ripped off his head in a WHA fight. And, after a great season, finishing just five points short of a division title, the Yotes lose to the San Jose Sharks in the first round of the 2002 playoffs.

THE ECSTASY: Back in the WHA, the Winnipeg Jets, led by Anders Hedberg, Ulf Nilsson and Bobby Hull, win three Avco Cup championships.

FANATIC: Record temperature in Phoenix in May: 113 degrees Fahrenheit.

Average ticket + parking + hot dog + beer:

$46.40

(30th highest in the NHL)

Clap for the Wolfman. Gary Bettman readies for a face-off with reporters. Note chipped podium—presumably a rental.

Coyote Ugly

In 2009, the Phoenix Coyotes file for Chapter 11 protection, slinking into an Arizona bankruptcy court, Judge Redfield T. Baum presiding. The jurist with the preposterous Looney Tunes name is to decide who owns the club. Coyotes owner Jerry Moyes has agreed to sell to Ontario billionaire Jim Balsillie for $212.5 million—shocking the NHL, which has been grooming Jerry Reinsdorf, the famously frugal owner of baseball's Chicago White Sox and basketball's Chicago Bulls. Ice Edge Holdings is also sniffing around for a deal. No one is sold on Phoenix. Balsillie plans a

move to southern Ontario. Ice Edge envisions the Coyotes playing some games in Saskatchewan—Runnin' Back and Forth to Saskatoon.

What will it be? The Phoenix–Saskatoon Border Collies? Jerry's Vultures? Judge Baum decided none of the above, tossing Phoenix back in the NHL's lap. Who owns the Coyotes? Ask any hockey fan, and he'll tell you: Gary Bettman, that's who.

Bettman is the least popular man in Canada—the butt end of a thousand small jokes. In fact, that's one of

them. He's portrayed as a litigious midget named Hairy Buttman in the 2006 Quebec murder mystery *Bon Cop, Bad Cop*:

Hairy Buttman: Don't you know who I am? We'll sue your asses. You can't put me in the trunk of a car.

Killer [slamming the trunk]: *Yes we can. It's a Quebec tradition.*

Canuck complaints? Bettman's a lawyer…a Yankee…a Yankee lawyer, and worst of all, a fool salesman trying to sell a winter sport into places that have no winter. Like Phoenix, where, come Stanley Cup time, temperatures soar above 100—what mom sets the oven at to keep roast beef warm for Sunday dinner! That's allegedly why Canadians dislike Bettman: because he put sunglasses on hockey.

That's a lot of bellyaching, even taking into consideration that, after hockey and folk singing, complaining is what Canadians do best. Especially when an ice-cold, hard look at the facts might suggest that Bettman's been the best (maybe the only) commissioner the NHL ever had. Yo Canada, anyone remember NHL hockey in the '90s? Skyrocketing salaries? Gretzky and Lemieux earned more than $1 million going into the 1989–90 season. Three seasons later, 25 players made at least that much. The Canadian dollar was trading at 73 U.S. cents. The great Edmonton and Calgary teams of the '80s hit the auction block. Winnipeg and Quebec were up for sale.

The NHL was in trouble. One guy had a plan. Not Gary Bettman, but Bruce McNall, the chatty charmer who bought Gretzky from Edmonton for $15 million in 1988. The Los Angeles Kings' owner was chairman of the NHL board of governors—the league's second in command. McNall wanted a salary cap and expansion—at $50 million for each new franchise, and keep 'em coming! And he coveted the deep-dish apple pie that was American TV sports revenue. The NFL had $3.6 billion worth of TV deals. Broadcasting—that's where the money was. McNall hooked the NHL up with Disney (via the Mighty Ducks of Anaheim) and Blockbuster Video (who became owners of the Florida Panthers). Breaking into the sunbelt meant the NHL finally had a national footprint in the United States. That meant national TV deals, right? Paydirt!

What the devil? Gary Bettman in Hamilton Spectator *after preventing Nashville from migrating north, in 2007.*

McNall's reverie was the business plan Gary Bettman inherited. San Jose, Anaheim, Tampa, Miami and Dallas were in. Over to you, Gary. Alas, while McNall's dreams had currency with NHL governors, he himself was broke. Hockey's Puck Finn ended up in jail for swindling California banks out of $236 million. The NHL's southern strategy had been authored by a cheerfully deluded confidence man.

Arguably, the best thing McNall did for the NHL was to bring in Bettman, a man constitutionally equipped to deal with the challenges ahead. Gary Bruce Bettman was born in 1952 in Queens, New York—Archie Bunker country. Except Gary had no Archie. "I didn't have a father to pass down the history of teams like the Rangers, Knicks, Yankees and Giants, so I rooted for the Islanders, Nets, Mets and Jets," he said.

Starting in 1993 as NHL commissioner, Bettman had a nursery of teams in their infancy—Sharks, Mighty Ducks, Senators, Panthers and Lightning, along with the transplanted Hurricanes, Stars, Avalanche and Coyotes. And before too long, under his watch, the Predators, Thrashers, Wild, and baby Blue Jackets were added to the stable. The last part is where Bettman blundered. If only a Father-Knows-Hockey-Best type had taken him aside and said, "When I was your age, there were six NHL teams. You're suggesting that, one generation later, we have 30. Imagine if baseball, with 20 teams in 1966, expanded 500 percent. That's right, there'd be 100 major-league teams. And the big leagues wouldn't seem so exclusive—so big league."

The NHL hasn't been good at managing its brand since the 1967

expansion. Teams coming and going (anyone remember the Cleveland Barons?). And of the first 11 expansion teams, only Philadelphia maintained their uniforms. Others go from one look to another, like anxious teenagers trying on different outfits before a party.

from the late '90s through 2002–03, teams in Edmonton, Calgary and Ottawa were drowning in red ink.

Growing into his job, Bettman figured out that a billion-dollar American TV deal was a mirage. And that the league had to consolidate, not multiply. So there have been no gypsy franchise flights since 2000. No franchise for the persistent Jim Balsillie, either—which was strike three in the minds of Canadian hockey fans (the first two whiffs being the 1994 and 2004 NHL lockouts—those stoppages hurt). But perhaps if a post-2004 salary cap had been in place in 1990, the Quebec Nordiques and Winnipeg Jets might still be in business. And Canadians should appreciate the importance of the NHL controlling team movement in the era of foreign takeovers. Imagine if George Gillett, the American businessman who owned the Montreal Canadiens, had been allowed to move the Canadiens to Wisconsin.

Anyone who thinks that Bettman's insistence on the Coyotes staying put betrays an anti-Canadian bias should remember that, from the late '90s through 2002–03, teams in Edmonton, Calgary and Ottawa were drowning in red ink. And that the NHL threw teams a life jacket in the form of the Canadian Assistance Program,

doling out more than $10 million in 1997–98.

But forget about salary caps and franchise security—Bettman's greatest service to hockey is aesthetic. No-interference rules enacted after the 2004–05 lockout ended the hooking and grabbing that turned stars into human rickshaws. The world's fastest sport is now faster still, especially during dizzying four-on-four overtimes, a welcome 1999 innovation. The elimination of center-ice offside has given hockey football's most exciting play: the long bomb touchdown pass. Shootouts eliminated kissing-your-sister ties. And NHL outdoor games, modeled after the 2001 Cold War between Michigan State and the University of Michigan, demonstrate that the NHL is finally alert to marketing possibilities.

According to *Forbes* magazine, the NHL showed a record profit in the 2008–09 season, due to new partnership deals with Honda, Bell Canada, Visa, Energizer and McDonald's. How did Gary get these corporations on board when the North American economy was tanking? No one in sports is more persuasive than Bettman, who can talk the ears off a field of corn. It's his upbringing, probably—what other family has ever boasted two sports commissioners? (Half-brother Jeffrey Pollack was once commissioner of the World Series of Poker. Can you imagine the arguments over who controlled the TV remote control on Sunday afternoons?)

And like every good lawyer (or billiards player), Bettman always sets himself up for the next shot. His league is in perpetual turmoil, it's true. McNall's sunbelt strategy, a crazy man's folly, remains Bettman's albatross. "Something has to change," you're thinking. Gary's already ahead of you. Bettman pulled NHL owners by the ears into the Olympics in 1998, growing the game everywhere, including at home. (The 2010 Canada–U.S. gold medal game was watched by almost 28 million Americans—more than any of the games in the 2009 World Series between the New York Yankees and Philadelphia Phillies.) Bettman also had a record six NHL teams—Columbus, Boston, Minnesota, San Jose, Phoenix and Carolina—opening their 2010–11 season in Europe. Maybe the NHL will eventually go international, establishing a satellite league involving Russia, Sweden, Finland, Germany, the Czech Republic and Slovakia.

"Yeah, but where's our new team?" Canadians ask. "This is our game, our league." Actually, no. For the last 80 years, Canadian teams have been outnumbered at least three to one. What's different is that northern teams somehow managed to win Stanley Cups. Between 1942 and 1990, Canadian-based teams won 35 Stanley Cups in 48 seasons. Bettman became commissioner in February 1993 and handed over Lord Stanley's punch bowl to Montreal later that spring. Since then—nothing. Canuck teams haven't won a championship in 18 seasons.

Ah, now we're coming to the real reason Canadian hockey fans dislike Gary Bettman: displaced rage. Who cares if he's made the sport better than he found it? That he guided the league through a recession, took hockey to the Olympics, introduced outdoor games and discovered heretofore-untapped revenue streams? For Canadian hockey fans, he's been nothing but bad luck. The guy who caused our Stanley Cups to runneth out. Hence the Yosemite Sam tantrum when in 2011 Bettman strolled onto Vancouver ice to hand Boston hockey's greatest prize. Where have you gone, Clarence Campbell? A nation turns its lonely eyes to you.

Wayne Gretzky behind the bench (and eight-ball) as coach of the Phoenix Coyotes.

Flight into Danger

At 17, Wayne Gretzky was attending David Letterman's old high school in Indianapolis, moonlighting as an Indianapolis Racer in the World Hockey Association. Weeks later, impoverished Racers owner Nelson Skalbania had to sell him. "Where do you want to go: Winnipeg or Edmonton?" he asked. Gretzky's agent, Gus Badali, recommended Edmonton, which had a new arena and, therefore, a better pro hockey future. A decade later, in 1988, it was Oilers owner Peter Pocklington who was in financial distress. Gretzky was for sale again. Plane tickets were being readied. Detroit or Los Angeles? It was up to Wayne. Had he chosen Detroit, Gretzky would have been part of the

team's storied '90s run—who knows, maybe an eight-time Stanley Cup champ and a member, like Steve Yzerman, of the executive training program with the league's best-run franchise. Instead, after fruitless sojourns with Los Angeles, St. Louis and New York, he ended up in Winnipeg after all. Or, at least, the team the Jets became—the Phoenix Coyotes. Gretzky's bad luck continued in Phoenix, where he became part owner and head of hockey operations in 2000. He coached the team from 2005–09. During Gretzky's time in Arizona, the team failed to win a playoff series.

PITTSBURGH PENGUINS

ALTERNATE NICKNAMES: Pens and 'Guins.

FRANCHISE STARTED: The Pittsburgh Pirates (1925–30) were the third NHL franchise to call the U.S. home, after the Boston Bruins and New York Americans. The team introduced Herculite glass along the boards. Unfortunately, Pittsburgh's economy wasn't shatterproof. The Pirates left for Philadelphia during the Depression. The Penguins waddled into town in the 1967 expansion.

UNIFORMLY SPEAKING: The team's first coach, Red Sullivan, hated the idea of penguin-colored uniforms, complaining, "After a bad game, sportswriters will say, 'They skated like a buncha nuns.'" So the original colors were changed to blue and white, after the Canadian Football League's Toronto Argonauts. The team went to black and gold in 1980. Their current alternate jersey is close to the 1968–72 home jersey.

HOW COOL?: Black and gold: 6.6. Light blue alternate: 8.7.

Pittsburgh fan wearing team's current alternate jersey.

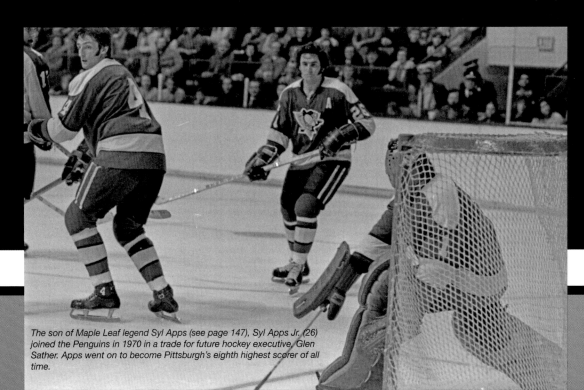

The son of Maple Leaf legend Syl Apps (see page 147), Syl Apps Jr. (26) joined the Penguins in 1970 in a trade for future hockey executive, Glen Sather. Apps went on to become Pittsburgh's eighth highest scorer of all time.

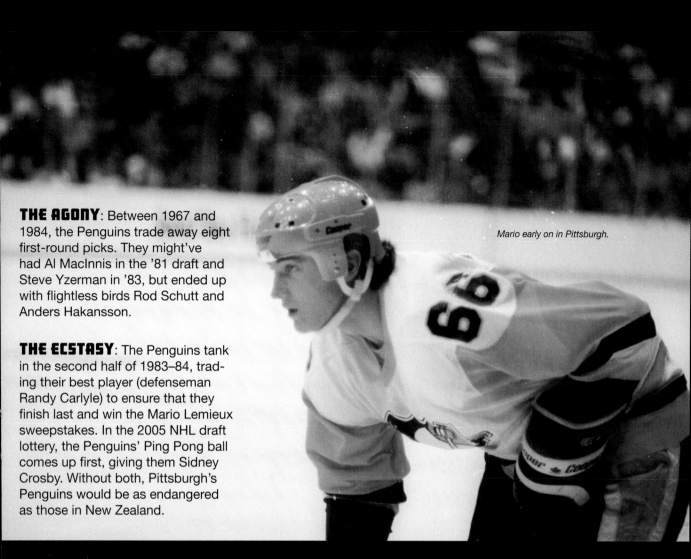

THE AGONY: Between 1967 and 1984, the Penguins trade away eight first-round picks. They might've had Al MacInnis in the '81 draft and Steve Yzerman in '83, but ended up with flightless birds Rod Schutt and Anders Hakansson.

THE ECSTASY: The Penguins tank in the second half of 1983–84, trading their best player (defenseman Randy Carlyle) to ensure that they finish last and win the Mario Lemieux sweepstakes. In the 2005 NHL draft lottery, the Penguins' Ping Pong ball comes up first, giving them Sidney Crosby. Without both, Pittsburgh's Penguins would be as endangered as those in New Zealand.

Mario early on in Pittsburgh.

FANATIC: A tie. Pittsburgh introduced the NHL's only live mascot, Pete, an Ecuadorean penguin, in 1967. They even had little CCM skates custom made for the little fella. Sadly, Pete succumbed to pneumonia (skaters' cough) in his rookie year. Andy Brown, a Penguin from 1972–74, was the last NHL goalie to play without a mask.

Average ticket + parking
+ hot dog + beer:
$82.54
(11th highest in the NHL)

Like Father, Like Son?

We never made enough of Sidney Crosby living with Mario Lemieux for five years. Think of the symmetry: Mario, the greatest Quebec junior ever, who at age 18 scored 133 goals in his final season with Laval (1983–84), including a couple off of a Verdun goalie named Troy Crosby. He's drafted by a bankrupt Pittsburgh franchise and moves into the home of Tom and Nancy Murphy—friends of the owner—in part to improve his English. He stays longer than anyone expected, keeping one skate back in childhood, easing into the rigors of NHL stardom by living with a happy, boisterous family, playing with kids. Chillaxing whenever.

Fast-forward a generation, and the next great Quebec junior, Sidney Crosby, arrives, scoring 66 goals (hey, isn't that Mario's number?) in 62 games for Rimouski in 2004–05. He is drafted by a bankrupt Pittsburgh franchise and moves into the owner's house—Mario and Nathalie Lemieux—in part to improve his French. He stays longer than anyone expected, keeping one skate…

And just as Mario popped a couple by Sidney's dad, Mario's hockey-mad daughter Stephanie fires them past Crosby during driveway ball hockey games in Sewickley, an affluent Pittsburgh suburb. (Sidney misses his own kid sister, Taylor, back in Cole Harbour, Nova Scotia.)

What were dinners like? It's Sunday. The Lemieuxs are having roast chicken. Potatoes Lyonnaise. Baby field-green salad. "Uh, Mario, pass the salt, please," Sidney asks. Without looking, Lemieux skims a shaker across the table, finding a sliver between the butter dish and a vase.

"Mario, pas à table," Nathalie hisses.

Superstars look the same from afar. You can find parallels in Mario's and Sidney's development—the whole prodigy thing. Sidney was skating at two; Mario, three. Mario had lessons with a neighborhood dad who took kids to the rink. He taught them to skate first. When Mario was four, the coach, Fernand Fichaud, threw a puck out. Mario raced in on the goalie, moved one way, pulling the netminder with him, and then abruptly changed course, skipping sideways, burying the puck in the abandoned side of the net.

Emperor Penguins: Mario Lemieux and Sidney Crosby.

No one taught the four-year-old how to deke. Coach Fichaud felt a shiver up his spine. "That was the greatest thing I ever saw," he told Lemieux biographer Lawrence Martin decades later. Fichaud might have felt the same tingle watching *The Tonight Show* in 2005, when Jay Leno showed a clip of Sidney playing atom hockey, moving in on a goalie, taking a peek, then whistling a wrist shot over the goalie's shoulder, just inside the post. A perfect shot.

Both children were indulged prodigies. Sidney turned his mother's laundry room, next to a practice net, into a bomb site, battering the clothes dryer, smashing a sink. When weather got too cold in

Montreal, Pierrette Lemieux, Mario's mom, brought snow in from the yard, trampling it on the floor and opening the front door wide, turning her home into a road hockey game.

At eight, Mario took a slapshot from center ice that sailed over the glass behind the net. At 15, he played golf for the first time, shooting 116. A year later, he was shooting in the 80s; the next summer, he was breaking par.

When Sidney was 16, he scored a goal for Rimouski that went viral on YouTube, rolling his wrists to scoop up a puck on his stick blade like a lacrosse player might pick up a loose ball, and then placing the puck just under the crossbar while still behind the net.

Both were 21 when they became national heroes. Mario in 1987 took a pass from Wayne Gretzky to beat Russia and win the Canada Cup. Sidney scored the overtime goal that gave his country an Olympic gold medal in 2010.

When you look closely, however, Lemieux and Crosby couldn't be more different. Don Cherry called Mario "a floater" early on. And it was true. It was almost as if Lemieux figured his surname ("the best" in English) was blessing enough. He never worked out. His first camp with Pittsburgh, Mario couldn't budge a 180-pound barbell and quit a three-mile run, exhausted.

He smoked cigars as a teenager and slept in till the afternoon. As a pro, he turned down product endorsements, preferring the sun to advertising executives' hands on his back. Off-days, Mario slept in and played golf. Twice, he didn't play for his country when asked. Just didn't feel like it. And some figured, compared to Gretzky, his lone reference point as a hockey talent, their numerals said it all. Wayne gave 99 percent; Mario, 66.

Is it possible that Lemieux's critics didn't know what they were talking about? That Mario knew what was the best for him?

Here's a guy who, playing without a body guard (unlike 99), with a bad back (others sometimes tied his skates) and various wounded limbs, led Pittsburgh to Stanley Cups in 1991 and 1992. The next season, Lemieux was challenging Gretzky's single-season records when he was diagnosed with Hodgkin's lymphoma, missed 20 games because of radiation treatments, then came back to win the scoring championship anyway.

Perhaps Mario Lemieux was precisely aware of his physical gifts and limitations—and knew what Muhammad Ali knew: even the deadliest bee needs to float like a butterfly once in a while.

Sidney Crosby is a different kettle of fish—a self-improvement machine. As a child, he was up before the break of dawn on weekends, practicing on Maritime rinks with his dad until league teams hogged the ice. Over the Christmas holidays, he'd phone friends to play ball hockey before their families had breakfast. "He's still in bed, Sidney," mothers would tell him. Sidney would phone back 30 minutes later: "He up now?"

Sidney had his own personal trainer at 13. One routine had the youngster straddling a seesaw—a plywood board riding an iron pipe—while the trainer threw medicine balls at him. These sessions helped Crosby develop an uncanny ability to stay upright through scrums.

When Sidney was 15, he astonished the hockey director at Shattuck–St. Mary's prep school in Minnesota, by practicing a bird-in-distress move where he'd pretend to lose the puck in his skates, luring the defenseman in, then kick the puck ahead and step quickly around the advancing checker.

But even self-improvement machines sometimes run out of energy. Between 2007 and 2010, Sidney Crosby played almost 400 hockey games, was named captain of the Pittsburgh Penguins, inked a $43.5-million contract, won a Stanley Cup and an Olympic gold medal and signed endorsement deals with Reebok, Bell, Tim Hortons and Gatorade.

Training like a Spartan warrior the whole time.

What could that be like? How draining? Sidney's dad told *Sports Illustrated* that, when Sidney returns to Nova Scotia, he likes to sit out in a boat in Grand Lake. "He can be out there for hours and not catch a thing," Troy Crosby reports.

Maybe that's the whole idea. Maybe living with Mario Lemieux was, for Sidney Crosby, a summer holiday from the winter game. Meditation time, too: an opportunity to contemplate one of sport's great success stories. How many other superstars have gone on to own championship teams?

Just Mario.

Ironically, the summer that Sidney moved out of Mario's house (2010), his kid sister, Taylor Crosby, left home in Cole Harbour. Mario's eldest daughter Stephanie also went off to school.

And where did the girls go? To the same prep school Sidney once attended: Shattuck–St. Mary's in Minnesota, where the Lemieux and Crosby girls will be hockey teammates, living together in the same dorm. "You could say we're like cousins," Taylor Crosby said.

You could indeed.

ST. LOUIS BLUES

ALTERNATE NICKNAMES: Bluenotes.

FRANCHISE STARTED: The original Ottawa Senators moved to Missouri in 1934, calling themselves the St. Louis Eagles. The Eagles' Scotty Bowman scored the NHL's first penalty-shot goal in 1934. Good Lord, just how old is Scotty? No, no, you're thinking of the other, more famous Scotty Bowman, coach of the St. Louis Blues when the team entered the NHL in the 1967 expansion.

UNIFORMLY SPEAKING: The team's first owner, Sid Salomon Jr., honored St. Louis's music tradition (Chuck Berry and Miles Davis were born here) by naming the club the St. Louis Blues, after the jazz standard by W. C. Handy.

HOW COOL?: Bluesy home outfit: 8.9. Newport Jazz Festival poster look coach Mike Keenan wisely banned in 1995: 0.0.

The Sporting News *called them the "Blues Brothers."*

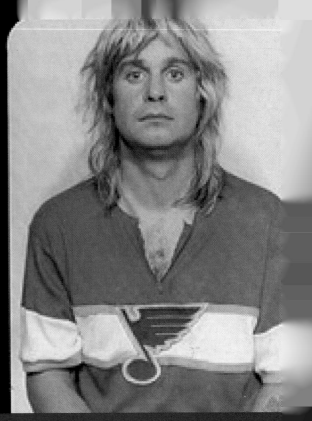

'05 1F 84
DATE

BOOKING NUMBER

SHELBY COUNTY
JUSTICE COMPLEX
MEMPHIS TENNESSEE

Bum note: Ozzie Osbourne's 1984 mug shot

THE AGONY: That famous photo of the Bruins' Bobby Orr flying through the air after scoring the Cup-winning goal in 1970. The goal was scored against Blues goalkeeper Glenn Hall, who got real tired of looking at it. Every time he sees Orr, he asks, "Didn't you score any other goals?"

THE ECSTASY: Brett Hull's stirring Hall of Fame induction speech, which ended with a Tom Joad–like tribute to the common fan: "I accept this honor for all of those playing pickup, beer league and senior hockey, who never got the opportunity I did. For every mom up at five, who drives to practice…every dad working overtime to buy equipment and a pair of tickets to take his kids to an NHL game, every teammate that sacrificed, every trainer that patched me up and every stick boy that brought me a cold one after the game. Nothing in life is worth a damn without friends."

FANATIC: Garry Unger didn't miss a game in nine seasons with the Blues (1971–79). All told, with Toronto, Detroit, St. Louis and Atlanta, he compiled an iron man streak of 914 consecutive games.

Headed for Trouble

In December 2010, speedy St. Louis center Andy McDonald was in full sail when his left skate caught a rut, causing him to crash headlong into the Oilers' Shawn Horcoff. He crumpled to the ice, rotating 180 degrees, unconscious, while everyone who knew him in the rink thought the same thing:

Concussion!

McDonald lost most of one season (2002–03) after big Adam Foote staggered him with an open-ice check. The year before, he'd fallen into the boards, missing three games with a concussion. In 2001, a hard check, headfirst, into the boards cost him 15 days.

McDonald, who would indeed miss two months with a concussion, wasn't the only Blues player to suffer a head injury early in 2010–11. David Perron, Cam Janssen and Carlo Colaiacovo also spent time on injured reserve with concussions. The Blues' Paul Kariya quit hockey prior to the season with post-concussion syndrome.

The McDonald–Horcoff mishap was just that, some hockey people argue. More proof that you can't legislate against injuries. Accidents happen. Getting your bell rung is part of hockey. Just like it was when Big Gordie and the Rocket played. Don't mess with the sport we know and love. Why ruin modern hockey?

Let's not kid ourselves. The sport the Rocket played no longer exists.

Players in the 1950s didn't quit with recurring headaches and nightmare depression. Teams didn't lose five players in two months with career-threatening head injuries.

The question then isn't, Why ruin modern hockey? but, rather, Why is modern hockey ruining its players?[1]

And let's be clear, hockey lives are being devastated by head injuries. Here's Marybeth LaFontaine, wife of Hockey Hall of Fame forward Pat LaFontaine, describing her husband's attempt to cope with his fifth concussion, in 1996:

> He was very emotional. I would walk into a room, and he would be crying. He cried a lot. Or he would be holding his head from the migraine headaches. They were terrible. He wouldn't leave the house for a week. He wouldn't change his clothes, wouldn't shower. It was all the classic signs of depression. I thought he was having a nervous breakdown.

LaFontaine retired the following season, after his sixth concussion.

Some statistics: in 1959–60, Rocket Richard and the Montreal Canadiens won the Stanley Cup in 82 games, including preseason and playoffs. One game went into overtime. In 2009–10,

some players on the championship Chicago Blackhawks had played 119 matches, including the Olympics. Three Hawks—Jonathan Toews, Brent Seabrook and Duncan Keith— who played for the Canadian Olympic team played 27 overtime games.

Toews, Seabrook and fellow Team Canada player Sidney Crosby all suffered concussions within 16 months of the Olympic victory.

In 1960, NHL teams took trains. In 2010, some NHL teams flew 50,000 miles.

In 1960, if a forward like McDonald played the Canadiens, he'd be going up against a defense averaging 5′11″ and 182 pounds. The Rocket himself tipped the Toledos at 180. On December 4, 2010, when McDonald played the Edmonton Oilers, he was skating against defenders averaging 6′3″ and 218 pounds.

If McDonald skated against the '60 Habs' second and third centers, he'd be up against Henri Richard or Ralph Backstrom, 160 pounds each. Nine players on the 2010 Canadian Olympic women's hockey team weighed more than that.

In 1959, between November 26 and December 4, the Montreal Canadiens played four games. Fifty-one years later, the Blues' McDonald played five games during the same stretch. In the 2010 games, teams handed out a total of 263 hits, averaging 53 collisions a game. There were six fights.

The NHL didn't record hits way back when, but I watched the final game of the 1960 Stanley Cup final between Montreal and Toronto and counted 14

hits, only one of which—Bob Pulford bowling over a wandering Jacques Plante—resembled your classic, modern-day rubout. The other 13 collisions were correctly described by play-by-play man Bill Hewitt as "bumps." Only one Montreal player fought in the entire 1960 playoffs: Albert Langlois.

Why is modern hockey ruining its players?

Going into the '70s, NHL teams rolled over three lines and two defense pairings. Shifts were longer, up to 90 seconds, and players preserved their energy, going at three-quarter speed until a scoring chance developed.

Teams today employ four lines. Players go all out for shifts that last just 30 seconds. Then the next bunch hits the ice, racing. Third and fourth liners hit everything they see.

Forwards in the '50s seldom traveled along the boards for the same reasons boxers were trained to stay away from the ropes—too easy to get hit. Today, all teams cycle the puck along the boards. They're courting trouble, sure. Drawing penalties is part of the plan.

In summary, then, today's players play many more games, with overtime—three pre-expansion seasons' worth every two years. The athletes are 50 pounds heavier, skate faster and hit far harder, four times as often. Also, the style of play is more dangerous. Shoulder pads, equipment that was meant to protect, have been turned into weaponry. Throw in travel fatigue, more fighting, and you have what you have: an NHL that too often stands for the National Hospital League.

---

[1] Thirty-nine NHL players have had to quit hockey because of head injuries in the last 16 years: Eric and Brett Lindros, Paul Kariya, Matthew Barnaby, Keith Primeau, Steve Rucchin, Rob DiMaio, Jason Botterill, Steve Moore, Scott Stevens, Jesse Wallin, Steve Dubinsky, Mark Moore, Stu Grimson, Adam Deadmarsh, Gino Odjick, Mike Richter, Cam Stewart, Brian Bradley, Brad Werenka, Paul Comrie, Kevin Kaminski, Petr Svoboda, Jeff Beukeboom, Geoff Courtnall, Warren Luhning, Jeff Kealty, Robin Bawa, Trevor Halverson, Pat LaFontaine, Jim Johnson, Steven Rice, Kaj Linna, Jay More, Dean Chynoweth, Dennis Vaske, Nick Kypreos, Michel Goulet and Dave Taylor.

SAN JOSE
SHARKS

ALTERNATE NICKNAMES: Fins, Fish and, when slumping, Guppies.

FRANCHISE STARTED: Got an hour? The California Seals were one of six NHL expansion franchises in 1967. The team stayed for nine seasons, playing under different names (Oakland Seals, California Golden Seals), before moving to Ohio in 1976. Two years later, the Cleveland Barons merged with the Minnesota North Stars. In 1991, the North Stars were effectively split in two, with George and Gordon Gund getting an expansion franchise for San Jose, while a group led by Norm Green took over in Minnesota (and moved to Dallas in 1993). San Jose sponsored a name-the-team contest. The fans chose Blades[1], but Gund figured that sounded like the name of a gang, so he went with Sharks (which was the name of the Puerto Rican gang in *West Side Story*, but never mind).

UNIFORMLY SPEAKING: There are 11 varieties of sharks in San Francisco Bay. None of them are black and teal, the dazzling color scheme San Jose chose for its NHL team. Sharks jerseys were the third-best sellers in sports (after the NBA's Chicago Bulls and the NFL's Oakland Raiders) in their first season. Princess Di had little William wearing a Sharks hat in 1994.

HOW COOL?: Home teal: 9.5. Away white: 9.0.

---

[1] Other San Jose name-the-team fan submissions: Fog Horns, Piranhas, Screaming Squids, Faults, Alcatraz Techs and Cansecos.

When you're a Shark you're a Shark all the way; from your first cigarette til your last dying day.

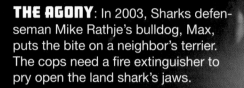

THE AGONY: In 2003, Sharks defenseman Mike Rathje's bulldog, Max, puts the bite on a neighbor's terrier. The cops need a fire extinguisher to pry open the land shark's jaws.

THE ECSTASY: In the team's third season, the Sharks make the playoffs, finishing eighth. Drawing conference champion Detroit, they shock the hockey world on April 30, 1994, by upsetting the Wings in game seven as Jamie Baker golfs in the winner. "Hey, this playoff thing is easy," Shark fans wrongly conclude.

FANATIC: A San Jose supporter throws a shark on the ice after Joe Pavelski scores against Detroit in the 2010 playoffs.

Average ticket + parking
+ hot dog + beer:
$76.96
(18th highest in the NHL)

Gag Reflex?

The idiom "jump the shark" refers to the moment when a TV show, musical group or even a politician is ruined by an absurd, credibility-destroying stunt. The pop culture specific is *Happy Days*, a hit TV series that went into rapid decline, so the story goes, after a 1977 episode in which the Fonz, wearing a leather jacket, water-skied over a great white shark.

It could be argued that San Jose's Sharks tripped over the particulars of their beautifully outrageous uniforms right from the jump. Talk about overbite: since 1993, when the club moved to the Shark Tank (the HP Pavilion), San Jose's pregame ceremony has been the same. A 17-foot great white, mouth open for business, drops from the rafters, its eyes flashing red— *Cripes, the shark has been drinking!* A creepy maritime fog drifts out of the creature's mouth. After that, heavy metal thunder—Metallica's "Seek and Destroy"—throbs over the sound system and Shark players spill, one after another, out of the big fish's jaws.

Predictably, San Jose's NHL debut wasn't so auspicious. On their first road trip, the team's jet couldn't get off the ground—flat tires. During a long wait, forward Paul Fenton slipped while using the water fountain and was hospitalized. When the team arrived east, Rick Lessard punctured his eardrum with a Q-Tip. The club quickly lost two games in a row, and

then three times as many players when half a dozen Sharks came down with food poisoning. (Weren't they supposed to be able to eat anything?) Their best player, Doug Wilson, did play—and dislocated a thumb in a 9–0 loss to New Jersey. After that, the equipment manager became sick. His replacement injured himself on the skate-sharpening machine.

What happens to San Jose in the playoffs?

The team finished the road trip 0–7, having been outscored 29–11.

Ah, well, an expansion team—what are you going to do? Plenty! Since 2000–01, San Jose has placed first or second in its division in eight of nine seasons. It finished second in the NHL's tougher Western Conference in 2003–04 and '07–08. From 2008–10, San Jose was reigning conference champ.

Playing to a full house every night at the Shark Tank, the team is a beautiful thing in the regular season, a perfect complement of savagery and skill— absolute Sharks!—with great players everywhere: Thornton, Heatley, Marleau, Clowe, Pavelski, Setoguchi, Boyle plus new kid Logan Couture.

If that's not sufficiently intimidating, they have Antero Niittymaki in net, who, when playing in Philly, wore a mask showing Al Capone enforcer Frank Nitti resolving a labor dispute.

All of which leads us to the uncomfortable question: What happens to San Jose in the playoffs? Every year, it's something, often a hot goalie— Calgary's Miikka Kiprusoff imitating a brick wall in 2004; four springs later, Dallas's sliding Marty Turco lifting a weary leg to swat away Patrick Marleau's third overtime try.

Still, the evidence is unflattering. In 2006 and '07, San Jose dropped three games in a row after taking commanding leads in conference semifinal series. In 2009, the Sharks won the President's Trophy after posting the league's best record, then lost four straight to eighth seed Anaheim in the first playoff round.

The team's best players, Thornton and Marleau, get too much of the blame. Perhaps the fault is not in San Jose's stars, but in their shelves. It's all the shark sweaters and gear. Having an apex predator as logo has been great for merchandise sales. Still, it could be argued that any team that delivers its players to battle with a Heimlich maneuver has a design flaw.

Joe Thornton proved in the 2011 playoffs that he was San Jose's Man of Teal, recording 17 points in 18 games, winning important faceoffs and playing gamely through a separated shoulder.

TAMPA BAY LIGHTNING

ALTERNATE NICKNAMES: Bolts.

FRANCHISE STARTED: Expansion team in 1992.

UNIFORMLY SPEAKING: Tampa is smack-dab in the middle of Florida's lightning belt—2,000 Floridians have been hit by lightning since 1959. Hence, Tampa Bay Lightning. Tampa's home uniform, appropriately, is night black with a bolt-from-above crest.

HOW COOL?: Night storm (home): 8.4. White lightning (away): 7.5.

Chain Lightning: Goal scorers are like home-run hitters in baseball. The bombs arrive in clusters. In 2009–10, Steven Stamkos (left) scored 4 goals in one 18-game stretch, then followed that with 17 goals in as many games. In his magical 1944–45 season—his 50 in 50 year— Rocket Richard got more than half his haul, 26 goals, in 10 games. The summer he swatted 60, in 1927, Babe Ruth hit 4 home-runs in April and 17 in September.

THE AGONY: For the team's first six seasons, Tampa was hounded by the Internal Revenue Service. Their Japanese owners never saw them play. Scouting amounted to Tony Esposito watching hockey on satellite TV. Rumor had it the team was being used to launder mob money. GM Phil Esposito explained how he'd fooled Japanese investors: "They were surprised to learn they invested in hockey. They thought we said 'sake.'"

THE ECSTASY: Taking advantage of high draft picks accumulated in lean years (Vincent Lecavalier, Brad Richards) and shrewd free-agent signings (Martin St. Louis and Dave Andreychuk), Tampa wins the Stanley Cup in 2004.

FANATIC: Cup-winning captain/mom Andreychuk ensured that players respect the team by fining anyone who stepped on the team logo on the dressing room floor. Failure to place one's game jerseys in the laundry cart cost players more money.

Average ticket + parking
+ hot dog + beer:
$54.73
(29th highest in the NHL)

The Man with

Seeing his ability to execute perfect one-timers, the Swiss watch makers, Tissot, selected Steven Stamkos to be their celebrity spokesman, and then gussied him up in a photo shoot with a James Bond evening suit and very butch Daniel Craig haircut. But who are they kidding? The hockey superstar didn't graduate from MI-6. His finishing school was teammate Gary Roberts's basement gym. At an even 6 feet and 180 pounds, Stamkos had a so-so rookie year in 2008–09. The game was faster, players bigger than he was accustomed to. After all, he'd been skating against 18-year-old Barrie Colts in junior the season before. Now, NHL bluebeards, brutes like 6′7″, 255-pound Zdeno Chara were catching and pushing him around.

In his first 40 games, the 19-year-old scored four goals.

In the old days, such a raw rookie would've been sent down. Instead, Tampa put him in the gym, under the supervision of strength coach Chuck Lobe. Home in Toronto the following summer, Stamkos drove to Roberts's country manor in nearby Uxbridge four days a week. There, Roberts, a veteran of 22 NHL winters, challenged the teenager with a punishing program designed to develop lower-body strength—increasing his on-ice speed and stability. After workouts, Stamkos sipped health elixirs: Fiji water and gray protein shakes. Lunch—the most important meal of the day, according to Roberts—was catered organic food. Stuff like high-energy, Inca-approved quinoa salads.

Don't let the Daniel Craig–James Bond look fool you.

the Golden Gun

"Not the best-tasting food," Stamkos reported, "but then the adjustment takes place in your body and you can feel how healthy you're eating."

Stamkos returned to the NHL 16 pounds stronger, but somehow lighter on his skates. The game seemed easier, especially after Martin St. Louis was placed on his left wing. A fluid, elusive skater with a giving nature, St. Louis broke down defenses like an accomplished basketball point guard, creating a tangle of confusion that allowed Stamkos to slip (more quickly now) into open spaces for what was suddenly hockey's best one-timer.

Like Brett Hull, Stamkos stripped the ready-aim-fire motion of a hockey shot down to one element: fire. Down on his right knee, he was three-quarters of the way through his shot when St. Louis's pass reached the blade of his stick.

And some of Stamkos's newfound strength went to his wrists, now seemingly energized by the lightning bolt on his jersey crest. Everyone was saying that he had the best shot in hockey.

At age 20, in 2010, Steven Stamkos scored 51 goals. Ready for this? According to *The Times* of London, that's the same number of lovers James Bond had going into Bond film number 23.

ALTERNATE NICKNAMES: Leafs, Buds, Leaf Nation, God's Team.

FRANCHISE STARTED: In February 1927, when a group led by Conn Smythe purchased the ailing Toronto St. Patricks.

UNIFORMLY SPEAKING: The road uniform is snow white with a blue crest and trim. The home jersey is the mirror image.

HOW COOL?: Still the prettiest blue in sports, but the old jersey, with the veiny crest, darker color and extra bands at the waist, had more character—and Stanley Cups! Current home: 7.5. Away: 7.0. Vintage jersey: 10.0.

The Big M, Frank Mahovlich.

TORONTO MAPLE LEAFS

Johnny Bower after letting in a goal. Even his mask looks sad.

THE AGONY: Go figure: The Leafs haven't reached the Cup final in 44 years, but ex-Leafs have coached in 12 Stanley Cup finals since then, winning 7. The winners: Al Arbour (1980–83), Pat Burns (2003), Randy Carlyle (2007) and Joel Quenneville (2010). The bridesmaids: Arbour (1984), Barry Melrose (1993), Pat Quinn (1980 and 1994) and Floyd Smith (1975).

THE ECSTASY: Darryl Sittler collecting a record six goals and four assists in an 11–4 win over Don Cherry's Boston Bruins in 1976.[1]

FANATIC: Mike Myers, whose first book report in a Toronto grade school was on Scott Young's *A Boy at the Leafs' Camp*, spends over $60 million making a movie, *The Love Guru*, that has the Leafs finally winning the Stanley Cup.

---

[1] Leafs go to town after Sittler's record performance, rewarding him with a special night and a silver tea set. Bruin coach Cherry pins newspaper accounts of the party on the bulletin board. Bruins never lose in Maple Leaf Gardens the next three years.

Average ticket + parking
+ hot dog + beer:
$147.23
(Highest in the NHL)

Maple Leafs Forever

A time line of how the Toronto Maple Leafs became Canada's Team

Green with Envy: 1812

Tired of being picked off by camouflaged Yankee snipers in the War of 1812, British troops stuff maple leaves in their scarlet tunics. Never good at spelling, Americans call them "maple leafs."[1]

Royal Approval: 1860

The maple leaf emblem is sewn into the badge of the 100th Regiment (the Royal Canadians). The maple leaf is everywhere during the Prince of Wales's 1860 tour of Upper and Lower Canada.

Symbol of Song and Story: 1866

Alexander Muir is strolling his Toronto property when a dancing maple leaf lands on his shoulder. A member of the Orange Lodge, a Protestant fraternal society, Muir is stricken with patriotic fever and writes "The Maple Leaf Forever," making the sugar maple an explicit symbol of Canadian exceptionalism.

---

[1] Another explanation: It is sometimes argued that the hockey team is named after the Canadian Army's Maple Leaf Regiment in World War I, and since the name of the regiment is a proper noun, the plural can be rendered ungrammatically. All of which makes sense, except there is no mention of such a regiment in Canadian military histories. Many World War I units did, however, wear cap badges in the shape of a maple leaf.

OFFICIAL HOCKEY PROGRAMME
ARENA GARDENS PRICE 10ᶜ
FASTEST SPORT IN THE WORLD.

Program from a 1930 Leaf game at the Mutual Street Arena (between Dundas and Shuter); (Above) illustration shows the Leafs scoring against the Montreal Maroons. (Opposite)"Nutsy Fagan" explains why Toronto's hockey team needs a new stadium. The Leafs would indeed move into Maple Leaf Gardens the following year.

In days of yore
From Britain's shore
Wolfe the dauntless hero came
And planted firm Britannia's flag
On Canada's fair domain
Here may it wave
Our boast, our pride
And joined in love together
The thistle, shamrock, rose entwined
The Maple Leaf Forever.

The song is English Canada's de facto anthem in the Confederation year of 1867.

Coining the Phrase: 1871

The maple leaf forever becomes a symbol on Canadian pennies in 1871.

Budding Sports Franchise: 1896

"Toronto" and "Maple Leafs" collide for the first time when an Ontario baseball team bearing that name is created. The Leafs win 11 pennants and 2 Junior World Series from 1902–67. Stars include Nap Lajoie, Carl Hubbell and Elston Howard.

Identity Crisis: 1906–27

Pro hockey arrives in Toronto in 1906, and is greeted by big yawns. The Toronto Hockey Club folds in 1909, but is revived in 1911. Over the next decade and a half, they're known as the Torontos, the Blueshirts, the Arenas and St. Patricks. Meanwhile, a second big-league team takes to the ice at the Mutual Street Arena in 1912. In three years, it goes through as many owners and operates under as many names: the Tecumsehs, Ontarios (wearing red-yellow sweaters and

Why We Need A New Arena

By Nutsy Fagan

It was last week when we were lining up for the Colborne and Canadien games, until we made Shipwreck Kelley look like a runner, that Frank Selke popped out from under his beaner and said "Mr. Fagan, why do we need a new Arena?"

"I will give up, Mr. Selke" I said, "Why do we need a new Arena?"

"I asked you first" says he, "You are a ghost writer, are you not?"

I replied "Sure, let me tell you about my apparition."

"Some other time" he protested, "But we are building a new Arena, willy nilly and perhaps you will have a few different slants on it?"

I did not relish this reference to a few "slant ons" I have had in the old Arena, but let it pass and now that they have brought the matter up I will tell you all why we need a bigger Arena in case you think we are building one just because some of the players are putting on weight.

Civic Pride demands it, that's what. Have we not in this grand and glorious hamlet the Canadian National Exhibition, the tallest skyscrapers in the British Empire, the most beautiful race track in North America (Woodbine not Dufferin), government control, the University of Toronto, and the Balmy Beach Canoe Club? The answer is "Yes, we have the Canadian National Exhibition, the tallest skyscrapers in the British Empire, the etc." We have all these and many more remarkable and prepossessing public institutions, and why, then should we be curtailed to a theatre of thump that will only hold eight thousand people with one foot in the aisle?

Toronto is the City of Homes and no one will stay in them. So bring on a new amphitheatre of action, a model indoor stadium that will seat at least fifteen thousand of our citizens in their overcoats. Make it so big that the standing room crowd will feel that they are out in the suburbs.

Is it right that every time the Canadiens or Bruins come to town we should be packed in so closely that we have to clap our hands up and down instead of sideways and that even in the box seats there is hardly room to swing a chair. Is it proper that during the intermissions you cannot reach the refreshment stand without gaining yards six times on plunges? The answer is no, no, no and a tiger.

Take the present press box, but bring it back, designed along tabloid lines, it is sometimes difficult for even a ghost writer, full of spirits, to write at all flowingly for there is only space enough for each scribe to scriven in short sentences. Then there is the radio to consider and unless we can rig up a more spacious balcony for friend Hewitt and give him some room to stickhandle up and down with the play, serious consequences may follow. Some night when he swings around the back of the net with Clancy, up to his own blue line, at centre, in on the defence, AROUND THE DEFENCE, IN ON THE GOAL and as HE SCORES, HE SCORES, Foster will find himself diving right through that microphone and what the stay-at-homes would then do without America's finest all round sports announcer is more than we can imagine.

And for the sake of big business as well, a new Arena is needed, one that will put seven thousand more tickets upon the market for each big match and thus allow the telephone service to get back to normal. At present on a Monday, Tom will phone Dick and say that he may be out of town for a few days but he would like a couple of tickets for Saturday's game and could Dick get them. Dick says he wants some himself and thinks he knows where he can land a few. So he rings up

Continued on Page 56.

WRESTLING

IVAN MICKAELOFF
matchmaker
ARENA ATHLETIC CLUB

MASSEY HALL
MARCH 20th.

AL. BAFFERT VS.
GEO. ZARYNOFF

TO A FINISH.
GEO. GALIZA VS.
JIM MALONEY

GOOD PRELIMINARY

Thanking you for past courtesys shown them.—IVAN MICKAELOFF.

courting the Orange Lodge) and Shamrocks (suddenly green and Irish as Paddy's pig). In 1915, Shamrocks owner Eddie Livingstone buys the Blueshirts and ditches his old club. Come World War I, the National Hockey Association admits the 228th Battalion, which has enlisted—literally—a handful of established pros to play in the team's khaki sweaters.

Conn Job: 1927–31

Constance Falkland Cary Smythe comes into the world carrying more baggage than names. His mom, Polly, is an alcoholic with a heartbreaking disappearing act. Dad Albert is a dreamy, impoverished socialist writer (*Poems Grave and Gay*, 1891). Conn discovers his identity in uniform, playing hockey and serving his country in the First World War, watching comrades die at Vimy. After 14 months in a German prison camp, where he learns to detest bridge, he returns home a fervent nationalist. Smythe

coaches the University of Toronto Grads, who go on to win the Allan Cup in 1927 and Olympic hockey gold in 1928.[2] After buying the Toronto St. Pats in February 1927, he changes their uniforms from kelly green to Great Lakes blue. For a new name and logo, he lifts the maple leaf insignia from his service uniform.

Roosevelt builds the Hoover Dam to lift America's spirit during the Great Depression. An unelected hero, Smythe erects Maple Leaf Gardens (1931), a winter cathedral where English-Canadians gather on Saturdays, while millions of others listen to Leafs games on CBC radio's *Hockey Night in Canada*. A new psalm enters the nation's prayer book. It begins: "Hello, Canada, and hockey fans in the United States and Newfoundland, this is Foster Hewitt from Maple Leaf Gardens…"

Smythe inspects every Leaf recruit, looking into his eyes for proof of character (read: humility). The Great Man has a credo, a philosophy of self-sacrifice that is as Canadian as taxes: stars win prizes, teams win championships.

---

[2] Although Smythe's team goes on to win a gold medal in the Olympics in 1928, he isn't behind the bench. He stubbornly refused to go after a disagreement over players who were late additions to the roster.

The biggest game in town: Maple Leaf Gardens on Carlton Street, 1934.

Minorities Report: 1936–67

Successive waves of immigrants learn to become Canadians by playing and watching hockey. And if they make a Canadian NHL team, chances are

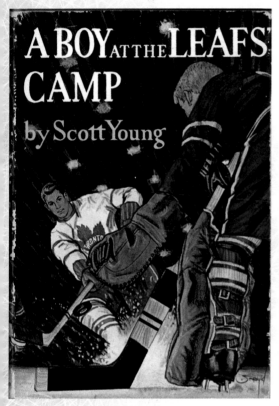

The fictional Leaf, Bill Spunska.

it's the Leafs. Turk Broda is the first Ukrainian to play in the NHL. In fact, for 40 years, Leafs always seem to have a Ukrainian in net—Johnny Bower (né Kiszkan) and Terry Sawchuk, Toronto goalies in the '50s and '60s, are Ukes. As is defender Bill Barilko. Wally Stanowski, Pete Stemkowski and Smythe's right-hand man, Frank Selke, are Polish. Superstar Frank Mahovlich is Croatian. Captain George Armstrong, a Cree. The Leafs even boast a skater from Mars: Eddie Shack. Scott Young (Neil's dad)

captures the Canadian immigrant's journey in his beloved hockey trilogy/civics lesson, *Scrubs on Skates, Boy on Defence* and *A Boy at the Leafs' Camp*. The juvenile series tells the story of multiethnic hockey-loving Winnipeg high schoolers Pete Gordon, Bill Spunska, Benny Wong, Grouchy DeGruchy and Horatio Big Canoe. Spunska eventually graduates to the culturally diverse Toronto Maple Leafs. There, he plays alongside fictional characters Buff Koska, Otto Tihane and Jiggs Mansicola.

The Age of Mythology: 1942–51

The Greatest Generation has a great team. The Maple Leafs win six Stanley Cups from 1942–51, often with a captivating story line. In the '42 final, the Leafs are down three–zip to Detroit. Coach Hap Day reads his discouraged troops a tearful letter from a 14-year-old girl, Doris Klein, begging them to pretty-please come back. Hearing the girl's urgent plea, the Leafs feel their sap rising and pile up four straight wins. In '51, Bill Barilko scores the

---

[3] Barilko's plane disappears in a storm, prompting weeks of front-page worry in newspapers. Conn Smythe offers a $10,000 dead or alive reward. A rumor spreads that Barilko, of Eastern European descent, has defected to the Soviet Union to aid their hockey program. Leafs stop accumulating Stanley Cups, not winning again until 1962, when Barilko's body is found. A mysterious circumstance which prompts The Tragically Hip to record a song in his honor, "Fifty Mission Cap," in 1992.

Cup winner in overtime, then disappears on a fishing trip, sparking the largest manhunt in Canadian history.[3] As per Smythe's design, the Leafs win championships without ever dressing an NHL scoring leader. They're peerless defensively, however. And seemingly cleaner than November snow. Team captain Syl Apps,[4] matinee-idol handsome, never drinks, smokes or swears. A Boston Bruin, Flash Hollett, attempts to take advantage of his good nature, knocking out his front teeth with a high stick. "By hum, thith hath gone on long enuth," Apps announces, flattening Flash with a right hook. Apps, Broda, Smythe and nine other Leafs go off to fight in the Second World War, leaving the team depleted. By comparison, the Montreal Canadiens are better than ever, replacing service-bound Joe Benoit and Paul Bibeault, their only wartime losses, with Hall of Famers Maurice Richard and Bill Durnan. For English Canada, this is kind of like in the movie *Robin Hood*, when Good King Richard goes off to fight in the Crusades, while Prince John stays home to live it up.

Flag Days: 1964–65

In 1958, a poll reveals Canadians want a new flag. In 1964, Parliamentary committees debate the flag issue, accepting 3,541 designs from Canadians. More than 2,100 submissions contain maple leaves (almost 400 depict beavers!) A historian, George Stanley, who played hockey at Oxford, comes up with the maple leaf design that, in 1965, becomes the Canadian flag.

---

[4] Apps's granddaughter, Gillian Apps, played on Canada's gold medal–winning team in 2006 and 2010.

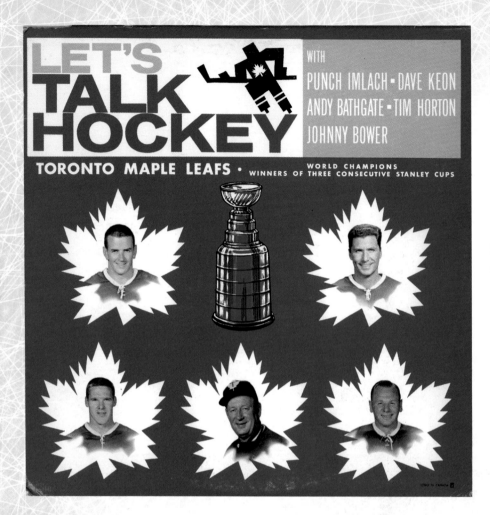

Record of achievement:
The Leafs put out a
long-playing album in
1964.

Turning Over a New Leaf: 1967

The Maple Leafs return the compliment prior to the 1967
playoffs, changing the traditional, jagged 35-point maple
leaf crest to a solid 11-point leaf that is closer to the Canadian flag.

Boomer Story: 1962–67

Baby Boomers have their own hockey team to cherish and
hold dear. The Leafs win four Stanley Cups in six years
in the mid-'60s, capping their historic run by upsetting the
star-studded Chicago Blackhawks and Montreal Canadiens in the centennial year of 1967. After that, for more
than 40 years, instead of counting sheep, Leaf fans go to
bed recalling this lineup: Bower and Sawchuk in net, Tim
Horton, Allan Stanley, Carl Brewer and Bob Baun (his
nickname was even Boomer!) on defense. Up front, Frank
Mahovlich and Red Kelly, Dave Keon, George Armstrong
…. ZZZZZZZZZZZZZZZ.

It's Only Make Believe: 1967–2010

And dat's dat, as Canada's team falls through thin ice, the
victim of plundering ownership and erratic management.
Empty the bandwagon. Cue the slurring trumpets. Now
they're the Toronto Make Believes, the Loafs, the Make
Me Laughs.

Except that, every decade or so, there comes a hockey
player with the right stuff—square shouldered, inde-
fatigable, courageous. With glowing hearts, we see thee
rise, Maple Leafs forever: Darryl Sittler, Wendel Clark
("Wennn-dellllll!") and Dougie Gilmour!

Cheer for Toronto? Never

How the Maple Leafs became the team everyone in Canada
(except Leaf loyalists) love to hate.

*Conn Smythe at a horse race,
telling the horse what to do.*

The Upper Canada Rebellion: 1946

Conn Smythe builds an airy bunker high in Maple Leaf
Gardens, from which he yells at his team with a sandpa-
pery growl. To ensure he is all-seeing, he films games—
something no one else is doing in the '30s. He is brilliant,
charismatic, with a conquering hero's energy and orga-
nizational skill. But that bunker—having God's point of
view—goes to his head. He figures he knows everything.
Makes trouble wherever he goes—and, too often, enemies

of friends. Major Smythe leads a company into World War
II. Wounded in France, the patriot who demands loyalty
decides he doesn't like how Canada is waging war, so he
attempts to overthrow Prime Minister King, dashing off
mutinous letters to newspapers. Back in Canada, he turns
against assistant Frank Selke, who arrives at his desk to
find a note advising him he needs permission to leave the
building. "Lincoln freed the slaves," Selke scrawls on the
note, then quits Upper Canada, seeking hockey asylum in
Montreal.

Not Ready for Prime-time Players: 1952–58

Television arrives in Canada on September 8, 1952. But this is a bad Hockey Decade in Canada for the Leafs. The team finishes out of the playoffs three times in the next five seasons, placing dead last the spring of 1958. The Rebellion is brewing.

Selke's Revenge: 1946–64

Frank Selke builds the Montreal Canadiens into the best team in hockey, enlarging the Montreal Forum and using the extra revenue to build a farm system controlling 750 teams—more than all other NHL teams combined. The Canadiens reach the Stanley Cup final 10 seasons in a row (1952–61), winning six times. Come the playoffs, Montreal is now Canada's team by default.

A Serpent in the Garden of Maple: 1961

Conn Smythe never recovers from his war wounds. His son Stafford, with a gang of millionaire's sons that includes Harold Ballard, takes over the Leafs by the late '50s. Conn gives the Silver Seven a $10,000 allowance. One year, the septet burned through $20,000 before the season has started. Parties are now an operating expense at the Gardens. Where Conn Smythe needed obedient followers, Stafford requires the reassurance of powerful cronies. In 1961, Smythe sells control of the Gardens to his son for $2.3 million. Then feigns shock when Stafford reveals that Ballard is in on the deal. But the Major must've known Stafford couldn't afford the Leafs on a $20,000 salary. Ballard is named vice president and alternate governor.

The Omen: 1962

Out drinking with Blackhawks owner Jim Norris, Ballard sells Frank Mahovlich to Chicago for $1 million. Conn Smythe has his son queer the deal, giving Stafford a good line for the papers: "We never rolled a drunk yet."

Rabbit Punches: 1958–68

A talented executive who can toot his own horn in any key, GM/coach Punch Imlach leads the Leafs to four Stanley Cups in the '60s. He is also hockey's first insult comedian. "The Canadiens . . . ha, they're mostly a

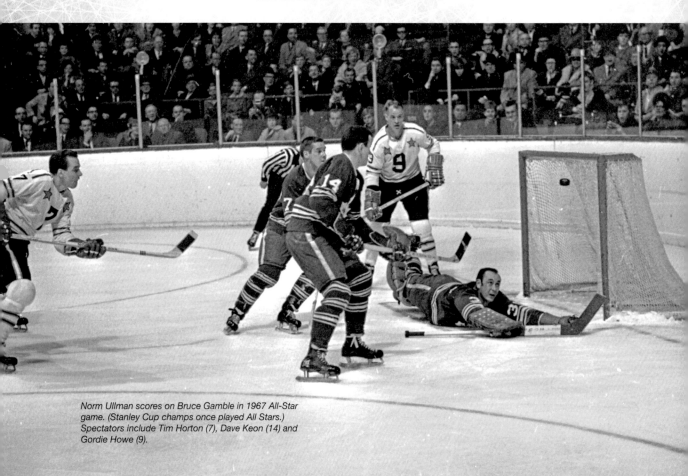

Norm Ullman scores on Bruce Gamble in 1967 All-Star game. (Stanley Cup champs once played All Stars.) Spectators include Tim Horton (7), Dave Keon (14) and Gordie Howe (9).

bunch a singers' midgets," he says before one playoff. Now the bleu-blanc-rouge half of Canada really hates the Maple Leafs.

The Omen II: 1967

Expansion arrives, bringing six new teams to the NHL. The Leafs perversely respond to the increased competition by selling their top farm clubs, the Victoria Maple Leafs and Rochester Americans.

Death and Taxes: 1971

Some trees grow so big that nearby saplings struggle to survive. Stafford Smythe oversees the farm system that provides Imlach with the resources to win all those Stanley Cups. Still, when *Hockey Night in Canada*'s Ward Cornell grabs him for an on-ice interview after the '67 Cup win, Stafford looks like a jailbreak escapee caught in a prison tower searchlight. It couldn't have been easy living in Conn Smythe's shadow, to feel eternally entitled and yet never quite worthy. Stafford bears that conflict like a lifelong illness. The executive who always felt underpaid

turns Ballard loose on a building that had never been exploited commercially. Ballard rips up the Gardens, throwing out Foster Hewitt's gondola; installing more seats, all of which are less comfortable. Stafford and Ballard renovate their homes, charging the expenses to Maple Leaf Gardens. That last maneuver costs them two years in a federal penalty box. Just 50 years old, Stafford dies on a hospital bed of a ruptured ulcer. "See, Dad? I told you they could never put me in jail," he tells his father. Ballard ends up with the Maple Leaf empire.

The Anti-Smythe: 1972–90

A millionaire's son, Harold Ballard never grows up into an affable blowhard, gravitating to the Peter Pan world of sports, where games go on forever. He is a cheerful presence, tobogganing a fat wallet from one managerial hockey job to another, serving without distinction, befriending the right people. Ballard's lovely wife, Dorothy, daughter of a Methodist minister and living proof that Harold must be an OK guy, succumbs to cancer in 1969. Harold takes to sitting by her graveside at night in a lawn chair, weeping. Until now, he's been a brilliant networker,

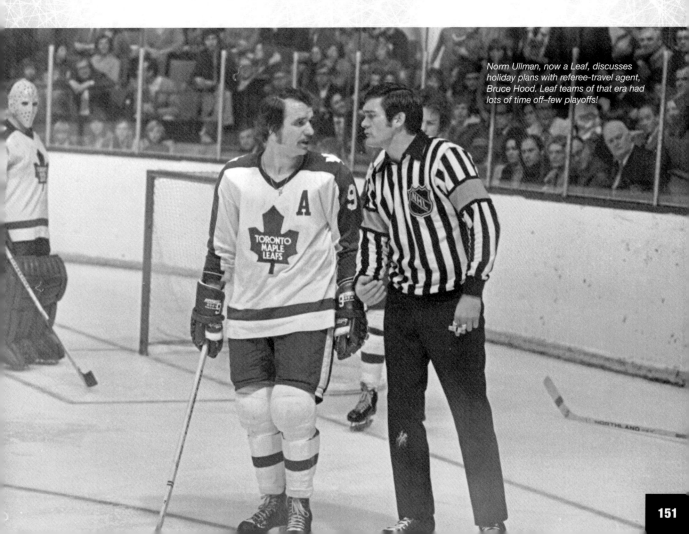

Norm Ullman, now a Leaf, discusses holiday plans with referee-travel agent, Bruce Hood. Leaf teams of that era had lots of time off–few playoffs!

151

with a born alternate governor's gift for appearing useful. But that graveyard—having Satan as a neighbor—goes to his head. The wounded hockey executive slips over to the dark side, finding pleasure in destroying all that frustrates him. The Maple Leafs are beyond his command. And so the emperor with no clue lays waste to his empire.

Angered that some of his Leafs are considering joining the rival WHA in the '70s, Harold refuses to negotiate, allowing 18 Leafs to defect. Most teams have 10 scouts; the Leafs, 3. The average pay for Gardens' workers in the '80s is $13,000—below the poverty line. The Leafs finish with a losing record every season that decade, leading the league in scandals. Comporting himself like a wrestling villain taunting the crowd, Harold fights the media, captain Darryl Sittler, his children and his ex-convict companion, Yolanda. The Gardens that Conn Smythe inspected the morning after every game, searching the aisles for discarded gum wrappers, is now a crime scene. Later, it's revealed that nearly 90 children have been sexually abused by lowlife Gardens' employees during the Ballard years.

The Cinderella Sisters' Syndrome: 1968–2011

There are great Canadian NHL teams between 1968 and 2011. Montreal and Edmonton enjoy championship runs. Calgary wins a Stanley Cup. Vancouver and Ottawa come close. Still, on

Man's best friend (T.C. Puck) with Toronto hockey's worst enemy (Harold Ballard). Rob Ramage (8) and Wendel Clark (17) look on.

Saturday nights in prime time, *Hockey Night in Canada* inevitably features a bad Leaf team—all because 20 percent of the country lives in Leafland (southern Ontario). Elsewhere, Canadian hockey fans develop a Cinderella-stepsisters' resentment toward the fabulously rich franchise[5]—a club that, for going on five decades, has often played as if its glass skates were tied together in a knot.

The Invisible Man: 2000

In the Leafs' horror-show pantheon, Harold Ballard is the Werewolf. And Richard Peddie, president and CEO of Maple Leafs Sports & Entertainment (2001–12) is the Invisible Man. Mr. Behind-the-Scenes leaves no puck unturned when it comes to making money. The net into which Mats Sundin scores his 500th goal is cut into 2,000 pieces and sold. Zamboni slush from the Leafs' final game in Maple Leaf Gardens is melted into plastic discs and raffled off for $50 a puck. Still, there's no getting around it: when it comes to sports—actually competing against other teams—the MLSE crew couldn't pour piss from a boot if the directions were written on the heel. Between 2008 and the spring of 2011, none of the MLSE teams—the Maple Leafs, the basketball Raptors or soccer's Toronto FC—make the playoffs.

A Nation's Skate-Goat: 2010

In 1999, the Leafs abandon the most famous building in Canada, moving to a new rink, gaining a new corporate sponsor—and stigma. They play in an arena named after a company whose name Canadians pronounce through clenched teeth. The Air Canada Centre and its hockey team are run by Maple Leaf Sports & Entertainment—more bad optics. Hey, wrestling is a sport and entertainment; hockey in Canada is life and death—except for wealthy Leaf fans, who never bother taking their platinum seats before the five-minute mark of any period. Watching the Leafs on TV in Halifax or Saskatoon, it's possible to believe that those empty seats represent the managerial indifference that has ruined the team. Hell, they're what's wrong with the country!

And so the Maple Leafs become Canada's necessary skate-goat.

The joke Canadians tell to cheer each other up. "What's the difference between the Toronto Maple Leafs and a cigarette vending machine? The vending machine has Players!"

The Bipolar Express: 2002–11

During his first season in Toronto, 2008–09, coach Ron Wilson called the Leaf media "bipolar," referring to a mental illness characterized by extreme, opposite moods. But that sounds more like a description of Leaf fans, who become intoxicated on a victory over the Ottawa Senators, then are reduced to Yosemite Sam tantrums when their guys lose two in a row. It's easy to understand why Leaf fans always loved manic shift-disturber Darcy Tucker. He's them.

---

[5] *Forbes* magazine named the Leafs the most valuable franchise in the NHL in 2009, with an estimated value of $470 million (U.S.).

VANCOUVER CANUCKS

ALTERNATE NICKNAMES: 'Nucks.

FRANCHISE STARTED: There is a long history of pro hockey in British Columbia. The Pacific Coast Hockey Association was launched in 1911. The Vancouver Millionaires won the Stanley Cup in 1915. The Victoria Cougars became the Detroit Red Wings. After World War II, the minor-league Vancouver Canucks started, taking their name from Canadian servicemen, who were nicknamed Johnny Canucks. The NHL Canucks began in 1970.

Heap of fashion trouble: All the old Canuck sweaters, including the two ugliest, the V-necked affair that looked like a Vancouver Pentecostal Choir robe and a Markus Naslund replica jersey illustrating the Ladies Mixed Drink top the team once wore.

UNIFORMLY SPEAKING: The Canucks came into the NHL with a uniform perfectly suited to their home between the sea (blue) and the mountains (green). That was followed by a series of ghastly makeovers. Their current blue-green alternate jerseys are a welcome return to the team's early days.

HOW COOL?: Blue home: 8.9. White away: 8.5.

Henrik Sedin.

THE AGONY: The 1986 trade that sent 50-goal scorer (and B.C. native) Cam Neely, along with the rights to Glen Wesley—a real good defenseman—to Boston for a wounded Barry Pederson.

THE ECSTASY: In the '94 playoffs, 'Nucks are down three games to one to Calgary in the opening round, then rip off three overtime wins on goals by Geoff Courtnall, Trevor Linden and Pavel Bure. Thus begins a thrilling playoff run that includes a half-dozen or so oh-my-God saves by Kirk McLean and a double-overtime victory over Toronto that gets them into the final. There, the team goes down 3–1 to New York before almost, nearly, not quite coming back.

FANATIC: In the 2008 film *Zach and Miri Make a Porno*, Vancouver native Seth Rogan sports a Monroeville Zombies hockey jersey. Monroeville, Pennsylvania, is where *Dawn of the Dead* was filmed in 1978. After the film, Monroeville Zombie merchandise does drop-dead business online.

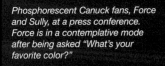

Phosphorescent Canuck fans, Force and Sully, at a press conference. Force is in a contemplative mode after being asked "What's your favorite color?"

Average ticket + parking
+ hot dog + beer:
$101.86
(3rd highest in the NHL)

O Brother, Where Art Thou?

Daniel and Henrik wait for teammates after scoring another goal.

No sport is more fraternal than hockey. No other pro athletic venture can be measured in family sextets (the Sutters) and quartets (Staals, Bouchers). The NHL has seen 20 three-sibling acts. Two-brother showings are hardly worth mentioning—228 so far, from Frank and Andy Bathgate to Ken and Gary Yaremchuk.

Pro baseball, football and basketball have, among them, one Hall of Fame brother combination: Paul and Lloyd Waner of the Pittsburgh Pirates. Hockey has seven: Max and Doug Bentley, Henri and Maurice Richard, Phil and Tony Esposito, along with the famous Conacher, Boucher, Cook and Patrick clans.

Breaking out an atlas to find the NHL's band of brothers, a pattern emerges. The Brotens—Neal, Aaron and Paul—are from Roseau, Minnesota, population 2,756 (see Winnipeg-Atlanta chapter). The Sutters come from Viking, Alberta, a town that dipped below 1,000 when they left. In actual Viking country, twins Henrik and Joel Lundqvist grew up in Are, a small Swedish ski village.

We can imagine their stories: northern towns, long winters. Hockey is a sustaining recreation, a way for villages to carve their names in the ice and say, "We were here." Children compete for joy and attention. Younger brothers want to be like (and better than) older siblings, who, in turn, emulate Dad or maybe a hockey hero on the next street over. Before long, the brothers are heroes themselves—small-town kids selected to take on the world, ready or not.

Such is the story of Henrik and Daniel Sedin, the NHL's third set of identical twins (after Peter and Chris Ferraro and Ron and Rich Sutter). The Vancouver Canuck stars were born six minutes apart in 1980 in Ornskoldsvik, a Swedish town of 28,617 tucked halfway between Stockholm and the Arctic Circle.

Legend has it that, in 1994, the Swedish king visited here. Children flocked to see him. As he moved through the crowd, though, kids seemed disappointed. "Oh, that king," one said, sagging. The youngsters figured Peter the Great (Peter Forsberg) had returned from NHL wars.

A Swedish mathematician calculated that Ornskoldsvik should have 12 million people to produce as many NHL players as it does. In the past 31 years, someone from the Baltic seaport has been the top scorer on the Canucks almost half the time. Thomas Gradin led Vancouver from 1980–82. His mom, Elsie, was nanny to Markus Naslund, top point-getter from 1999–2006. It has been either Daniel or Henrik Sedin ever since.

Other townies to make it in the NHL include Anders Hedberg (Bobby Hull's favorite linemate), Anders Eriksson, Tomas Jonsson, Lars Molin, Niklas Sundstrom and Tampa Bay's young star, Victor Hedman. The Columbus Blue Jackets' Sammy Pahlsson lives just down the street from Daniel Sedin.

It's skold in Ornskoldsvik—there's lots of ice. Winters are dark. In December, the sun rises after 10 a.m. and remains a crack on the horizon for a few hours before calling it a day.[1] Lighted outdoor rinks summon kids from all over. Cold is never a worry. There is a saying around town: "There is no such thing as bad weather, just bad clothes."

Nowhere is hockey taken more seriously than here. A local high school, working with the town's famous sports club, Modo, has a specialty class for elite players called Hockey 401. Twelve to 15 students are chosen annually, attending lectures on everything from nutrition to injury prevention and media training. Forsberg and Naslund attended classes. So did Henrik and Daniel Sedin. The twins wouldn't think of skipping. Their father, Tommy, was the Modo school's vice principal.

In junior, playing for Modo, the Sedins were nicknamed "The Red Ants" because of their tenacity and coloring. The twins are not exactly identical. Henrik (right) is an inch taller and five pounds heavier. Modo has produced 25 percent of all Swedish players in the NHL. In 2007, when Modo won the Swedish national championship, Peter Forsberg phoned from the States with instructions to buy 30 bottles of Dom Pérignon for the team's celebration at the club's local hangout, Mammamia. Former Canuck, Marcus Naslund is currently GM of the team.

---

[1] On the other hand, Ornskoldsvik is one of the rare places in the world where you can book tee time for golf at twelve o'clock and be asked, "Will that be afternoon or evening?" The sun never quite sets some weeks in summer.

Being identical twins, sharing every physical and emotional growth spurt, not to mention vacation, school, soccer and hockey games, gave the Sedin boys a great, but (some argued) fragile advantage. It was as though they shared a common brain that delegated authority for the common good. Daniel, the more assertive twin, evolved into the goal-scoring left winger. Studious Henrik was the playmaking center who worried about defense.

On the ice, they displayed a fabulous rapport. "I always know where Henrik is and most of the time what he's thinking," Daniel said. Telepathy made for gorgeous offensive moves—no-look passes and complex double give-and-goes that left defenders feeling like they'd stepped off a merry-go-round.

Detroit's Henrik Zetterberg remembers playing against them as a teenager in Sweden. "They won, like, 10–9 and the Sedin line scored all their goals," he said.

The twins were both ranked in the top five in their draft year (1999). But what would a team get with only one Sedin—half of a great player? Their agent, Michael Barnett, sent NHL clubs a letter that read in part, "Undoubtedly, the Sedin brothers could have long and successful pro careers apart. But the benefits of them playing together, for everyone involved, are obvious . . . We will support the efforts of the NHL club that shows itself to be the most desirous of obtaining both Daniel and Henrik . . . Our role may evolve into something more than passive."

Vancouver GM Brian Burke did some fancy stickhandling and ended up with two top picks, choosing Daniel second (giving him number 22) and Henrik third (33).

The twins started slowly in the NHL. For a while, they were called the Sedin sisters by a wisenheimer on Vancouver radio. But after the lockout season, 2004–05, the players emerged vastly improved, perhaps the NHL's best

cycling team, circling in corners and along the boards, playing catch with the puck, waiting for someone, usually Daniel, to spin into the clear in front of the net.

In 2009–10, the hockey world had a chance to see what a Sedin could do alone when Daniel broke a foot early on. Left to his own devices, Henrik went on a scoring tear, securing his first NHL hat trick a few games later. When Daniel returned, they were better than ever, scoring goals with magical flips and feints. Henrik's backhand no-look pass to a speeding-to-the-net Daniel was now hockey's most exciting play.

That old expression, "He must have eyes at the back of his head," seemed literally true of both Henrik and Daniel, who could always envision (without looking) where the other was going.

At season's end, Henrik collected the league's MVP award and delivered a humble, funny, properly appreciative acceptance speech. Although he was on stage alone, he used the plural pronoun—us. The Hart Trophy winner also got to the heart of the matter regarding how the twins got so good, thanking his two older siblings "for letting us play with you despite being rather annoying younger brothers."

VANCOUVER'S FIRST HOCKEY BROTHERS

If the Sedin twins follow their career trajectory into the Hockey Hall of Fame, they will not be the first Vancouver brothers to get there. Frank and Lester Patrick arrived long before them, and changed hockey along the way. Lester won Stanley Cups for the Montreal Wanderers as hockey's first rushing defenseman in 1906 and 1907. In 1911, he and Frank built Canada's first artificial-ice rink (in Victoria) and organized a west coast professional league, the PCHA. Frank was playing coach of the Stanley Cup–winning 1915 Vancouver Millionaires. Lester guided the 1925 champion Victoria Cougars. Frank Patrick is often called the inventor or modern hockey. His innovations include goalies being allowed to fall to the ice, the forward pass, blue lines, playoffs, changing on the fly and the penalty shot.

WASHINGTON CAPITALS

ALTERNATE NICKNAME: Caps.

FRANCHISE STARTED: Added as an expansion team in 1974.

UNIFORMLY SPEAKING: Red, white and blue colors, befitting a team representing America's capital. They originally wore white pants with their away uniforms, but retired that look because of unsightly sweat stains.

HOW COOL?: Angry electorate red home uniform: 7.5. Snow white away: 7.2.

THE AGONY: In their debut season of 1974–75, the Capitals are the worst team in NHL history, going 8–67–5 and losing 37 road games in a row. Comments coach Jim Anderson, "I'd rather find out my wife is cheating on me than keep losing like this. At least I could tell my wife to cut it out."

THE ECSTASY: The Capitals win the 2004 draft lottery, selecting Alexander Ovechkin with the first-overall pick.

FANATIC: The Caps' theme song, "Let's Go Caps," is by Washington heavy metal band Darkest Hour.

Alexander Ovechkin (left) and Nicklas Backstrom (right).

Ovechkin rewards Washington's investment, winning the NHL MVP trophy in 2008 and 2009. In June 2009, Superman gets his screen test. Ovie is selected to star in the NHL 2K10 video game. He wears retroflective markers during a Las Vegas shoot outside Caesars Palace.

Average ticket + parking
+ hot dog + beer:

$63.66

(24th highest in the NHL)

Tatyana and Alexander Ovechkin.

Mother Russia

Love dies. Empires fade. In 1975, 28 percent of all major-league baseball players were African-American. By 2008, that percentage was down to 8. Lacrosse was Canada's most popular spectator sport in the 19th century. Now it lags well behind curling and NASCAR.

And hockey, a sport the brutish Soviet regime somehow made beautiful, has wasted away in Mother Russia. The Big Red Machine has fallen into disrepair.

During the 1960s, 1,500 kids attended tryouts for the Red Army hockey program every year. Only 39 showed up in 1985. Going into the 2009–10 season, 25 Russians were playing in the NHL, down 60 percent from 2004.

From 1963–90, the Soviet Union won 20 of 28 world championships. Since then: 3 wins, 17 losses.

Anti-Western dictators Leonid Brezhnev, a hockey fanatic who ruled the USSR from 1964–82, and Viktor Tikhonov, the tyrant who coached the Central Red Army forever (1977–96), would be horrified to learn that the best remaining argument for Russian hockey supremacy plays, at $8 million a year, for the NHL's Washington Capital-ists.

At least it's a good argument. When primed, Alexander Ovechkin, Tikhonov's most famous star, is the best hockey player in the world. If he doesn't ruin his talent with reckless play (on and off the ice), he may

become the best winger ever. How'd he get that way? Indeed, how did the Big Red Machine dominate hockey for three decades—then suddenly, and without warning, grind to a shrieking halt?

The answer to the first question is easy: breeding. When in 1946 the Soviet Union decided to compete in hockey, its ministry of sport took to creating a team as if they were scientists conducting a lab experiment. They were hardly starting from scratch. Before the NHL was founded in 1917, 34 teams in six Russian cities played competitive bandy. In fact, Russians had been playing a sport like hockey since the 1700s, when Peter the Great stickhandled on the frozen Neva River.

Two and a half centuries later, Joseph Stalin put his government's propaganda department in charge of athletics. Sports schools created superheroes to inspire the proletariat. Children skilled in athletics began training seriously at age eight. Muscle biopsies determined their optimum sport.

Four thousand sports schools trained 1.3 million athletes. The best hockey players made their way to Moscow Dynamo, sponsored by the KGB (secret police), or Red Army. Players for Red Army—even married, adult stars like Valery Kharlamov—trained 11 months a year, six days a week in an isolated barracks 20 kilometers west of Moscow. Players slept two to a room. No phones, women or booze. Lights out at 11.

A Russian hockey player's training program was varied. He played soccer. Ran. Lifted weights long before NHL pros did. On-ice workouts pro-moted strength, flexibility and impro-visational skills. Players stickhandled on one leg. Practiced three-on-two rushes with five pucks.

In 1974, Gordie Howe and Bobby Hull watched the Russians work out. Soviet captain Boris Mikhailov shouted, "Let's show them what we can do." The Big Red Machine began moving like a carnival Tilt-a-Whirl.

"Hey, Bobby, put your eyeballs back in your head," Gordie whispered.

Red Army produced great athletes. After scoring 52 goals his first NHL season (2005–06), Ovechkin spent the off-season making promotional ap-pearances for the Capitals. One week, he threw out the ball at a Washington Nationals' game and co-hosted a golf tournament. Ovie, it should be made clear, had never thrown a baseball or swung a club. He fired a strike into the catcher's mitt, and, playing with a borrowed 4-iron, hit a 160-yard, three-hop hole-in-one. After acing the hole, he shouted, "I hit. I swear Gaa. I swear my mom . . . my home."

One play from Ovechkin's second season became a YouTube sensa-tion. Hurtling toward the net against Phoenix, Number 8 was thrown to the ice by defenseman Paul Mara. Sliding with his back to the net, the winger managed a one-hand backhand swipe, guiding the puck into the net from an impossible angle.

"HE MAY HAVE BEEN THE ONLY GUY WHO COULD SCORE THAT GOAL!" the rink announcer shouted. "ALEXANDER THE GREAT!"

Sitting in the Verizon Center among the fans (she doesn't like corporate boxes), Alexander's mom had a low-ercase response to The Goal. Tatyana Ovechkin told Washington reporter April Witt that, as fans screamed, she contemplated a Soviet sports song celebrating individual sacrifice: "We

In North America, stars can easily be captured in action figures for a hero-hungry fan base.

need one victory, one for all, regardless of the price."

Here lies the paradox of Alexander Ovechkin—the conflict that makes him so dangerous (perhaps even to himself). Ovechkin is a product of the Soviet Union, a gone-but-not-forgotten land where God, mother and home amounted to the same thing. He attended Soviet sports schools. So did his parents. Tatyana was captain of the national basketball club at 19. She would go on to win two Olympic gold medals and a slew of national honors—such drab citations as the Order of Friendship of the Peoples.

The 8 on Alex's back is his mother's number. Ovechkin promises to represent his country if the NHL skips the 2014 Moscow Olympics.

At the same time, Alex's public life is a response to his upbringing. There was, as they say, no party in the Communist Party. (Comedian Lenny Bruce likened communism to "one big phone company.") Russian players didn't draw attention with garish celebrations. Rough play was cowardice that disturbed a team's "musicality," according to Anatoli Tarasov, father of Russian hockey. The puck carrier, he said, was "the servant of other players."

Tarasov believed in constant motion and misdirection: players hopping lanes at full speed, making passes to open spaces suddenly filled with charging red jerseys—until all that was left was an open player with an empty net.

Theoretically, there were no Soviet superstars. Russian coaches were cool to the NHL's marquee players. Surveying the Montreal Canadiens lineup of the mid-

'70s, Tikhonov preferred diligent Bob Gainey to spectacular Guy Lafleur.

Ovechkin, though, is servant to no one. A superstar, he shoots and scores more than anyone. And when the red light shines, he throws himself high against the glass, as if trying to crash a frat party through the second-floor window.

Canadian TV hockey commentator Don Cherry, Washington coach Bruce Boudreau and, via a two-game suspension in 2009, the NHL have all told Ovechkin to be more careful. He doesn't care. "I just play my game," he said after the suspension. "I play risky. I won't try and hit and make some people get hurt, but ... what can you do? You can do nothing?"

The nihilism is what's most frightening. Here's an English translation of Alex talking with Anna Nasekina, a Russian journalist:

Q: There's probably no place left on earth where you can sit in peace?

A: Come on! Some places they know me, some places they don't. It's not hard to sign autographs and pose for pictures.

Basically, my philosophy is "what the hell"…

Q: So a star can never be captured?

A: The illness of fame can be lost just as quickly as it is found.

Q: Well, it seems to me that the reputation of "caveman" flatters you.

A: They call me caveman because I don't care what others think of me. I couldn't care less about anyone or anything.

Q: If you didn't care, then you couldn't play the way you do?

A: Well, maybe I play the way I do only because it's all the same to me.

Q: You mean to tell me that your manly, unshaven face, your nonchalance, your missing tooth and yellow skates aren't part of your image?

A: You want some wine?

Ovechkin is an X-game onto himself. Accepting the ceremonial key to Washington from mayor Adrian Fenty

in 2008, Alex jokingly revoked the city's speed limits. That same year, a camera caught him racing a utility cart just under a closing Verizon Center garage door, nearly losing his head.

The last bit is disturbing. Alex's older brother Sergei died in a crash. His mother was nearly killed by a car while walking home from school as a girl. The great Valery Kharlamov, Russia's greatest forward before Ovechkin, perished on the highway. So did Russian stars Anatoly Fetisov, Vladimir Durdin and Boris Alexandrov. The death rate on Russian roads is four times higher than in Sweden. Alcohol consumption has tripled since the Soviet Union dissolved in 1991.

That same year, the government-sponsored sports academies closed. The Big Red Machine ran out of gas. Coaches and players fled. Five Russian stars—Slava Fetisov, Alexei Kasatonov, Vyacheslav Kozlov, Igor Larionov and Sergei Fedorov—migrated eventually to Michigan, helping the Wings to championships in 1997 and '98. The famed Soviet national club was suddenly a pickup team drawn from players scattered worldwide.

For 60 years, Russian hockey has been Russia. Viktor Tikhonov played defense for Joseph Stalin's son, Vasily, the Soviet minister of sport, and then coached Alexander Ovechkin. For all its success, the Central Red Army never escaped its country's troubles. Igor Larionov's dissident grandfather was banished to Siberia. Igor learned English by committing

treason, listening to Voice of America radio broadcasts. Slava Festisov passed the puck, but never secrets, to his defense partner, Vladimir Konstantinov, a known KGB informant.[1]

Alexander Ovechkin is Russian, but he doesn't play Russian hockey. Growing up, he dreamed in North American, wondering what it would be like to confront his favorite player—Owen Nolan, then with the San Jose Sharks. Not being able to see them on TV, did he think San Jose played like the monsters on their jerseys? "He's like the shark in *Jaws*, circling in the water for blood," St. Louis Blues president John Davidson says of Ovechkin. "They should play that music from the movie—da-duh, da-duh, da-duh—when he's out on a shift. He doesn't just go after loose pucks, he hunts them down."

Ovechkin's game is a repudiation of those critics who allege that Russians never show emotion or can't play tough. He honors Russian and North American hockey. This from Gordie Howe, who met Alex in 2009: "There's 18 guys sitting down, and he's the only one who jumped up to shake my hand," Big Gordie says. "He shows respect for the older players."

There is a hell-bent, Cossack-like quality to Ovechkin's game. Scoring, he says, is as exciting as "being chase by big dog." But it's not true that he doesn't care. Rather, he cares too much. He's the first hockey player

> ## There is a hell-bent, Cossack-like quality to Ovechkin's game.

with the weight of two worlds—Russia and North America—on his shoulders.

That pressure makes him do wonderful, dangerous-looking things. In 2008, against Montreal, he played as if being pursued by a wolf pack. He hit, and was hit by, Canadiens all night; at various points had his nose broken and mouth stitched. Still, he was incredible, skating miles while collecting four goals—two on spectacular plays—and an assist in his team's 5–4 win.

At various points, he was Vsevolod Bobrov and Bobby Hull; the Russian Rocket, Pavel Bure and his more flammable antecedent, Rocket Richard.

He was all of the above. And he was himself, Alexander Ovechkin.

AFTERWORD

The preceding was written in January 2010. A lot has happened since. Russia did not medal in the 2010 Olympics, and the Capitals were upset in the first round of the playoffs by Montreal. Afterward, Ovechkin drowned his sorrows on a Love Boat *cruise around Turkey, accompanied by helpful Moscow nightclub hostesses. And there's no getting around it: Ovie looked out of gas through the early months of 2010–11—Mike Tyson hanging on against Buster Douglas in their 1990 championship fight. Can he regain his status as the world's greatest player? Yes—he's only 25. Is he willing to work harder than Sidney Crosby to ensure that happens?*

Who knows? As Alex himself says, "The illness of fame can be lost just as quickly as it is found."

---

[1] Konstantinov was seriously injured in a car accident after Detroit won the Stanley Cup in 1997. He would never play again.

WINNIPEG-ATLANTA THRASHER-JETS

Thrashed!

THRASHERS · T.O.I. · PENGUINS · 0

The NHL pulled the Atlanta Thrashers off life support during the 2011 playoffs, moving the team to Winnipeg. That's twice the NHL has test-marketed a team in Georgia, decided un-unh and sent the club packing to western Canada. The Atlanta Flames became the Calgary Flames in 1980. If Winnipeg names its club after Manitoba's provincial bird, they will be the Winnipeg Great Gray Owls. Our condolences to Atlanta hockey fans, several hundred of whom protested the team's move by gathering together in a May 2011 tailgate party. Many carried signs. One hopeful placard read, "Dewey Defeats Truman," referencing the Chicago *Daily Tribune* front page that got the 1948 American election wrong. A few angry fans blamed NHL chief, Gary Bettman, waving signs quoting Bob Dylan's 1965 song, "Desolation Row": *"Now here comes the bl commissioner, they've got him in a trance . . ."*

ALTERNATE NICKNAMES: None.

FRANCHISE STARTED: The Atlanta Flames were Georgia's first NHL team, lasting eight seasons before flickering out to Calgary in 1980. (How dumb was it to commemorate Sherman's sacking and burning of Atlanta in the Civil War?) The South rose again, hockey-wise, with the Thrashers in 1999.

Atlanta Flames mascot with Colonel Sanders's perm.

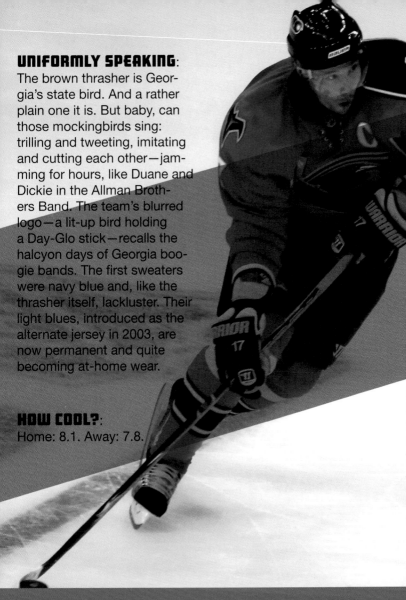

UNIFORMLY SPEAKING:
The brown thrasher is Georgia's state bird. And a rather plain one it is. But baby, can those mockingbirds sing: trilling and tweeting, imitating and cutting each other—jamming for hours, like Duane and Dickie in the Allman Brothers Band. The team's blurred logo—a lit-up bird holding a Day-Glo stick—recalls the halcyon days of Georgia boogie bands. The first sweaters were navy blue and, like the thrasher itself, lackluster. Their light blues, introduced as the alternate jersey in 2003, are now permanent and quite becoming at-home wear.

HOW COOL?:
Home: 8.1. Away: 7.8.

FANATIC: Hollywood actor Glenn Ford (his dad was born in Glenford, Alberta) tried unsuccessfully to buy the Atlanta Flames for $8 million in 1980. Singer Kenny Rogers became a Thrashers fan in 2005. He's currently the team's honorary captain.

THE AGONY: The Thrashers never got over a horrible start that saw three straight lottery draft picks fly away. In 1999, Thrashers picked first and bypassed the Sedin twins for Patrik Stefan, an underachiever whose NHL career ended in Dallas, fanning on an empty-net breakaway, only to see the other team tie the game. In 2000, Atlanta picked star Dany Heatley second. He asked to be traded in 2005 after a tragic car accident that killed teammate Dan Snyder. Thrashers got Marian Hossa in return, but couldn't sign him and had to trade the high-scoring forward in 2008 to Pittsburgh for tenacious Colby Armstrong, whom they again couldn't sign, losing him eventually to free agency. In 2001, the team picked the fabulous Ilya Kovalchuk first overall, whom they couldn't sign, resulting in… *"Such a rainy night in Georgia / Lord, I believe it's rainin' all over the world."*

THE ECSTASY: Upon moving to Winnipeg, Dustin Byfuglien's team sells all their season tickets (13,000) in less than four days.

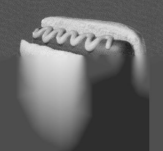

Big Cargo from Fargo

He is the answer to the question, "What would Charles Barkley have been like as a hockey player?" The 6′ 5″, 265-pound Dustin Byfuglien led the Chicago Blackhawks to the Stanley Cup in 2010, settling in on the right side of the big line with Jonathan Toews and Patrick Kane, making it enormous, knocking everyone he felt like off the puck, collecting easy rebounds (just like Sir Charles), then flipping the puck into the net, scoring 11 goals, many of them game-winners.

All of that with hands as cool and soft as Minnesota snow.

Weeks later, in an effort to squeeze under the salary cap, Chicago shipped the 25-year-old to Atlanta, where he instantly became star of a team that always seems to be losing its best player. What's more, he did so as an All-Star defenseman specializing in barging, end-to-end rushes.

Can he lead the success-starved franchise to playoff respectability? Who knows? Nobody has ever been sure how good a hockey player Dustin Byfuglien can be—least of all, maybe, Dustin.

He was born in Roseau, Minnesota, a six-hour drive north from Minneapolis-St. Paul. (Ten more minutes and you're in Canada.) There are 713 families in Roseau—mostly Norwegians and Swedes. This is Fargo country. Dustin's mom, Cheryl Byfuglien—pronounced Bye-foog-lee-ann—could've gone to school with Jerry Lundegaard and Minnesota-nice Sheriff Marge Gunderson, characters in the Coen Brothers' 1996 film.

Dustin stuck out like a bruised thumb in Roseau. His mother had gone away to beauty school in St. Cloud, returning with the child of a black college football player. She moved into a trailer behind her parents' 17-acre spread, taking a job as a forklift operator at the nearby Polaris snowmobile factory.

Differences are conspicuous in a prairie town. I once drove across Canada, stopping in Shell Lake, Saskatchewan for gas. After grabbing lunch in a diner, I wandered back to find some kids crouched and staring at my parked car.

They'd never seen Quebec plates before.

In some ways, Byfuglien's story is the same as Gordie Howe, another reluctant prairie giant. Like Gordie, Byfuglien grew up too fast and far, a big-for-his-age hulk stared at in school—"Look, there's Paul Bunyan!" Howe repeated grades, earning the nickname "Big Dummy." (He was dyslexic.) Dustin towered over the teachers he avoided. Like Howe again, he was superbly coordinated—Dustin's grandfather recalls him trick-riding a car in the backyard at age seven, standing on the steering wheel with his head sticking out the sunroof.

All Dustin wanted was to play hockey for the Roseau Rams, the seven-time Minnesota high school state champs. The Brotens—NHLers Neil, Aaron and Paul—had been Rams. So had Dustin's stepfather, Dale Smedsmo. As of 2011, there was still a Broten and a Byfuglien—Chase and Derian—on the Rams.

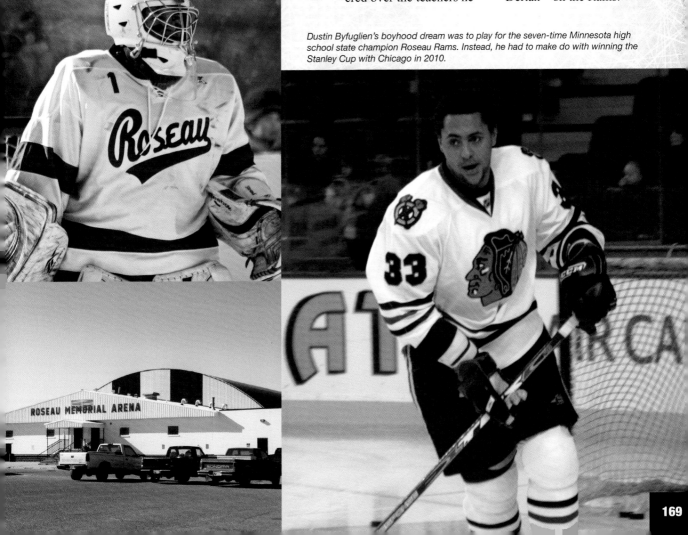

Dustin Byfuglien's boyhood dream was to play for the seven-time Minnesota high school state champion Roseau Rams. Instead, he had to make do with winning the Stanley Cup with Chicago in 2010.

Dustin never made the team, though—because of academic ineligibility. In a town with one movie screen and three arenas, being unable to play for the school team was a crippling blow. Dustin was Paul Bunyan without an axe.

He quit hockey at 14. Still, Dustin hung around the Memorial Auditorium, where he had lived on hot dogs and hot chocolate for 10 years. Occasionally, he crossed the street to the American Legion, where his grandmother, a former figure skater who worked the kitchen, slipped him warm plates of food. That was his routine from the time he was a squirt through bantam age. Dustin even made a touring midget team, playing with an $80 aluminum stick his mom paid for in two installments from the True Value Hardware store near the rink.

Though he'd stopped playing, his mom still couldn't pry her boy out of the Aud's brackish, sweat-soaked dressing rooms. Dustin would sit on the green benches late into the evening, listening to adult-league players talk hockey, enjoying their easy camaraderie.

"Dustin, we gotta go."

"Coming."

Minutes later, his mother would lose her patience. "I'm coming in," she'd yell. Only then would Dustin scramble for the door. And off they'd go into the slap-in-the-face cold Minnesota night.

Mom would have to go to bed soon after getting home. Her morning shift at the factory started at 5:45. Dustin stayed up late, watching TV with the volume down, emptying the fridge.

This couldn't go on. His mother finally talked to him. "Son, it's time to fish or cut bait," Cheryl Byfuglien said. A triple-A midget team in Illinois wanted him. He'd have to move to another state and family, go to a different school. Gordie Howe faced the same challenge as a young teenager,

moving from Saskatchewan to Ontario.

"It's up to you, but I think you should go," his mother said.

Everything started to move fast now, like at the end of a close hockey game when both teams play to win. Dustin was 15 years old and 281 pounds when he joined the Chicago Mission. Way too big. And the big defenseman who just took the puck in his own end and flew in bantam, knocking past defenders as if they were swinging doors on a saloon, had little sense of positional play.

Coach Darren McClusky put Dustin on a diet and showed him the weight room. In the summer of 2001, Dustin was drafted by the Brandon Wheat Kings, a Canadian junior team. Eventually, he was a Prince George Cougar, a high-scoring, highlight-reel defenseman with issues—fluctuating concentration and weight.

The Chicago Blackhawks gambled an eighth-round pick on him in 2003. He was a B prospect—a big kid with lots of heart, but maybe too much stomach and hips. He lost weight, got stronger, became a minor-league All-Star in the American Hockey League and played pretty well in a couple of seasons with the Blackhawks, earning a reputation as a third-line banger who could score—a fan favorite who sometimes

ran off with the crowd's imagination, trying to do too much.

The transformation took place under an assumed name. Bye-foog-lee-ann was now Buff-lin—Big Buff. The kid wasn't the first prairie ethnic to have cosmetic surgery on his name. North Dakota's Roger Maras, a Croatian-American, changed his name to Roger Maris before becoming a home run–hitting hero. Saskatchewan's John Kiszkan, a Ukrainian-Canadian, turned himself into Johnny Bower before taking on NHL shooters.

Big Buff became an ESPN SportsCenter regular in 2010. Suddenly he wasn't like Gordie Howe; he was Big Gordie. "Buff-lin" collected hat tricks in consecutive playoff series. He tallied three game-winners against San Jose, including the deciding marker in the pivotal third game—a three-overtime marathon. Like Gordie, he was harder to move than a parked car. And he was putting the puck in from everywhere—in close with delicate chip shots; far away with devastating one-timers that snapped the twine taut, sending water bottles jumping from atop the net. Like a circus strongman ringing a bell.

And after every goal at home, the seven-year-old who rode a car no-hands back in Roseau materialized, cruising past boards

on one skate, his arms in the air like a football referee signaling a touchdown.

Against Philadelphia in the Stanley Cup final, he discouraged the Flyers with a series of body blows, tossing aside big Chris Pronger one game, and then rolling a strike, bowling Kimmo Timonen into a referee.

Afterward, there was the Heart Trophy moment—returning to Roseau with the Stanley Cup, taking the trophy into the Memorial Auditorium, in the presence of his mom, stepdad, grandparents and everyone in town. "This means so much to me, I'm so happy to be able to do it," he said, his voice breaking. Then Big Buff pointed to the Cup. "Here it is."

Can he bring the team a Cup? Everyone says no. The franchise has been one of the league's perennial underachievers. A tomato can for the rich teams to knock over.

It's doubtful that Atlanta's number 33 feels that way, however. For a kid who couldn't make his high school team yet has already won the Stanley Cup, nothing is impossible. And the only thing in hockey that can knock over Dustin Byfuglien is a Zamboni.

Share your photos!

Do you have a funny or unusual hockey photo from past or present? You can add it to the *Double Overtime* photostream at www.flickr.com/groups/doubleovertime. Your photo could be chosen for the next edition of *Double Overtime*.

www.doubleovertime.ca

Acknowledgments

I'd like to thank my family—wife, Jacquie and my two boys, Harry and Lewis, for their technical support (ferrying drinks and sandwiches to my third-floor office), as well as my agent, Dean Cooke, and his assistant, Mary Hu, editor, Lloyd Davis, and all the great, much-appreciated support from the folks at Simon & Schuster Canada, including Kevin Hanson, Alison Clarke, Cailen Swain, Lynda Kanelakos and Paul Barker.

Sources

I read the sports section of *The Globe and Mail*, *The Toronto Star, The New York Times* and *The Boston Globe* before brushing my teeth in the morning, and regularly listen to podcasts of W-Fan in New York and The Fan, in Toronto. ESPN and *Sports Illustrated* are other frequent entertainment-information stops. My favorite show is The Fan's *Hockey Central at Noon*, with Daren Millard, Nick Kyrpreos and Doug MacLean. When a big story breaks, I make a point of catching *Prime Time Sports*, with Bob McCown and Stephen Brunt. For Vancouver sports, I turn to Cam Cole. And I regularly read Greg Wyshynski's Puck Daddy blog along with the *Hockey News*; much of the material on uniforms comes from the latter magazine's special issue on uniforms from a couple of years ago.

Here are sources for individual chapters in the book:

Anaheim Ducks: The three Mighty Ducks films from Disney (the last one was a mighty slog), as well as *Sports Illustrated* reports of the Ducks' 2007 Stanley Cup win. And the book, *Total Hockey*.

Atlanta Thrashers: Stories from Michael Russo and Brad Schlossman in the *Grand Forks Herald*, David Hugh of the *St. Paul Pioneer Express*, and Tris Wykes of *The Virginian Pilot*. Also, *Sports Illustrated* reports from Michael Farber.

Boston Bruins: The books *Total Hockey, Hockey! The Story of the World's Fastest Sport*; Trent Frayne's *The Mad Men of Hockey, All You Have to Do is Win* and *Famous Hockey Players*; Stephen Brunt's *Searching for Bobby Orr*; George Plimpton's *Open Net*. Also, stories by E.M. Swift in *Sports Illustrated* and Bob Ryan in *The Boston Globe*. Paul Quarrington's story on Eddie Shore in *Original Six* is the best hockey story I have ever read. Special thanks to Paul Patskou for the Don Cherry poems.

Buffalo Sabres: Stories in *The Buffalo News*, Calvin Trillin's essay, "An Attempt to Compile a Short History of The Buffalo Chicken Wing" from a 1980 issue of *The New Yorker*. Also, the book *Total Hockey*.

Calgary Flames: Research by Paul Patskou and Norm Pawluck. Also, the book *Total Hockey*.

Carolina Hurricanes: I watched three episodes of *The Andy Griffith Show*, my favorite show as a kid (although I remember it mainly from syndication). Also, Michael Farber, *Sports Illustrated* stories on the team's Stanley Cup win in 2006 and the book *Total Hockey*.

Chicago Blackhawks: The books *Total Hockey* and *Hockey! The Story of the World's Fastest Sport* and Trent Frayne's *Famous Hockey Players*. Also, Michael Farber's *Sports Illustrated* stories on Chicago winning the 2010 Stanley Cup, as well as articles from Mike Spellman in the Chicago *Daily Herald* and Adam L. Jahn in the *Chicago Sun-Times*. Special thanks to my main man in Chicago, Paul Haizman for taking me to so many reindeer games.

Colorado Rockies: The book *Total Hockey* and stories by Eric Duhatshek in *The Globe and Mail*. Special thanks to Kirk Makin, Haliburton summer tour guide.

Columbus Blue Jackets: The blog, The Columbus Blue Jackets' Civil War Hockey from 2007, by Benzion Chinn.

Dallas Stars: The book, *Brett: His Own Story*, by Brett Hull and Kevin Allen, and stories by Michiko Kakutani in *The New York Times* and Jerry Crowe in the *Los Angeles Times*.

Detroit Red Wings: The books *Total Hockey; Hockey! The Story of the World's Fastest Sport*; Trent Frayne's *Mad Men of Hockey; The Gods of Olympia Stadium*, by Rich Kincaide; *Gordie: A Hockey Legend*, by Roy Macskimming; *Yzerman: the Making of a Champion*, by Doug Hunter; *The Road to Hockeytown,* by Jim Devallano and Roger Lavoie; as well as stories by Gare Joyce in *The Globe and Mail*, Vartan Kupelian and Mike O'Hara in *The Detroit News*. I've also stored away many things Doug MacLean has said about working for the Wings on *Hockey Central at Noon*. Special thanks to my old pals, Bill Anderson and Andrew Meeson.

Edmonton Oilers: The books *Total Hockey; The Game of Our Lives*, by Peter Gzowski, *Gretzky's Tears*, by Stephen Brunt; *I'd Trade Him Again*, by Terry McConnell and J'lyn Nye with Peter Pocklington; *Outliers,* by Malcolm Gladwell; along with Terry Jones's accounts of the Oilers from the *Edmonton Sun*. Special thanks to James Adams at *The Globe and Mail*.

Florida Panthers: Stories by Mike Phillips in *The Miami Herald* and Steve Gorten in *The South Florida Sun-Sentinel*, and Michael Farber, *Sports Illustrated*.

Los Angeles Kings: The books *Total Hockey* and *Tales from the Los Angeles Kings*, by Randy Shultz and Bob Miller.

Montreal Canadiens: The books *Total Hockey; Hockey! The Story of the World's Fastest Sport; Lions in Winter*, by Chrys Goyens and Allan Turowetz; *The Rocket: A Cultural History of Rocket Richard*, by Benoit Melancon. The CBC TV special, *The Montreal Canadiens: 100 Years–100 Stars*, hosted by George Stroumboulopoulos. Special thanks to Chris Murray for taking me to so many Montreal hockey and baseball games.

Minnesota Wild: The book *Big Man: Real Life & Tall Tales*, by Clarence Clemons and Don Reo, as well as stories from Michael Russo in the Minnesota *Star Tribune*, Rob Vanstone in the *Saskatoon Star Phoenix*, Bob Duff in the Regina *Leader Post*, and Jeff Klein in *The New York Times*. Thanks for research and assistance help from Paul Patskou.

Nashville Predators: I've been to Nashville several times, for country music as well as hockey. Stories by James Mirtle, *The Globe and Mail* and Bruce Ward, Canwest News Service. Thanks to Geoff Pevere for the last Nashville trek.

New York Rangers: The books *Total Hockey* and *Hockey! The Story of the World's Fastest Sport*. I was living in New York and attended the game where Bob Probert took on Tie Domi, sitting a few rows behind the Detroit bench. Special thanks to Ted Riley for getting me to the game.

New York Islanders: The books *Total Hockey* and *Ladies and Gentlemen, The Bronx Is Burning*, by Jonathan Mahler. Stories by Michael McEnanay of *Long Island Press*, and Jack Dellapina, New York *Daily News*.

New Jersey Devils: The books *Total Hockey* and *Brodeur: Beyond the Crease*, by Damien Cox and Martin Brodeur.

Ottawa Senators: The book *Total Hockey*.

Philadelphia Flyers: The book *Total Hockey* and the documentaries, *NHL History of the Philadelphia Flyers and The Broad Street Bullies* (HBO), along with Bill Meltzer's Heroes of the Past at www.flyershistory.net.

Phoenix Coyotes: The books *Total Hockey* and Stephen Brunt's *Gretzky's Tears*, along with stories by Garth Woolsey in *The Toronto Star*, Stephen Brunt in *The Globe and Mail* and Dean Bonham in *Rocky Mountain News*.

Pittsbrugh Penguins: The books *Total Hockey* and *Hockey! The Story of the World's Fastest Sport; Mario*, by Lawrence Martin and *Sidney Crosby: Taking the Game by Storm,* by Gare Joyce.

St. Louis Blues: The books *Total Hockey* and *Hockey! The Story of the World's Fastest Sport*, along with stories on concussions by Dave Washburn, Canwest News Service and Leigh Montville in *Sports Illustrated*. Special thanks to *The Globe and Mail* for assigning me to do a feature on hockey concussions in 2003. In addition, I watched the fourth game of the 1960 Stanley Cup finals between Toronto and Montreal, along with a Toronto-New York and two Toronto-Detroit games from the 1950s and 1960s on Leaf TV in researching this story.

San Jose Sharks: My editor, Lloyd Davis, contributed a great deal to the opening section on San Jose's early franchise history. I consulted *Total Hockey* and found material in an uncredited 1991 story on the team, "When you're a Shark, life is tough on and off the ice," from the *Houston Chronicle* News Service. Other stories used include a piece by Rick Sadowski in *The Los Angeles Daily News*.

Tampa Bay Lightning: Stories by Allan Maki in *The Globe and Mail*, Dave Scheiber in *St. Petersburg Times*, George Johnson in the *Calgary Herald*, Sunaya Sapuri in Yahoo Sports, John Bingham in *The Telegraph* and James Duthie's TSN column, "Going 1-on-1" with Steven Stamkos.

Toronto Maple Leafs: The books *Total Hockey* and *Hockey! The Story of the World's Fastest Sport*; Trent Frayne's *Mad Men of Hockey*; William Houston's *Inside Maple Leaf*

Gardens: The Rise and Fall of the Toronto Maple Leafs; Scott Young's *If You Can't Beat Em in the Alley*; Dick Beddoes's *Pal Hal*; *Leaf AbomiNation* by Dave Feschuk and Michael Grange; Damien Cox's columns on the Leafs over the years, along with *Maclean's* magazine's 2008 story, "Why Leafs Stink," by Steve Maich.

Vancouver Canucks: The books *Total Hockey* and *Hockey! The Story of the World's Fastest Sport*, along with the story "Finding Forsberg" in *ESPN The Magazine*, as well as articles by Roy Cummings in *The Tampa Tribune*, Jan Gradval in the *Chicago Sun-Times* and Cam Cole in the *Vancouver Sun*.

Washington Capitals: The books *Total Hockey* and *Hockey! The Story of the World's Fastest Sport*; *The Red Machine*, by Lawrence Martin and April Witt's magazine story on Alexander Ovechkin in *Washington Post Magazine*.

Winnipeg-Atlanta: Stories from Michael Russo and Brad Schlossman in the *Grand Forks Herald*, David Hugh of the *St. Paul Pioneer Express*, and Tris Wykes of *The Virginian Pilot*. Also, *Sports Illustrated* reports from Michael Farber.

HOTO CREDITS

hotography indicators: t = top, b = bottom,
= left, r = right, c = center

ppearing throughout
   Ice with skate tracks, Shutterstock
   Hot dog and bun, iStockphoto

OREWORD
   x. *Hockey Heroes* cover, From the personal
   collection of Stephen Cole
   xi. *Hello Canada!* cover, From the personal
   collection of Stephen Cole

NAHEIM DUCKS
   2. Kid in Duck Jersey, Scott Henderson
   3. (t) George Parros and fan, LiberalArtist/
   Flickr
   3. (b) Ducks' fans standing, Mark Muano
   4. George Parros, Ivan Makarov/Flickr
   5. Ryan Getzlaf Stanley Cup, AP Photo/Mark
   Avery

OSTON BRUINS
   6. (t) Kid in Bruins gear, www.murphhockey
   .com
   6. (b) Kids with Bruins mascot, michael
   .gratton@fmr.com
   7. (t,l) Bobby Orr in wheelchair, © Bettmann/
   CORBIS
   7. (t,r) Bobby Orr in white uniform, Michael
   Hasenstein
   7. (b) Marco Sturm, Zdeno Chara, Patrice
   Bergeron, Tim Shahan/Flickr
   8. Kennedy Family, © Bettmann/CORBIS
   9. Bobby Orr in dark uniform, Michael
   Hasenstein
   10. (t) Ray Bourque, Françcois Couture
   10. (b) Terry O'Reilly, Nick DeWolf
   11. (t) Don Cherry woodcarving, Lisa Brawn/
   lisabrawn.com
   11. (b) Tim Thomas, cool09/Flickr

UFFALO SABRES
   12. (t,c) Paul Gaustad, Maureen Landers
   12. (c,r) Sabres fan in red uniform, kgigante/
   Flickr
   12. (c,l) Sabres fan with foam puckhead,
   Maureen Landers
   12. (b) Ryan Miller, Maureen Landers
   13. Buffalo Memorial Auditorium postcard,
   vaviabuffalo/Flickr
   14. Tyler Myers, Zane Haserot
   15. (l) Alexander Mogilny, sabre11richard/
   Flickr
   15. (r) Rob Ray, sabre11richard/Flickr
   16. (t) Ryan Miller, Joel Stuckey/Flickr
   16. (b) Dominic Hasek, Alexei Zhitnik, Bill
   Wippert/Sports Illustrated/Getty Images
   17. (l) Sabres/Soviet cartoon, Mike Ricigliano
   17. (b) René Robert and Gilbert Perreault,
   Steve Babineau / NHL via Getty Images

ALGARY FLAMES
   18. (t) Flames fans outside arena, Live and
   Basic/Flickr
   18. (b) Willi Plett—Atlanta Flames, gatsbyiris/
   Flickr
   19. (t) Old fan in Flames toque, Morgan
   Briggs/Flickr
   19. (c) Flames fan wearing balaclava, Brett
   Ketler—Melissa Kwan/Flickr
   20. Jarome Iginla and Dion Phaneuf, Bruce
   Bennett/Getty Images
   21. Foster Hewitt, Archives of Ontario, C
   3-1-0-0-472 / Gilbert A Milne fonds / Image
   I0020097

   22. Neil Colville, Gjon Mili//Time Life Pictures/
   Getty Images

CAROLINE HURRICANES
   30–31. RBC Center All-Star game, Lalitree
   Darnielle-http://lalitree.com
   30. (b) Sergei Samsonov and Cory Stillman,
   Dan4th/Flickr
   31. (b) Home of the Staal Brothers, Kevin
   Carlson
   32. Andy and Opie, Joanna Shere
   33. Barney Fife, Lz
   35. Glen Wesley Stanley Cup, Richard
   Spence/Flickr

CHICAGO BLACKHAWKS
   36–37. Blackhawks Parade, ifmuth/Flickr
   38. Bobby Hull towel, Francis Miller//Time Life
   Pictures/Getty Images
   40. Jonathan Toews and Patrick Kane vs Red
   Wings, Dave Sandford/NHLI via Getty Images
   41. (t,r) Chicago Blackhawk players, Randy
   Sanders/sandersphotoart/SandersPhotoArt@
   yahoo.com
   41. (c,l) Michael Jordan statue wearing
   Jonathan Toews Jersey, Dale Ahrens/Flickr
   41. (c,r) Wrigley Field sign, Nick Angeloni
   41. (b,l) Lion with Blackhawk helmet, Ernesto
   Rios
   41. (b,r) Lion with Blackhawk helmet, Rich
   McDowell/e15rimac/Flickr

COLORADO AVALANCHE
   42. (t) Quebec Nordiques fans, Jonathan
   Guyon © www.jonathanguyon.com
   42. (b) Joe Sakic, Matthieu Masquelet
   43. (t) Peter Forsberg, Håkan Dahlström/Flickr
   43. (b) Avalanche Ale, Aubrey Laurence
   44. Matt Duchene and Anze Kopitar, cikiri/
   Flickr
   45. (t) Matt Duchene and Paul Stasny,
   Dannielle Browne
   45. (b) Haliburton, James H. G. Redekop

COLUMBUS BLUE JACKETS
   46. (t) Kris Russell, Dannielle Browne
   46. (b,l) Columbus Blue Jacket beer, Ken Falk/
   DerDrache/Flickr
   46. (b,r) Cannon, Mike Smail
   47. Blimp, Stephen Blanzaco
   48. Rick Nash, Jamie Sabau/NHLI via Getty
   Images
   49. Rick Nash with puck, Gail West

DALLAS STARS
   50. (t) Gump Worsley, Archives of Ontario,
   C 193-3 Julien LeBourdais photographic
   negatives, 1963–1995, Envelope 70065,
   Image 42
   50. (b) Jason Arnott, Ronald Martinez/Getty
   Images
   51. Steve Ott, Andy Martin Jr., andymartinjr
   .com
   52. Brett and Bobby Hull, Bruce Bennett
   Studios/Getty Images
   53. Bobby Hull goal, Archives of Ontario,
   C 193-3 Julien LeBourdais photographic
   negatives, 1963–1995, Envelope 70064,
   Image 37

DETROIT RED WINGS
   54. Gordie Howe, W. T. Helfrich
   55. (t) Al the octopus, Ed Frank/clutchpics
   .com
   55. (b) Statue with Red Wings jersey, M.
   Cowan
   56. Steve Yzerman billboard, Jennifer DiSano
   57. Red Wings banners, Wylie Poon
   58. (t) Jack Adams and Terry Sawchuk, ©
   Bettmann/CORBIS
   58. (b) Gordie Howe in alone, W. T. Helfrich

   59. Red Wings vs Flyers, Robert Lane/Flickr
   60. (t) Gordie Howe, Stan Wayman//Time Life
   Pictures/Getty Images
   60. (inset) 1949 Cadillac Sedanette, www
   .robidaconcepts.com
   63. Nicklas Lidstrom, Maureen Landers

EDMONTON OILERS
   64. Oiler jerseys painted on fence, Simon Law
   65. (t) Wayne Gretzky, Dave Madeloni
   65. (b) Edmonton Oilers Fanboni, rgoshko/
   Flickr
   66. Wayne Gretzky coffee table, Paul
   Kennedy/Sports Illustrated/Getty Images
   68. Wayne Gretzky holding the Cup, THE
   CANADIAN PRESS/Mike Ridewood

FLORIDA PANTHERS
   70. (l) Cory Stillman, Jamie Kellner
   70. (r) Florida Panthers Mascot Stanley C.
   Panther, Reto Kurmann/Flickr
   71. Patrick Roy rats, AP Photo/Rick Bowmer

LOS ANGELES KINGS
   72. Garry Desjardins, Archives on Ontario,
   C 193-3, Julien LeBourdais photographic
   negatives, 1963–1995, envelope 68037, image
   44
   73. (t) Cover image taken from *Gretzky: An
   Autobiography* by Wayne Gretzky with Rick
   Reilly © 1990 by Wayne Gretzky. Cover
   Design © 1990 by HarperCollins Publishers
   Ltd. All rights reserved.
   73. (b) Fan with Kings announcers, Ramidogg
   74. Drew Doughty, Harry How/Getty Images
   75. Don Cherry and Ron Maclean, Dave
   Olson/uncleweed/Flickr

MINNESOTA WILD
   76. (t) Wild fans, J. Hinrichs/Flickr
   76. (b) Snoopy's home ice, Wally Gobetz/
   wallyg/Flickr
   77. Derek Boogaard, Bruce Kluckhohn/NHLI
   via Getty Images
   79. Player scuffle, Archives of Ontario, C
   193-3 Julien LeBourdais photographic
   negatives, 1963–1995, Envelope 72067,
   Image 42

MONTREAL CANADIENS
   80. Guy Lafleur wall painting, Susan
   Thompson-Flickr.com/photos/sue90ca
   81. Viggo Mortensen, Karen Seto, Toronto
   82. Maurice Richard, Michael Hasenstein
   83. Bernie Geoffrion Phillips ad, Denis Goulet/
   Flickr
   84. Mario Lemieux (head), Bruce Bennett
   Studios/Getty Images
   84. Montreal Canadien lifting Stanley Cup
   (body), MONTREAL GAZETTE/AFP/Getty
   Images

NASHVILLE PREDATORS
   86. Sabretooth entrance, Paul Nicholson
   87. (t) Shea Weber, Gosha Images
   87. (b) Nashville Predators blowup player,
   Olivia Lind/Flickr
   88–89. Downtown Nashville, Chuck Kramer-
   Flickr.com/ckramer
   90. (t) Shea Weber, Jamie Kellner
   90. (b) Carrie Underwood and fan, Danielle
   Pope
   91. Nashville neon, jtdiego/Flickr

NEW JERSEY DEVILS
   92. (t) NJ Devils sculpture, Susan Kane
   92. (b,r) Martin Brodeur, Andy Martin Jr.,
   andymartinjr.com
   93. Patrick Roy and Martin Brodeur, Bruce
   Bennett Studios/Getty Images
   95. Martin Brodeur, Elsa/Getty Images

NEW YORK ISLANDERS

96. Kid in Islanders jersey, sydandsaskia/Flickr
97. (t) Islanders with Stanley Cup, Bruce Bennett Studios/Getty Images
97. (b) Islanders fan wearing two jerseys, Mike Durkin/Flickr
98. NYR/NYI brawl, Tobias Neubert
99. (b) PTVSX license plate, Alessandra/Aoife City Womanchile/Flickr
101. Rick DiPietro and Al Montoya, Tobias Neubert

NEW YORK RANGERS

102–103. Madison Square Garden, Ludovic Bertron/Flickr
102. (inset) Rangers fans, Dean Ayres/Flickr
104–105. Tie Domi and Bob Probert, AP Photo/Ron Frehm

OTTAWA SENATORS

108. Alfredsson/Spezza/Heately, Lucas Powell (http://www.linkedin.com/in/lucaspowell)
109. (t) Coke pixel art, Sue Novotny
109. (b) Kids in Senators jerseys, Chris Wightman
110. Dany Heatley, Andre Ringuette/NHLI via Getty Images

PHILADELPHIA FLYERS

114. Flyers wedding cake topper, www.magicmud.com
115. (t) Flyer flyer, Huggie! (temporary trade impasse)/Flickr
115. (b) Flyer fan with sign, David Krikst
116. Dave Schultz cover, *Philadelphia Magazine*
117. Flyer fan with Fred Shero, Jerry Klein
118. Bobby Clarke *Sports Illustrated* cover, Tony Triolo/Sports Illustrated/Getty Images

PHOENIX COYOTES

120. Coyotes entrance, Mike Robbins/Flickr
121. (l) Peter Mueller, Mike Robbins/Flickr
121. (r) Coyotes logo, Nicki Miller/Flickr
122. Gary Bettman, Christian Petersen/Getty Images
123. *Hamilton Spectator* cartoon, Graeme MacKay / artizans.com
125. Wayne Gretzky, Mitchell Fluhrer

PITTSBURGH PENGUINS

126. (t) Penguins fan, Nedra Isenberg
126. (b) Syl Apps Jr., Archives of Ontario, C 193-3, Julien LeBourdais photographic negatives, 1963–1995, enveloped 72082, image 1a
127. Mario Lemieux, Dave Madeloni
128. Mario Lemieux and Sidney Crosby, Brian Bahr/Getty Images for NHL

ST. LOUIS BLUES

130. Brett Hull and Wayne Gretzky, Michael Desjardins/Getty Images
131. Ozzy mug shot, Shelby County Sheriff, 1984
132. Andy Mcdonald and Aaron Rome, AP Photo/Bill Boyce

SAN JOSE SHARKS

134. (t) Fan with Shark head, Nikole Harlan/Flickr
134. (b,l) Fan with Sharks beanie, Elliot Lowe
134. (b,c) Kid on street in Sharks jersey, Wendy Tienken
134. (b,r) Older Sharks fan, Elliot Lowe
135. (t) Sharks entrance, Bill Hage
135. (b) Sharkie on ATV, Elliot Lowe
137. Joe Thornton, Morgen Sagen/morgen/Flickr

TAMPA BAY LIGHTNING

138. Steven Stamkos goal, Sonny Del Monte
139. Steven Stamkos with puck, Sonny Del Monte
140. Steven Stamkos, 25stanley.com
141. Daniel Craig, Fred Duval/FilmMagic

TORONTO MAPLE LEAFS

142. Frank Mahovlich, © Library and Archives Canada/Weekend Magazine collection/e002505650. Reproduced with the permission of Library and Archives Canada,
143. Johnny Bower, Archives of Ontario,C 193-3 Julien LeBourdais photographic negatives, 1963–1995, Envelope 68022, Image 18
144,145. Toronto Maple Leafs program 1930, City of Toronto Archives, Series 306, Sub-series 1, File 21
146. Maple Leaf Gardens 1934, City of Toronto Archives, Fonds 1244, Item 3185
147. *A Boy at the Leafs Camp* by Scott Young, © 1963, 1985. Used with permission of McClelland & Stewart Ltd.
148. Toronto Maple Leafs record, From the personal collection of Stephen Cole
149. Conn Smythe, Yale Joel/Time & Life Pictures/Getty Images
150. All-Stars vs. Leafs, Archives of Ontario, C 193-3 Julien LeBourdais photographic negatives, 1963–1995, Envelope 68033, Image 31
151. Norm Ullman, Archives of Ontario, C 193-3 Julien LeBourdais photographic negatives, 1963–1995, Envelope 72070, Image 12
152. Harold Ballard, Toronto Star-Frank Lennon/The Canadian Press.
153. Darcy Tucker, THE CANADIAN PRESS/Adrian Wyld

VANCOUVER CANUCKS

154. Canucks jerseys, Lisataime Powell
155. (t) Henrik Sedin, Jamie Kellner
155. (b,l) Green Men press conference, Ariane Colenbrander/ariane c design
155. (b,r) Monroeville Zombies, S. King/Flickr
156–157. Henrik and Daniel Sedin, Jessica Haydahl/NHL via Getty Images
158. Henrik and Daniel Sedin in Modo jerseys, CP PHOTO/stf-Ryan Remiorz
159. Canucks pennant, CORSIWORLD

WASHINGTON CAPITALS

160. (l) Alexander Ovechkin, James Patterson/Flickr
160. (r) Nicklas Backstrom, Dan4th/Flickr
161. Alexander Ovechkin, Ethan Miller/Getty Images
162. Alexander Oveckin and mother, Simon Bruty/Sports Illustrated/Getty Images
163. (l) Alexander Ovechkin slapshot, mrtoxikk/Flickr
163. (r) Alexander Ovechkin action figure, Malabooboo/Flickr
164. Alexander Ovechkin, mrtoxikk/Flickr

WINNIPEG-ATLANTA THRASHER-JETS

166. (t) Thrashers Jumbotron, Cathy Stikes/Flickr
166. (b) Atlanta Flames patch, Nick Allin
167. Ilya Kovalchuk, D. Wedford Turner
168. Dusten Byfuglien, Scott Cunningham/Getty Images
169. (t,l) Roseau Rams goalie, Brandon Vizenor/Flickr
169. (b,l) Roseau Memorial Arena, ©2010 Cory Shubert Photography
169. (b,r) Dusten Byfuglien, Aticia Ayers-Fischer
170. Dusten Byfuglien in scrum, Curtis Miller

ENDPAPERS

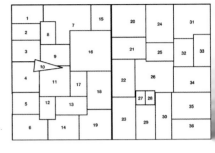

1. Mascot, Harry Schaefer/Flickr
2. Edmonton Eskimos, public domain
3. Florida Panthers player, TRAVISDEICHL/Flickr
4. Crosby fan, Dan4th/Flickr
5. 1946 Montreal Canadiens, Mick Bailey
6. Ovechkin giving an interview, Jamie Kellner
7. Brind'Amour with Cup, Richard Spence/Flickr
8. Leafs fan, PGBee
9. "Jussi the Finnisher," Jamie Kellner
10. Atlanta Flames pennant, slade1955/Flickr
11. Julien LeBourdais, Archives of Ontario C193-3/Photographic Negatives 1963–1995/Envelope 75254/Image 12
12. Gretzky, Håkan Dahlström
13. "Laurie Heart Kessel," Dan4th/Flickr
14. Statue with Detroit jersey, Angela C. Williams (Word Nerdy/Flickr)
15. Pavel Bure, Håkan Dahlström
16. Family in jerseys, Rick Harris
17. NYR wedding piece, www.magicmud.com
18. Nordiques fan with binoculars, Jonathan Guyon
19. Tim Thomas, Dan4th/Flickr
20. Madison Square Garden, www.mattluce.com
21. Victoria Cougars, public domain
22. Detroit fan at Winter Classic, George Hradecky
23. Jean Beliveau, Archives of Ontario C193-Photographic Negatives 1963–1995/Envelop 72060/Image 16
24. Calgary fan, Victor Lai
25. Sens Army, Sue Novotny
26. Crosby model, Phillip Rosson
27. Oilers fan, Randy Pond Photography (www.randypond.ca)
28. San Jose fan, www.sanjosebikeblog.com Flickr
29. Vincent Lecavalier, www.andymartinjr.co
30. Detroit player, Archives of Ontario C193-Photographic Negatives 1963–1995/Envelop 68038/Image 5
31. 1960s Wings Oldtimers, W. T. Helfrich
32. Oilers monkey, Wendy Leslie
33. Frank Fredrickson, public domain
34. Chicago Blackhawks line, Hattie Trott/Flickr
35. Marc Tardif, Archives of Ontario C193-3/Photographic Negatives 1963–1995/Envelop 75237/Image 8
36. Toronto Maple Leafs flag, George Balogh

BRIND'AMOUR 17

JUSSI THE FINNISHER

ATLANTA FLAMES

CROSBY #87

NY

LAURIE HEART KESSEL

GO WINGS! THIS IS ... HOCKEYTOWN 2009

BRUINS